THE ALLAGASH

THE ALLAGASH

BY LEW DIETZ
ILLUSTRATED BY GEORGE LOH

THE THORNDIKE PRESS · THORNDIKE, MAINE

Library of Congress Cataloging in Publication Data

Dietz, Lew, 1906-
  The Allagash.

  Reprint of the ed. published by Holt, Rinehart, and Winston,
  New York, in series: Rivers of America.
  Bibliography: p.
  Includes index.
  1. Allagash River.   I. Title.   II. Series.
F27.A4D5 1978   974.1'1   78-8326
ISBN 0-89621-001-6 lim. ed.
ISBN 0-89621-000-6 pbk.

Reprinted by arrangement with Holt, Rinehart and Winston, Inc.

The kings of England formerly had their
forests "to hold the king's game," for sport
or food, sometimes destroying villages to create
or extend them; and I think that they were
impelled by a true instinct. Why should not we,
who have renounced the king's authority, have our
national preserves, where no villages need be
destroyed, in which the bear and panther, and some
even of the hunter race, may still exist, and not
be "civilized off the face of the earth"—our
forests, not to hold the king's game merely, but
to hold and preserve the king himself also, the
lord of creation—not for idle sport or food,
but for inspiration and our own true recreation
or shall we, like the villains, grub them all
up, poaching on our own national domains?

—HENRY DAVID THOREAU

CONTENTS

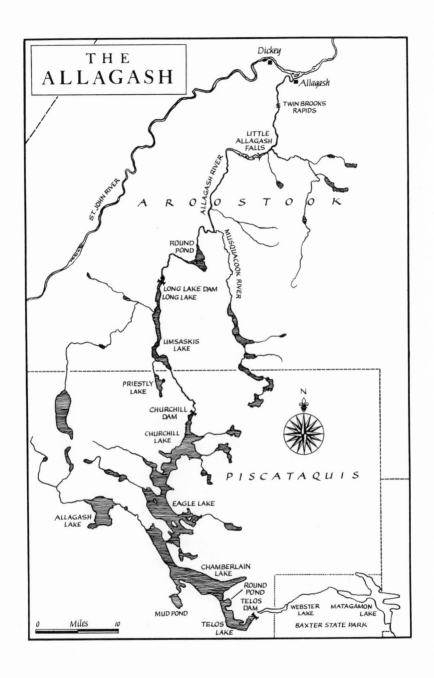

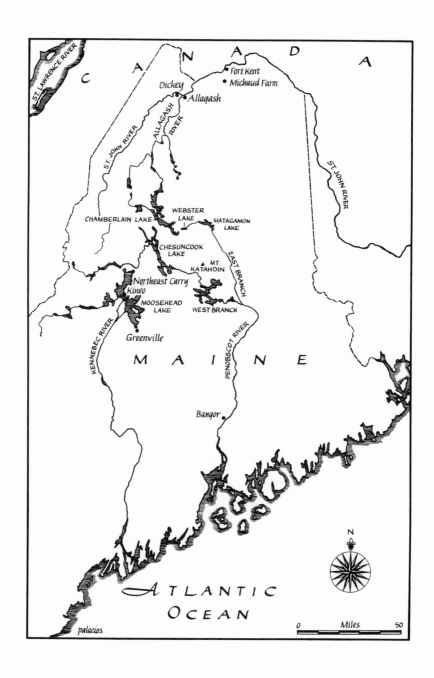

CANADA

ST. LAWRENCE RIVER

C A N A D A

Fort Kent
Michaud Farm

Dickey
Allagash

ST. JOHN RIVER

ALLAGASH RIVER

ST. JOHN RIVER

WEBSTER LAKE

CHAMBERLAIN LAKE

MATAGAMON LAKE

CHESUNCOOK LAKE

MT. KATAHDIN

EAST BRANCH

Northeast Carry
Kineo

MOOSEHEAD LAKE

WEST BRANCH

KENNEBEC RIVER

Greenville

PENOBSCOT RIVER

M A I N E

Bangor

A T L A N T I C

O C E A N

palacios

N

0   Miles   50

FOREWORD

BY SENATOR EDMUND E. MUSKIE

THE ALLAGASH is not a spectacular river, but it is unique. Shielded from urban expansion and industrial development by its location and by the economics and landowning patterns of Maine's long lumber and pulp companies, the Allagash survived as a free-flowing and unpolluted stream long after similar rivers in the northeast had been degraded.

Now, under a cooperative federal-state program, the Allagash will be protected in perpetuity as an unspoiled link with our past and as a natural beauty area for future generations. The Allagash was saved for several reasons. Naturalists and conservationists appreciated its special qualities. Sportsmen wished to preserve its attractions as a canoeing and fishing river. Public officials understood the importance of protecting the Allagash against threats of flooding by hydroelectric dams, overcutting of its forests under increasing pressure for pulp and long lumber, and excessive recreational land use through subdivision of shore acreage.

President Kennedy launched the federal effort to protect the Allagash in April, 1963, as part of the review of proposed flood control and hydroelectric projects on the upper St. John River. He instructed Secretary Udall to consider the preservation of the Allagash as part of the overall resource development plan for the area.

The initial preservation plan would have incorporated the Allagash in a national wild rivers program. Objections from landowners and others in Maine made it clear the route of national acquisition could leave the Allagash a bruised symbol of another heated conservation fight. With the cooperation of Secretary of the Interior Stewart L. Udall, and the skillful legislative leadership of Maine State Senator Elmer H. Violette, Maine developed its own program under which the state would acquire, protect and administer the Allagash, aided in the acquisition by matching federal grants from the land and water conservation fund.

Thus, the Allagash has become a symbol of sound conservation, balanced resource development and federal-state cooperation. But it will always be more than this, as a source of pleasure and recreation for those who cherish the close relationship between man and the natural environment. It is that affinity, continued through centuries of exploration, use and enjoyment, which Lew Dietz has captured in his book. His writing is true because he has known the Allagash as others—famous and infamous, noted and unremembered—have known it.

I hope this book will inspire other efforts to conserve those examples of the natural environment which remain in our too often overcrowded and abused land.

Washington, D.C.
January 1968

INTRODUCTION

A wilderness river trip is always memorable. At a time when man has wandered too far from his biological beginnings, a visit to a wild river calls forth a response that is in a sense a recognition. It is a returning, a fulfillment of a hidden need for life-renewing communion with the vapors of the earth.

I have made many happy journeys to the woods and rivers of Maine, but there was one that was infinitely more than a pleasure: it was a privilege. I was with not one, but three, Allagash men, "Moosetowners" born and bred in this region where the Allagash River flows into the St. John. For John Sinclair, Bud Gibson and Dave Dow, this river country was home.

Moreover, this was to be a circuit trip which would entail running up the Upper St. John, carrying across to the Allagash Waterway, then down the Allagash and returning to our point of departure, a closing of the ring that John, a surveyor by training, termed "tying in our traverse."

Ideally, perhaps, this circuit should be made by going up the Allagash and down the St. John. On this June day there was what Allagashers term "a fair pitch of water" on the St. John. It was thought wise to take advantage of good water on the St. John while we had it. The St. John is broader and more shallow than the Allagash and the spring runoff is swift and often violent. You can have wild, daunting water one day and be bumping on the rocks the next. You definitely have to pick your time to run the St. John.

What lent this trip an edge of poignancy was the very real .possibility that this might be the last time I'd ever see this wild

piece of river. The Allagash had had a last minute reprieve
when public outcry had quashed the plan to build a power
dam on the St. John downriver from the Allagash Plantation.
Now the Upper St. John was under sentence. At the time, the
proposal to build a dam at Dickey, just upriver from the Allagash settlement, was moving swiftly beyond the talking
stage. If the engineers were to have their way, the Upper St.
John would be flowed back for almost fifty miles to form a
lake. It would, a certain "progressive" segment of the citizenry
insisted, be a boon to the economy of the state.

To say that economic imperatives demanded that an irre-
placeable wild river be killed was much like saying, it seemed
to me, that the technological age we live in demanded the air
we breathed. The new affluent society has given us ease and a
parade of wonders. It has also drained our swamps, polluted
our rivers, defiled our cities and fouled our air. When modern
Prometheans travel into space they take with them a balanced
system of oxygen, clean water and controlled temperatures. If
this industrial economy is to play the tune, it may well be that
in some bleak and not too distant future spaceships will be the
last hospitable places on earth for man to live.

All that idyllic week, these thoughts were with us like ghosts
at a banquet.

We put in that June morning on the St. John, a few miles
upriver from the plantation at the old Oullette Farm, the staging area for many a log drive in the days when timber took the
river road. We had three twenty-foot canoes, powered for the
upriver push by five-horsepower outboards. It was a warm,
misty day with a threat of rain in the gathering clouds.

I was paired with Bud Gibson, a big, slow-moving, easy-
going man with a florid Irish face. There is something refresh-
ingly anachronistic about an Allagash man. He seems to
belong in another time. Until very recent years the Allagash
people have been isolated, islanded where the rivers meet in a
sea of trees. They speak a language of their fathers, a speech

cleansed of vulgarities. They are soft-spoken and conduct themselves with an old-world courtliness. It is as though a hard life and a close feeling of identification with nature had shorn them of conceits and pretenses. They are by general agreement the finest woodsmen and rivermen in the state.

Riding the rips a good waterman can "read the water." He finds the channel among the rocks by what appears to be an innate sense, but it truly is no more than a knowing refined by years of experience. Traveling the dead water where there is no current to betray the dangers of hidden rocks is a by-guess-and-by-God-affair. A bump would call forth from Bud no more than a softly uttered "oh." A little harder bump would warrant an "oh, oh," and upward to as many as six "ohs," depending on the severity of the contact. As a measure of Bud's river sense, there were no more than two "six-oh" rocks during the course of that week on the rivers.

There are few human experiences that can match the joy and deep peace of traveling the course of a wild river. No two stretches of river are alike. Every turn and twist offers a new prospect and delight. One moment the water runs with a white-flecked roar, then, of a sudden, the river is still and clear, so clear, despite the pale-tea tincture from leachings in the conifer swamp headwaters, that one can see the cobbly bottom slide away and the sinuous ribbon grasses streaming out in the current.

For four days we pushed up the river, fishing when and where we pleased, rendezvousing at Nine Mile Bridge. Lionel Caron, a Forest Service man and a friend of John's, met us with a Chevy truck and bore us, our canoes and gear across to the Allagash Waterway via the old LaCroix road. Built by "King" LaCroix in the early 20s, the road was the first access to the vast Allagash wilderness.

We put in below Chase's Rapids at Umsaskis Lake. The section of the Allagash between Churchill Dam and Umsaskis is the most challenging piece of river on the waterway, but we had had our white-water thrills running Big Black Rapids on the St. John and wanted some time for leisurely downriver fishing.

We had had two days of intermittent rain. Now the skies were lifting with low mists still shrouding the encircling hills. The Allagash Lakes are superlatively beautiful, but rivermen are not truly at home until the trees close in and they feel the lift of a current under their canoes. Technically, the Allagash Waterway begins at Telos Dam and includes Chamberlain, Eagle and Churchill lakes. In the view of the Allagash man, the "true" river begins at Churchill Dam. Both the Upper St. John and the Allagash flow roughly northward, a fact that is often confusing to outlanders. Thus, when the Allagash man speaks of the "lower river" he is referring to that northern section of the river that begins at Round Pond and ends at his dooryard where the Allagash flows into the St. John. The "Upper river" is that piece of water from Round Pond south to Churchill Dam. In short, when Allagashers go upstream, they go south and when they travel downriver, they go north.

When we arrived at Long Lake Dam—or what remains of this relic of the river-driving days—we met a party of four that had earlier been a party of sixteen. The group had attempted to run Chase's Rapids without sufficient white-water experience behind them. All but two canoes had been lost, along with food and gear. The survivors had been flown out of the woods sadder and, hopefully, wiser for the experience.

We soon learned of one good reason for the disaster. The party carried no setting poles and would not have known how to use them if they had had them. The setting pole is as important as a paddle to an Allagash waterman. In running the rips, the seasoned riverman uses his pole to "snub" his canoe, thereby keeping his craft under control at all times.

In upriver passage, the pole is employed to push over bars and shoals. The pole serves to beach a canoe in an onshore wind to avoid taking water or damaging the canoe on rocks. At night camp the Allagash man drives his pole into the earth at an acute inshore angle and lashes his canoe to it for safekeeping. The setting pole serves admirably as a stake to which to tie his canoe stern when fishing in the rips.

There are no two river trips alike, and few that fail to bring some new learning. And there are few men, no matter how woodswise, who cannot learn a thing or two from Moosetowners. Once again, I was amazed at the ease and speed with which men bred to the woods can make camp. The division of labor is arranged without words and seems almost instinctual.

Once the gear was unloaded, Bud went for dry hardwood, cutting and fetching in ten-foot lengths of sound dead trees. John arranged the cooking gear and Dave began axing up the logs into usable billets, enough for the night fire and the morning. The lug pole was set on forked sticks. This frame built over the cookfire is called by Allagash men the "spunhungan," or at least this is as close as my ear could ever catch it—I've never seen the word in print. Crotched green sticks are hung from the lug pole with a nail tacked at its end to hold the bailed teakettle. This is variously called a lug stick, pothook or wangan stick. The pole driven into the ground at such an angle as to extend over the fire is a wambeck.

Each night, rain or shine, it was no more than a matter of fifteen minutes before the tents were up and camp arranged and trout were sizzling in pork fat over the coals.

Curiously, the hardest lesson to learn in packing for river traveling is the knack of simplifying, to take only what you need and yet to forget nothing that is essential. Next to his canoe, the Allagash man's most treasured and important item of gear is a sharp axe. Moreover, it is as personal as his toothbrush. One learns quickly on the river road that light wool clothing is more comfortable and serviceable than cotton. Wool sheds water, cotton remains clammy. This is true of sneakers. Much better is a pair of low moccasins for camp wear and a short pair of soft-soled leather boots for travel. And you learn painfully that clothing should be light in color. Black flies and mosquitoes, those first citizens of Allagash country,

are attracted by dark cloth and will bite right through a dark
shirt to get a man beneath it.

All men who live close to nature have their superstitions. I
learned around night fires on this trip that an Allagash man
takes pains not to leave an axe sticking into a log or stump. You
lay an axe flat. If an axe is left driven into a tree no one will rest
that night. If you lodge a tree in felling it, there will surely be
a storm on the morrow. It is bad luck to leave the spunhungan
standing once the tea had boiled. You never leave a canoe
belly up on the shore. As do many superstitions, this one is
rooted in reason. In bear country, a tyro learns sadly that a
bear doesn't investigate or satisfy his curiosity with the delicacy of a raccoon. He will smash his way in and investigate
afterward.

Perhaps the most beautiful section of the river is the stretch
between Round Pond and Allagash Falls. I was particularly
struck by the contrast between two beautiful wild rivers, the
Allagash and the Upper St. John. The Allagash was deeper and
narrower, the ridges steeper. The conifer forest pressed closer
upon you, lending a more somber aspect to the eye. The water
of the Allagash is colder and clearer, for the river rises, not in
the swamps, but in spring-fed highland lakes.

All along the sinuous river route solitary old-growth pines,
spared by the early loggers, stand like lonely sentinels, their
terraced crowns rising high above the spruce canopy. Many of
the spires of these ancient giants are riven by lightning strikes,
the price they pay for their lordly vantage.

We saw wildlife at almost every turn in the river. Deer were
everywhere. As Bud and I fished late one afternoon, a great
bull moose stood at the river's edge and watched us for a full
fifteen minutes. One night, a bear cub came into our camp and
began banging the larder box around until he was sent packing. We saw three eagles on the last stretch of river, heartening
evidence that these majestic birds are holding their own in the
Allagash fastnesses.

On the last night we stopped to fish at Rosie's Rock, near the mouth of the Musquacook. This was one of Bud's favorite fishing holes. The name appears on no map and it is unlikely that it ever will, for fishermen are not given to advertising a productive fishing spot. Rosie, Bud told me, was the wife of a Forest Service towerman who spent many happy and fruitful hours fishing from the rock while her husband manned his lonely station.

Our final lunch stop on the downriver run was at Cunliffe Depot, once a bustling base logging camp. Now all that remains are the rusting old carcasses of two Lombard log-haulers.

As we approached Twin Brooks, the first intrusive manifestations of encroaching civilization reached out for us. The sound of a logging truck, on the lumber road just beyond the border of trees, was shocking to our senses, lulled these many days only by the sound of a running river or the morning song of a white-throated sparrow.

We went ashore at the Forest Service station just above Twin Brooks. There was something I might like to see, John said. There on the banks was a grave of an Allagash trapper. He had lived his life on the river and asked only that he be buried at the river's edge. No coffin was available so they fitted him into two sugar barrels nailed end to end. And there he lies.

"There's a story there," John said.

I nodded. "So many I would hardly know where to begin."

When I first addressed myself to the task of writing the story of the Allagash it seemed a simple enough matter. After all, here was a river region, then and now a wilderness; its history would surely be uncluttered, dealing largely with trappers, hunters, loggers, beasts and birds. No great cities have grown up on the river's banks nor telling battles fought at its crossings. The Allagash can boast of no Frontenac, LaSalle, nor even a Henry Hudson. It was then, it seemed to me, merely a matter of gathering the essential facts of its history, recording the adventures of those men who have known the river and been tested by it, culling through the massive body of recollections; all this, together with my own experiences in this wilderness country, would suffice to spin out the tale.

Rivers have a way of wandering from their beds and overflowing their banks; never yet has a river taken the shortest route from headwaters to mouth; a hill turns it aside here, resistant rocks divert it there, and a spring torrent may send it rampaging to scour out a new and unexpected channel.

I had not proceeded far down the river's story before I realized that a river, like history itself, can have a mind of its own. Further, I discovered that no amount of facts can make a history; that facts are no more nor less than the gross material from which questions are posed, answers suggested and a point of view established.

For example: it is a fact that the Allagash is a wilderness river. In terms of history, this bare statement has little meaning unless reasons for its so being are explored. As there are reasons for a civilization, so there are reasons for the absence of one. The quest for such answers might lead, as indeed it did, to London or Paris and turn on such extraneous events as the beheading of Charles I or the Edict at Nantes.

In fact, towns might well be flourishing along the Allagash today had not the great stands of virgin pine stood there at a time when man's need for them was critical. To breach this wilderness required capital and men who thought, not in terms of acres of timberland, but in baronies of many square miles. The search for the reasons for Maine's unique wildlands ownership arrangement, which discouraged homesteading and fixed the shape of the future of the Allagash region as a wilderness with timber its one-crop resource, led far afield and to such unlikely places as the Salem counting house of one David Pingree and a social wedding in Philadelphia.

Why, one might ask, was the pine there in the first place: Here again, the quest for answers lures the storyteller afield, requiring an ecological exploration, a harkening back to the glacial ages, indeed, to the beginning of time.

Thus, it soon became not so much a matter of gathering fact and evaluating events as carefully choosing among the mass of material only those pieces and fragments that lent meaning to the whole and following only those beckoning avenues that promised to enrich and illuminate the story.

Even so, I found myself writing the story of the North Woods of Maine, for clearly, any smaller canvas would have failed to give meaning to the river which lies at its heart. Moreover, I discovered that this river country, where no mills have ever turned and whose population might be placed handily in a middling-sized hall, had a truly human story to tell, and all the more human for its dearth of humankind, for even an ordinary man who stands alone with space and air around him acquires stature by his very aloneness.

I am making neither a disclaimer nor an apology when I say I am not by temperament nor trade an historian. Nor do I suggest that this story is purely and scrupulously objective. This would be the same as saying that facts speak for themselves. Place a set of facts before one hundred honest men and you may have as many interpretations of those facts. As to my interpretation of certain facts I take full responsibility, feeling as I do that it is the honorable prerogative of a storyteller-cum-historian to exercise his creative faculty and seek the larger truth which bare facts too often obscure.

Possibly, it was this storyteller attitude that dictated my footnote methodology. The notes are relatively few, and except in those cases where it seemed awkward or diverting, I have placed ancillary material in the running text. Samuel Johnson, in his heavily annotated edition of Shakespeare, wrote that "notes are often necessary, but they are necessary evils." The footnotes I have placed at the end of the book are not in any true sense necessary at all. They are there for incorrigible foot-note readers who enjoy meaty tidbits much the way some women enjoy gossip.

Then there is the matter of taxonomy. There are, for example, at least a dozen acceptable ways to spell "Abnaki," and as many renderings of "Algonquian." My choices have been more or less arbitrary, for in each case I chose the usage that appealed to me. Nor is the appended bibliography intended to be anything more than a listing of my main sources of material, for a complete catalog of all sources, snippets of facts, recollections, observations that were drawn from hundreds of dusty files, would have required more space than any scholarly value would have warranted.

As for acknowledgments, aid came from a hundred gracious sources, both in supplying grist for the project and research, and staffs of both the Maine State Library and the Bangor Library were ever helpful, as were the representatives of the timberland owners, in particular, John Sinclair, of the Pingree Heirs.

Finally, of course, there are the living Allagash rivermen who like their fathers still take the river road. For them the story of the Allagash is not so much history as recollection.

Many of their stories are skewed by personal prejudice or colored by the agency of a thousand tellings. But exaggeration is merely an extension of the truth of how it once was and will never be again.

Let me add only that I have enjoyed my long voyage of exploration. Hopefully, the reader who embarks upon the story of this engaging and uncommon river will find a like pleasure.

L.D.

Rockport, Maine
October 1967

PART ONE

THE RIVER   I

IN THE heart of Maine's North Country the Allagash River
flows northward a hundred miles through uplands of
unbroken forest. It flows backward, one might say, for reasonable rivers of the continent tend to southern courses. And
backward it flows in time, for there is no river in the Eastern
United States that remains so nearly as it was when the first
white man faced the trees with his back to the sea.

A region as well as a river, this vast watershed springs from
a half-hundred lakes, countless streams and rills, forming the
heart of the wild land that blankets northwestern Maine. This
serpentining waterway, in turn serene and brawling, links
seven major lakes on its northerly course, tapping the legendary North Woods of pine and spruce and fir that once
stretched in unbroken ranks west and north into Canada.

The Allagash is much more than a river: it is a symbol. Since
the aboriginal Indian guided his fragile birch along this dark
corridor, the waterway has been a classic canoe route, a beckoning byway into an age-old dimension of human experience.

It is only the remoteness of these half-million acres that has,
thus far, preserved their integrity. The Allagash remains a
woodsman's world of paddle and portage, of wild trout and
night-crying loon. Its trails, cut by lumbermen and trappers,
have, since the days when Henry David Thoreau tramped
them, been followed only by the few who feel, as did the
Concord naturalist himself, that the wilderness is for those who
make the bone effort to find it.

It is not a great river by the measure of the Nile, the Missis-
sippi or the Amazon. From the Telos Dam to the St. John

River is a middling ninety miles. But, much as there are men who are all man, the Allagash is all river.

Allagash stream, winding down from the watershed's ultimate sources, flows out of Allagash Lake white and tumbling. Round Pond detains the trout stream; then it plunges over Little Allagash Falls to deepen in quiet bends and still waters as it nears the central lakes of the Allagash country.

The eighteen-mile-long waters of Eagle and Churchill lakes form the central links in the Allagash waterway. Embayed, islanded, fed by a network of tributaries, these sequestered lakes were the favorite camping grounds of the nomadic forest tribes. Today, artifacts and charred remains of ancient campfires can be found in the shoreside midden heaps.

Below Churchill Lake, the main Allagash begins with a roar. That mile and a half at Chase's Carry demands the skills of a seasoned waterman. Then, some seven miles beyond, the river slows to enter the hill-set length of Umsaskis and Long lakes. To the west, Priestly Mountain rises above Priestly Lake, one of the lovely waters of the Allagash region.

Below Long Lake, the Allagash once again becomes a river, majestic now, wide and unhurried as it passes ranks of dark spruce and fir, relieved at intervals by stands of bright, arching birch.

The basin of Round Pond holds the river by the mountains for a spell. Then the river flows on. Downstream from the abandoned Michaud Farm, where once woods teams were summered, bosky islands divide the river into fingering channels. The river reforms again for one final glorious climax to chute in roaring foam over Allagash Falls.

Then, in alternating calms and rapids, the river sweeps on through a new world of maples to the settlement of Allagash and the pleasant villages of the St. John valley.

The river's sinuous journey is both the heart and the frame of the Allagash story. Born of a cataclysm before man appeared, its primeval history, recorded in its rocks, is there for man to read. The brief human history of the Allagash began

with the ancient people of the mists who left only graves and
stone-age tools to mark their long residency. The red man
came, and he, too, departed, leaving the wilderness much as he
had found it. His record remains, imperishable, in legends and
a thousand place names.

Then upon the Indian's haunted trails strode the *coureurs de
bois*—white savages they were called by those who tried to
tame them. When the French dream of empire was shattered,
the English wilderness man, who was already losing his Eng-
lishness, began to write his story with axe and trap line. Later,
the "lumberers" rode the river, the calk-booted "Moosetowners," weaned on rum and dedicated, as the saying went, to
letting the sunlight into the swamp.

They, too, left their names upon the region of the river.
Years later, an early geologist digressed from his scientific report long enough to deplore such thoughtlessness. "No one
would wish to give a child a name of which the youth would
be ashamed in after years," he wrote. "Nor can we suppose
that a community would desire such uncouth names to remain
attached to beautiful natural objects in their vicinity as always
provokes a smile upon the lips of strangers. Nor can inelegant
names ever appear in poetry. Such designations as Hogback
Mountain, Tumbledown Dick, Bull Hill, Quaggy Joe, Jockey
Cap, Singepole, Ben Barrows Hill and Hedgehog Mountain,
are certainly inelegant, both in Poetry and prose."

Would the Allagash be the same had some later chronicler,
whose delicate ear was offended, changed its name to Pleasant
River? Language is a repository of history; place names have
their story to tell to those who come after.

The early white man, venturing into the sea of trees, listened
to the name. There was a lake the Indian called *Allagask-
wiganmook*, "Bark Cabin Lake,"(1) and the river that issued
from it, *Allequash*. The Indian's tongue being strange and the
white man's ear impatient, the river's name knew many variations. In time it came to be written "Allagash." Then, as now, it
was a hidden, distant place of beauty and legend.

Allagash Falls

Nor would a gazetteer satisfy to capture its essence. An early report of water power in Maine states bleakly: "The Allequash is the second largest tributary of the St. John in Maine and drains about 1650 square miles. Chamberlain Lake furnishes the headwaters of the stream which, with smaller lakes in its basin gives the river comparatively constant flow throughout the year." Or a later report: "The river proper starts at the outlet of Churchill Lake, although waters as far south as Allagash Lake and Chamberlain Lake drain into the system."

To grasp the truth of the river is to accept that it was not designed for man alone. Now, as then, this is domain for the majestic moose, the beaver, otter, and hunting cat. Now, as then, along Allagash trails grow the fragrant twinflower, the wood sorrel, the lovely orchid known as the lady-slipper. In profusion, too, grow the creeping snowberry, the bunchberry and dwarf dogwood.

Symbols are signs by which one perceives the inexpressible. The Allagash is a loon crying at night on a lonely lake; the Canada jay, the friendly camp companion known affectionately by Allagash men as the moosebird, whisky-jack or gorbie; the white-throated sparrow which evoked from Thoreau this memorable passage in the journal of his Allagash journey. "I lay awake very early and I listened to the clear, shrill *ah-tette-tette-te* of the white-throated sparrow, repeated for half an hour, as if it could not enough express its happiness."

It can be said that the Allagash is merely a river in Maine that flows from here to there to join a larger river on its flow to sea. In the context of today this small wilderness river has become vast for there are few rivers in America that remain to give some small hint of how it once was in another time.

A river that can serve not the demands of man's material needs but as a sanctuary of the human spirit is a large river indeed. And not Maine's but America's river.

IN THE BEGINNING 2

HIGH UP on the bleak, inhospitable summit of Mount Katahdin lives a small Arctic mouse. There is truly no beginning to any story, but merely a point of departure. The mouse that lives on Maine's loftiest peak will serve as a taking off place in the story of a wilderness river, for the same primordial events that marooned this tiny rodent created the river and, indeed, fashioned the landscape of all that vast region through which the river flows.

This cataclysmic event is recent history in terms of the earth clock. One hundred and fifty million years ago the region that was to be the State of Maine appeared as a typical peneplain, a nearly flat, gently rolling topography broken only by occasional masses of resistant igneous rock. Rivers flowed through broad shallow valleys.

Over this placid landscape flew toothed birds and flying reptiles. In the swamps lived the herbivorous, helmeted Corythosaurus, a creature that fled in terror into deep water when pursued by the fearsome Tyrannosaurus, a complete engine of destruction measuring up to fifty feet and whose clawed feet and fanged jaws could tear anything in its path to shreds. The landscape was dominated by forests of conifers. Primitive mammals were just beginning to emerge.

The first events of Tertiary history saw a re-elevation of the land that had been worn down by eons of erosion in the course of the Jurassic period, a movement accompanied by a gentle tilting toward the southeast. This new cant of the land rejuvenated the rivers. Waters quickened and over the ensuing millennia the cutting edge of rivers incised deep valleys in what is

9

now the Moosehead Plateau. The dinosaur disappeared and the small fur bearers, equipped to withstand the increasing cold, took its place. Flora of modern recognition began to develop, the oak and maple, and the ferns assumed the forms they hold to this day.

With the dawn of the age of mammals emerged the ancestors of the animals that still roam the deep forests, the deer, weasels, otters, raccoon, the first true cats, and the precursors of the true bear. And the revived rivers cut deeper and deeper over the planed-off roots of the eroded mountains.

Then, a mere million years ago, came the great and cataclysmic happening that was to alter the landscape of the region that was to become Maine. The Great Ice Age dawned.

For some millions of years the continent had been slowly rising, causing a creeping refrigeration. Ice formed at the top of the earth. As it thickened, the growing pressures caused by its weight began to push the ice mass outward and southward. Imperceptibly and irresistibly it invaded the northerly reaches of the continent, gouging out valleys, sheering off mountaintops.

The ice retreated only to invade again and again, and in each advance it mangled the landscape and sent fleeing before it whatever forms of life had sprung up in the warm intervals between the encroachments.

So it was that a sea of ice covered Maine and to a depth that engulfed Mount Katahdin. The earth sank under the burden and seas rushed in. Carratunk, deep in Maine, knew the lapping of salt seas; the St. Croix and the region of Mattawamkeag on the Penobscot stood at the brink of the ocean.

When the ice retreated nothing remained of the preglacial landscape. Valleys, deepened and dammed by debris, became lakes, and with the re-elevation of the land the rivers quickened, cutting out gorges to carry runoffs to the sea. This erosive action carried off some of the glacial debris which covered the land, and the filling of the lakes with stream-borne litter began. Some lakes were drained in a twinkling when their outlets cut through the dams of glacial rubble.

Maine, the North Country, the Allagash began to assume a semblance of what the animal called man was to see and perceive as he emerged to inherit the earth.

The marine invasion after the last ice age occurred a mere 12,000 years ago and lasted but 700 years. And when the seas departed, an Arctic mouse was left stranded on the crest of Mount Katahdin.

The recovery was amazingly fast. Favorable temperatures and the proximity to the sea were probable factors in the quick resurgence of life. Recent carbon-14 dating tests reveal that it took but eight centuries for organic life to regain a foothold in this battered region with the recovery skipping the usual tundra stage and the great conifer forests making the first headway in the development of plant life.

From the vantage of the present, the eons of nature's work appears as a culmination rather than a ceaseless and continuing process. The river's geological history is timeless only because man has not the mind to comprehend primordial time. Man's tenancy of the earth is no more than a matter of seconds by the cosmic clock. In his narrow view, the river did not exist in any meaningful way until he arrived and found it.

History is the record of peoples. The people were about to arrive.

THE CHILDREN
OF THE MYTHS

3

IN RECENT times an old chief of the Penobscot tribe
said, "All the Indians between the Saco and the St. John
were brothers . . . each tribe was younger as we passed east."

There is no record of the first to come but only dim race
memory. Memory became legend and the legends the clues to
prehistory. That remote time of this first migration from the
west toward the rising sun was so long ago that the tribes that
met the first white men from across the sea could not themselves guess how long ago it was.

Nor is there a clear knowledge of who they were. And only
because the logic is persuasive is it presumed that they came
to this continent from Asia across the bridge of land that is
today severed by the Bering Strait. Did they come with long
coarse hair and coppery bodies? Or was their physical aspect
an adaptation to the harsh environment with which they were
forced to contend? Their movement over the continent was
glacial in pace, some moving southward paralleling the spines
of the mountains; others moving east and southeast into the
great unoccupied spaces made habitable by the retreat of the
glacier.

They were hunters and they brought with them their simple
tools and weapons. And their history.

The earliest group to occupy New England drifted in from
the west. The evidence of artifacts suggests that they were
unacquainted with agriculture, but their simple tools and
weapons were efficient. Some seventy-five years ago, a slate
semilunar knife was plowed up out of the muck where it had

been protected from erosion for possibly three thousand years. Its cutting edge was perfect and could be used today almost as effectively as a modern steel knife for butchering meat and splitting fish for drying, the task for which it was primarily designed by these pre-Algonquian people.

Curious tools whose use has never been conclusively established have been uncovered in the Penobscot valley and on the shores of Lake Chesuncook. These people of prehistory knew the art of fire making. Fire-making sets were among the most common implements unearthed from pre-Algonquian graves. Each set consisted originally of two lumps of iron pyrites or one lump of this material and one of flint from which sparks could be struck to light dry moss or some punky material which could be cosseted into a blaze.

The almost universal use of red ochre by these early nomads has, for want of a better identification, led to the use of the designation "Red Paint People." Some modern anthropologists offer the theory that the now extinct Beothuk of Newfoundland were remnants of this early race who were driven from New England by an ensuing tide of migrants. The theory is supported by the fact that the Newfoundland Beothuks were called "Red Indians" by the ancient navigators who touched in at that island in the sixteenth century. These European explorers were not referring to the natural hue of their skin, but to their lavish use of red ochre which they plastered not only upon their persons but on many of their belongings.

Late in the seventeenth century the French imported Micmac warriors and began a war of extermination against the Beothuk. By the middle of the eighteenth century the tribe was reduced to a few small groups, and by the dawn of the last century they were gone from the earth.

The theory that the Beothuk was the direct descendant of Maine's "Red Paint People" is intriguing, but it is unlikely that clinching evidence of the kinship will ever be uncovered.

Whoever first knew the region of the river were here over a great span of time. They were a primitive race, yet artful and cunning in their ways of survival, and few stone age people on the continent made more finely finished tools. That they used canoes, both birch and dugout, to transport themselves over the lakes and rivers of northern and central Maine, there is little doubt, for their tools were designed for boat making.

And the region of Moosehead Lake was their Mecca, as it was for later tribes. The outcrops of red oxide of iron that still exist near the Katahdin Iron Works was a bountiful source of this precious material. From hundreds of miles away they came by stream and through the forests to mine the mineral and carry it off to their encampments in skin bags.

And to the "Big Lake" they came for flint, jasper and chalcedony for the cutting edge of their tools and weapons. They would mine "blanks" of portable size and bear them off to their camps for final fashioning.

These early people made no pottery. Their food was cooked in birchbark vessels. A square piece of birchbark, properly folded and bound with split roots at the rim to a thin strip of bent wood, made a seamless, waterproof vessel that served reasonably well if filled with sufficient liquid and not hung too close to the fire.

So, for perhaps a thousand years, these mysterious aboriginal tribes roamed the woods and plied the streams of the North Woods, moving, hunting, fishing, in an unceasing quest for food. There was little time for anything else.

The second wave of migrants moved in from the west. Again, there are only artifacts as evidence of their cultural springs. Possibly they were outlying tribes of the mound builders whose culture was centered in Ohio. Yet, moving east, they built no mounds east of central New York. But with them they brought a new and revolutionary way of life.

From time out of mind primitive peoples had moved ceaselessly, seeking fish and game and eking out their diet with nature's bounty of roots and berries.

Then came a perception of the mystery of the seed. Fruiting plants matured into seed. Seeds could be planted, nurtured and harvested. Some of the seeds of the harvest could be saved and borne to a new bed of earth and planted.

The Indian legend that tells of this awakening is significant, for, as in all legends, this folk tale grew from a kernel of truth. "Long ago," the old men said, "a crow brought our eastern Indians a grain of corn in one ear and a bean in the other from the field of the great god, *Kautantouwit,* in the southwest from whence came all our corn and beans."

These new wanderers became agriculturists. And having learned to plant and harvest, wandering lost its necessity and their history was changed. Indian corn (maize) became the staff of life; agriculture brought a new stability and a more complete form of social organization.

For now there were established villages. They had learned the art of living together, the advantages of division of labor. There was time for play, a social life, and an esthetic and spiritual enrichment. True, some seasons the crops failed and often the game was scarce; but it was a better life.

It was with these people that the axe first appeared. Curiously, the precursors of these early Algonquians knew only the adze, a tool with its cutting edge set at right angles to the haft. They acquired the ceremony of smoking pipes and, in a limited way, the art of working copper.

The third migration from the west was an outgrowth of the second. Algonquians they were for a certainty, for these were the tribes the first white men found, and there was tribal memory to piece together the story of their past.

The Algonquian stock dominated the continent in this period. Its nation was spread across the continent, extending from the Blackfeet of the Rockies, north to Hudson Bay and south to the Carolinas, a sway broken only by the Sioux and the encroaching wedge of the Iroquois. It was this thrust of the Iroquois southward from the St. Lawrence and the Great Lakes and across New York that was to isolate these eastern Algonquians from their parent stock. And, cut off, they became a new people.

Later in historic time the Maine Indian was to be called Abnaki, or, in his own tongue, "Dawnlander," for his nearness to the rising sun. The tribal composition of the Maine Abnaki has never been clearly defined. To begin with there was a lack of precision in the Indian tongue and the words the red man spoke were mauled and hauled between the French and English languags. The Indians adopted words from both these languages and compounded the confusion by uttering them in strange and corrupt forms. Scholars and anthropologists seeking precision found ambiguity in a sea of contradiction.

It is probable that the historic Abnaki group was a loose confederacy made up largely of the old Malecite group that inhabited central and southern New Brunswick and the shore of Passamaquoddy Bay, with small tribal subdivisions in the region of the Kennebec and Penobscot rivers. These latter river tribes were affected early by the retreat of the more southerly tribes into Maine before the advancing tide of European settlement. As a result the Penobscot and Kennebec Indians lost their original tribal purity and became a part of the group to be bundled under the loose designation, Abnaki. The Passamaquoddy Indians, on the other hand, remained wholly Malecite and closely attached themselves to those tribes living along the St. John River in New Brunswick.

Francis Parkman, in his massive work on the French in Canada, made a brave attempt to throw some light on taxonomic confusion. "The name *Abenaki* is generic, and of very loose application. As employed by the best French writers at the end of the seventeenth century, it may be taken to include the tribes from the Kennebec eastward to the St. John. These again may be subdivided as follows: First, the Canibas (Kennibas), or tribes of the Kennebec and adjacent waters. These, with kindred tribes on the Saco, the Androscoggin, and the Sheepscot, have been held by some writers to be the Abenakis proper, though some of them, such as the Sokokis or Pequawkets or the Saco, spoke a dialect distinct from the rest. Secondly, the tribes of the Penobscots, called Tarratines by early New England writers, who sometimes, however, give this name a more extended application. Thirdly, the Malicites (Marechites) of the St. Croix and St. John. These, with the Penobscots or Tarratines, are the Etchemins of early French writers. All of these tribes speak dialects of Algonquin, so nearly related that they could understand each other with little difficulty."

Later, included in the Abnaki group were the St. Francis Indians, fragments of many tribes decimated by the white settlers, who fled northward to live under the protection of the French on the St. Francis River on the Maine-Canadian border.

The consolidation of the Abnakis into this concord was natural enough. There existed a linguistic bond: they could understand one another. They embraced the same gods and knew the same myths. But, primarily, it was necessity that dictated the union. Against common enemies there was no alternative but to make common cause. First, there was their ancient and mortal enemy to the west, the Iroquois, and the Abnakis' fear of these aggressive and arrogant tribes was deep and abiding.

Then, from across the ocean, came the strangers in ever increasing numbers.

THE STRANGERS   4

WITH THE white man's advent the written record began. The first confrontations between the white settlers and the aboriginal people of the world that was old but was soon to be called "new," were propitious, for they were characterized by a mutual curiosity and open wonder.

John Verrazano, the Florentine who explored the New England coast in 1524, expressed delight in his account. "There were amongst these people 2 kings, as of so goodly stature and shape as is impossible to declare. . . . Their apparel was on this manner: the elder had upon his body a harts skin, wrought artificialie with divers braunches like Damaske, his head was bare, with the hair tied up behind with divers knottes: about his neck he had a large chaine garnished with divers stones of sundrie colours. . . . This is the goodliest people, and of the fairest conditions, that wee have found in this our voyage. . . . The women are of like conformitie and beawtie, verie handsome and well favored, they are as well mannered and continente as any woman of good education."

All this was to change as the few strangers became hordes and the irresistible tide of English colonial expansion pushed in from the sea. The Protestant English brought with them their women, a race pride, and a yeoman hunger for land. And a sense of destiny.

The Abnakis allied themselves with the French. Frenchmen, or their half-breed sons, led the attacks on the English settlements. The Indian wars that were to spread across a hundred years, were sparks of European wars, but here in the new

wilderness the contention for empire had strong religious over-
tones. French priests, under orders, joined in the battles for
dominion and for souls.

The Abnaki alignment with the French was understandable.
The French expressed interest in their souls, while the English,
they suspected, were interested only in their furs and their
land. The French leaders, both temporal and spiritual,
shrewdly addressed the Indians as "their children," while the
English, even in their most conciliatory interludes, satisfied
themselves with the infinitely less binding term, "brothers."
The Abnakis were a deeply religious people. They had their
spiritual leaders, or powwows, and tribal life was governed by
them. They were amenable to the discipline and the mysticism
of French Catholicism whose teachings they readily compre-
hended.

To match the French alliance, the English exploited the
Mohawks' hatred of the French. The Mohawks, of the Iroquois
confederacy, were easily incited to fight the eastern Abnakis.
And this they did with characteristic ferocity. The north Maine
woods and the region of the river abide with unmarked battle-
grounds of these blood enemies.

Steel and European guns took the New England Indian
quickly out of the stone age. Never numerically strong (esti-
mates of the time put the Indian population of all New England at the beginning of the seventeenth century at no more
than 35,000, and perhaps 16,000 fighting braves), the Indian
race was foredoomed to crumble under pressures of a new and
marching civilization.

And what the scourge of war did not accomplish, pestilence
mopped up. The great smallpox epidemic, which reached its
peak in the winter of 1617, wiped out whole Indian villages.
In some cases there were no living left to bury the dead. The
strange fact that the English were, for the most part, untouched by the disease which they brought with them, has led
some scholars to suspect that this contagion was not smallpox

at all but a form of measles or chicken pox, a mild affliction
to the white man, most of whom were immunized against it
as children, but deadly to the vulnerable Indian.

The red man's stewardship of the region of Maine, of its
forests, lakes and streams, was as honorable as it was long.
They left it much as they had found it, for they were a forest
people and their castles were of nature. Of the Abnaki tribes,
it was the Penobscots, most probably, who called the region of
the Allagash their own at the time of the white man's coming.

The eastern tribes knew themselves by the river that was
their homeplace. The Penobscots were "The People of the
White Rocks," or, "The People Where the River Broadens."
They occupied not only the Penobscot but the Mattawamkeag
and Passadumkeag rivers as well. They spread westward to the
Katahdin country, and the watershed of the St. John and Allagash was their hunting ground.

Now the beam and the focus narrow down to The River.
Then, as now, it was a distant and sequestered place, a place
of mystery, myth and legend.

The woodland tribe of the Penobscots was special in a number of ways. Few other tribes in the loose Abnaki group had
their tribal integrity, social organization or moral discipline.
Physically, they were of medium height, erect in bearing, with
black brilliant eyes and ivory white teeth. They were quick
and alert. Their way of life had accustomed them to hardship
from childhood. They possessed marvelous powers of physical
endurance. To contend, to test themselves, was a deep part of
their religious nature.

Survivors write the histories. The white man, in his relationship with the Indian, has ever been prone to rationalize his
ruthlessness by dismissing the red man as a howling barbarian;
then, having exterminated him, sentimentalized his victim as a
Noble Savage. There was savagery and treachery on both
sides, savagery begot savagery. In the heat of the conflict, the
Indian killed, pillaged and burned. White bounty hunters, for

their part, were offered up to a hundred dollars for Indian scalps, of man, woman or child—and they collected with righteous satisfaction.

The Indians knew the English as "split tongues"—liars and double-dealers. The English invented the term "Indian giver" as a reflection upon the red man's honor. The truth, the reality, once lost, ever eludes recovery. It can only be said that the Indian was a man and therefore human; and, being close to nature, there was with his savagery an innocence, the like of which was never again to be seen upon this continent.

In a time and a place where distance was measured by a day's paddling, this region of the Penobscots was vast. And over this domain they moved in seasonal rhythms. The spring was spent up the river at the head of the tide to take alewives, shad and salmon on their spawning runs. It was time to plant corn and beans "when the oak leaves were the size of mouse ears." In early June, when the black flies and mosquitoes swarmed, the Indians escaped to the sea and the estuaries to take seal and porpoise for food and skins. They collected the eggs of nesting sea birds and dried quantities of clams and lobsters to be stored for the winter. With the first cool night in September, they moved back up the river to harvest their crops. Then, once again, the hunters returned to the woods to hunt deer, the moose and the caribou. In March, with the first intimations of spring, it was time to make catches of beaver and otter until the ice was out of their home river. Then, flashing paddles returned them to their home place, to the children, the squaws and the old men who waited. Twelve moons, a year, and it was time to begin again.

The "Lazy Indian" was a figment of the white man's prejudice, for merely to exist, to keep himself in food, clothing, shelter, weapon and fire, in a climate as harsh as this north country, called for unceasing application. It required long and patient labor to build a good birch canoe with stone tools. It was a prodigious task to fell a giant oak.

The tree was first girdled with a stone axe. Above the girdle

the trunk was daubed with clay or wet mud. Then a blazing
fire was built at the base of the tree. When the fire died the
char was chipped away. Again this process of fire and chipping
was repeated until the great tree tottered and fell.

Later, when a few skins could be bartered for the white
man's guns and steel knives, then a change did come for the
brave. His burden of work became lightened and male prerog-
atives proliferated, assuming social acceptance. Many tasks the
men had once joined in accomplishing with their spouses became "squaw's work."

The Penobscot, in common with his brothers of other
Abnaki tribes, was an obsessive gambler, frequently risking all
he owned on a cast of the dice. In the matter of physical
courage the Penobscot brave's constant testing of his manhood
betrays his fear of failing. The Abnaki's fear of the Mohawk
went far beyond a rational emotion: It was a naked terror.
The white settlers were inclined to consider their Indian
enemies cowardly. Courage is difficult to assess; but it
cannot be denied that in their attacks upon the white settlements, their courage was in direct proportion to their numbers.

The Indian considered pity a weakness and in his relationships with his enemies suppressed any manifestations of it as
unbecoming a man. Revenge was taken as a moral right. The
Old Testament "eye for an eye and tooth for a tooth" were
exacted with biblical fervor.

John Gyles, whose story of his Indian captivity was published in 1736, saw his Indian captors without sentimentality.
For the best part of a decade he lived with the Penobscot
tribesmen deep in the Maine woods in the region of the St.
John which is fed by the Allagash. The Penobscots had taken
him as a boy at Pemaquid and had killed his father and tortured his brother to death.

Wrote Gyles, ". . . when any great number of Indians met, or
when any captive deserters are retaken, they have a dance and
torture the unhappy people who have fallen into their hands.
An unfortunate brother, who had been taken captive with me,

after about three years of captivity, deserted with another Englishman . . . and [they] were retaken at New Harbor . . . they were both tortured at the stake by fire, for some time; then their noses and ears were cut off, and they made to eat them. After this they were burned to death at the stake."

Of his own personal experience just after his capture, Gyles wrote, "I was whirled in among the circle of Indians, and we prisoners looked upon each other with sorrowful countenance. Presently one was seized by each hand and foot, by four Indians, who, swinging him up, let his back fall upon the ground with full force. This they repeated until they had danced, as they call it, round the whole wigwam, which was some thirty or forty feet in length. But when they torture a boy they take him up between two. This is one of their customs of torturing captives. Another is to take up a person by the middle, with his head downward, and jolt him until one would think his bowels would shake out of his mouth. Sometimes they will take up a captive by the hair of his head, and stooping him forward, strike him on the back and shoulder, till the blood gushes out of his mouth and nose. Sometimes an old shriveled squaw will take up a shovel of hot embers and throw them into a captive's bosom. If he cry out the Indians will laugh and say, 'What a brave action our old grandmother has done.'"

That the English settlers were themselves a tough breed of cats is amply revealed in Gyles's account of the aftermath of an Indian hunting trip. A mere lad at the time, his matter-of-fact relation suggests he possessed courage and fortitude of the highest order.

One winter, as we were moving from place to place, our hunters killed some moose. One lying some miles from our wigwams, a young Indian and myself were ordered to fetch part of it. We set out in the morning, when the weather was promising, but it proved a very cold, cloudy day. It was late in the evening before we arrived at the place where the moose lay, so that we had no time to provide materials for fire or shelter. At the same time came on a storm of snow, very thick, which continued until the next morning. We made a small fire with what little rubbish we could find around us. The fire, with the warmth of our bodies melted the snow upon us as fast as it fell, and so our clothes were filled with water. However, early in the morning we took our loads of moose flesh, and set out on our return to our wigwams. We had not gone far before my moose-skin coat (which was the only garment I had on my back, and the hair chiefly worn off), was frozen stiff around my knees, like a hoop, as were my snow-shoes and snow-clouts to my feet. Thus I marched the whole day without fire or food. At first I was in great pain, then my flesh became numb, and at times I felt extremely sick, and thought I could not travel one foot further, but I wonderfully revived again.

After long traveling I felt very drowsy, and had thoughts of sitting down, which had I done, without doubt I had fallen on my last sleep. My Indian companion, being better clothed than me had left me long before. Again my spirits revived as much as if I had received the richest cordial. Some hours after sunset I reached the wigwam, and crawling in with my snow-shoes on, the Indians cried out, 'The captive is frozen to death'. They took off my packs, and the place where they lay against my back was the only one that was not frozen. They cut off my snow-shoes and stripped off the clouts from my feet which were as void of feeling as any frozen flesh could be. I had not sat long by the fire before the blood began to circulate, and my feet to my ankles turned black, and swelled with bloody blisters, and were inexpressibly painful. The Indians said one to another 'His feet will rot and he will die'. Yet I slept well at night. Soon after, the skin came off my feet from my ankles, whole, like a shoe, leaving my toes naked without a nail, and the ends of my great toe bones bare, which, in a little time turned black, so that I was obliged to cut the first joint off with my knife. The Indians gave me rags to bind up my feet, and advised me to apply fir balsam, but withal added that they believed it was not worth while to use [such] means, for I should certainly die. But, by the use of my elbows and a stick in each hand, I shoved myself along as I sat upon the

ground over the snow from one tree to another, till I got
some balsam. This I burned in a clam-shell till it was of a
consistence like salve, which I applied to my feet and
ankles, and, by the divine blessing, within a week I could go
about upon my heels with my staff.

The estimable young Gyles had more to say about the
Abnakis' folkways and their apparent need to work themselves
up emotionally to war pitch.

When the Indians determine on war . . . they kill a number
of their dogs, burn off the hair, and cut them to pieces,
leaving only the dog's head whole. Then the dog's head that
is left whole, is scorched till the nose and lips have shrunk
from the teeth, leaving them bare and grinning. This done,
they fasten it on a stick, and the Indian, who is proposed to
be chief in the expedition, takes the head into his hand and
sings a warlike song, in which he mentions the town they
design to attack, and the principal man in it, threatening
that in a few days he will carry this man's head and scalp in
his hand in the same manner. When the chief has finished
his singing, he so places the dog's head at him who he
supposes will go his second, who, if he accepts, takes the
head in his hand and sings but if he refuses to go he turns
the teeth to another; thus from one to another till they have
enlisted their company.

The Indians imagine that dog's flesh makes them bold. I
have seen an Indian split a dog's head with a hatchet, take
out the brains hot, and eat them raw with the blood running
down his jaws.

Although there is little evidence that the Abnakis resorted to
cannibalism except *in extremis,* the Mohawks, on the other
hand, had no compunction whatever in this regard, stating
that because of the salt in the white man's diet his flesh had a
delicate saline taste. Parkman offers an account of a wilderness
skirmish between an English force, commanded by Peter

Schuyler, and a band of priest-led mission Indians, which included some Maine Abnakis, a grisly notation which tends to
explain why the Abnakis considered the Mohawks fearsome
barbarians.

Three times the French renewed the attack in vain; then
gave over the attempt, and lay behind their barricade of
trees. So also did their opponents. The morning was dark
and stormy, and the driving snow that filled the air made
the position doubly dreary. The English were starving.
Their slender stock of provisions had been consumed or
shared with the Indians, who on their part did not want
food, having resources unknown to their white friends. A
group of them squatted about a fire invited Schuyler to
share their broth; but his appetite was spoiled when he saw
a human hand ladled out of the kettle. His hosts were
breakfasting on a dead Frenchman.

Strangely, there are few indications of sexual excesses among
the Eastern tribes, nor reliable documentation of sexual attack
upon their white captives. The Abnaki was naturally modest
and continence was regarded as a cardinal virtue. Gyles observed, "If a young pair have a child within a year and nine
months, they are thought to be forward and libidinous persons."

Mrs. Suzanna Johnson, who was taken by the St. Francis
Indians in New Hampshire in 1754 and marched across the
wilderness to their village, related that she discovered herself
naked when the marauders broke into her cabin. A brave,
having plundered three gowns, quickly gave her one of them
to put on.

Of her long and arduous march though the wilderness with
her children, husband and fellow captives, Mrs. Johnson,
whose childbirth was imminent, furthers the image of the
Abnakis' respect for womanhood.

In the morning we were roused before sunrise: the Indians struck up a fire, hung on their stolen kettle, and made

us some water gruel for breakfast. After a few sips of this
meagre fare I was again put on the horse, with my husband
at my side to hold me on. . . . I was taken with the pangs of
childbirth. The Indians signified to us that we must go on to
a brook. When we got there they showed some humanity by
making a booth for me. My children were crying at a distance, where they were held by their masters, and only my
husband and sister to attend me. The Indians kept aloof the
whole time. About ten o'clock a daughter was born. They
then brought me some articles of clothing for the child
which they had taken from the house.

The Indians had a simple method of establishing proprietary
rights to their captives. A brave had merely to be the first to
touch a white settler at the time of attack and the victim was
his to kill, keep or sell to the French, who were offering twenty
crowns for prisoners. The fact that the bounty on scalps was
only ten crowns explains why some settlers were spared to tell
the tale. The French motive was not one of humanity; it was
simply that when the Indians presented scalps for bounty there
were grave doubts in the minds of the French if they were
indeed all from the heads of their English enemies. The scalp
of the Frenchman was indistinguishable from the scalp of an
Englishman and French scalps could be come by a good deal
easier.

Mrs. Johnson related that her Indian master was quite delighted with the new baby. She wrote, "He clapped his hands
with joy, crying, 'two monies for me! Two monies for me!'"

However it was the whole company of Indians that set
about making a stretcher on which the new mother might be
carried and another booth to serve as a private bedroom for
the remainder of the journey. "They brought me a needle and
two pins, and some bark to tie the child's clothes, which they
gave my sister, and a large wooden spoon to feed it with."

By the fifth day of the journey the food was gone. Hunters
were dispatched, but returned without game. Mrs. Johnson
continues her account, "As we had in the morning consumed

our last morsel of our meal, everyone now began to be seriously alarmed; and hunger, with all its horrors, looked us earnestly in the face. Before dark we halted: and the Indians by help of their punk, which they carried in horns, made a fire. They soon adopted a plan to relieve their hunger. The horse was shot, and his flesh was in a few moments broiling on embers. . . . To use the word politeness of this repast, may be thought a burlesque; yet their offering the prisoners the best parts of the horse certainly bordered on civility."

It happened long ago in this immense wilderness through which the river flows—this and an endless skein of human happenings, unrecalled and unrecorded.

THE PEOPLE OF THE WHITE ROCKS 5

THE PENOBSCOTS maintained a firm social structure: there was law and there was order. There was a war chief and a civil chief as well. The grand council consisted of these two chiefs and a leader chosen by each family. Unlike many of the most southerly tribes where descent was reckoned through the female line, the Penobscot titles were handed down from father to son.

The basic unit of tribal organization was the family, a loose gens composed of persons related by blood and owning hunting and fishing grounds marked by traditional bounds. Each family was known by its totemic emblem, the origin of which went back to a story that became a legend. Family hunting grounds were well defined geographically by lakes or rivers and the rights were passed down to the active hunters in the family—sons, nephews, sons-in-law—and such possession was precious.

But these rights could never lie fallow. They were held by "naked possession," usufruct tenure; which is to say, there was no title conveyed or privilege bestowed beyond continued usage. If the hunting territory was not utilized, the title to it lapsed to be taken up by others.

So long as a hunting territory was exploited the right to it was inalienable and strictly respected. It was customary for a cruising party first to ask permission before crossing the district of another family.

"Posted Land" of our present culture has an honorable lineage. In the Allagash wilderness there were signs at every crossing and carry, fixed with the totemic mark of the owner family.

29

The region was crisscrossed with marked trails, making it unlikely that even the most inept hunter could get lost.

Out of this consciousness of property rights grew responsibility. The Penobscots were profoundly aware of their past and
correlatively had faith in and a vision of the future. The tribesmen husbanded their resources. Conservation was a basic tenet
of their philosophy of survival. It was their prudent way to
hunt but one quarter of the family preserve each season, leaving the remainder to increase. And in the utilized section seed
was left to perpetuate the precious stock of beaver, moose,
deer and caribou.

The first English settler was more farmer than woodsman.
He took the Indian furs in trade for knives, guns and fabrics.
Later, when a new breed of wilderness men evolved, the white
trappers went deep into the woods, matching the Indian's
knowledge of woods lore. They trespassed on the Indian
trapping grounds and took what they could without much regard for the future. This was the beginning of an anger that
was destined never to be cooled.

The Penobscot was a lover of the expressions of nature
about him. And, as with all lovers of nature, there was wonder
and a sense of awe, and a nonseeking of answers to the unan-
swerables that is religion. There was fear, too. As is true of all
preliterate peoples, the Indian believed that supernatural
powers were constantly threatening him, that the world was
filled with forces he could not see. Many were evil, vengeful
and capricious. His tribal powwows, part priest, part healer,
had taught him to fear the wrath of his gods and to appease
them.

The Abnaki believed in one great spirit; but he was basically
polytheistic. "Manitou" was little more than a symbol of perva-
sive mystery. His gods were demigods, human, feckless. The
chief god was *Glooskap* (variously, *Glusgahbeh, Kuloskap*),
the first created man. The word had an Indian meaning close
to "liar," a designation more indulgent than critical. *Glooskap*

Mt. Katahdin

had promised to return to earth and had never kept his promise.

Glooskap's messenger was the loon. He had caused the loon to call like a dog and when the loon cried at night on a lonely lake he was calling with a message for his master.

Everything in nature and every manifestation of it had a spirit form. The thunder spirits were two brothers with cheeks and brows of stone who dwelt high in the crags of Katahdin. There, too, on Katahdin, lived the dread Pamola whose thirst for Indian blood was never sated, and not even the bravest of the brave dared venture near this lofty precinct.

The Penobscot hunters who traveled west from their home place into the Allagash region were ever aware of the brooding presence of this mountain. Its sway over the dominion of the river was complete and unassailable. Gyles in his account of his Indian captivity, relates a legend of the mountain, *Teddon,*(2) and speaks of the awe in which the peak was held by the Red Man.

There is an old story told among the Indians of a family who had a daughter that was accounted a finished beauty. . . . She was so formed by nature and polished by art, that they could not find her a suitable consort. At length, while this family were once residing upon the head of the Penobscot river, under the white hills called *Teddon,* this fine creature was missing, and her parents could learn no tidings of her. After much time and pains spent, and tears showered in quest of her, they saw her diverting herself with a beautiful youth, whose hair, like her own, flowed down below the waist . . . ; but they vanished on their approach. This beautiful person, whom they imagined to be one of those kind spirits who inhabit the *Teddon,* they looked upon as their son-in-law; and according to their custom, they called upon him for moose, bear, or whatever creature they desired, and if they did but go to the waterside and signify their desire, the animal would come swimming to them! I have heard an Indian say that he lived by the river at the foot of the *Teddon,* the top of which he could see through a hole of his wigwam left for the smoke to pass out. He was tempted to travel it, and accordingly set out on a summer morning, and labored hard in ascending the hill, all day, and the top seemed as distant from the place he lodged at night as from his wigwam where he began his journey. He now concluded the spirits were there, and never dared to make a second attempt.

I have been credibly informed that several others have failed in like attempts. Once three young men climbed towards its summit three days and a half, at the end of which time they became strangely disordered with delirium . . . and when their imagination was clear, and they could recollect where they were, found themselves returned one day's journey. How they came to be thus transported they could not conjecture, unless the genii of the place had conveyed them.

The institution of marriage held a high position in the life of the Abnaki. Polygamy was rare and practiced only by an occasional high chief. Physical attraction doubtless played a part in the initial choice, but parental agreement, which was decisive, was based on more material consideration.

The parents of a marriageable daughter sought for her husband a brave who was a good hunter. His character was considered, but equally important was the extent of his personal estate. If he possessed a gun, a canoe, a spear and hatchet, crooked knife, pipe and knot bowl for tossing dice, he was considered a good catch and in an advantageous bargaining position. The parents of the marriageable son sought an educated bride for their son: that is to say, she should be versed in the arts of making *monoodah* (Indian bags), birch dishes, shoes, wampum belts, and if she could cook and sew birch canoes, so much the better.

Although solemnly ritualistic, the courtship and marriage were essentially simple. The young brave having set his eye on a nubile young maiden would seek a private opportunity to test her feeling in the matter. This was accomplished by toss-

ing at her feet a chip of wood or a pebble. Should the girl
ignore the offering, the affair was concluded. If, however, she
should pick up the offering, this was the signal that she would
accept his attentions.

The ensuing official courtship became somewhat more elaborate. The young brave would appoint a go-between, an uncle
or respected elder. Bearing a few gifts, the emissary would
proceed to the habitation of the girl's parents and, presenting
the gifts, speak the brave's petition, and then retire to permit
time for consideration of the proposal.

The emissary would return after a reasonable lapse of time
to hear the verdict. If the answer was "no," then the matter
was forgotten; there was no higher court of appeal. If the
answer was favorable, then immediate plans were arranged for
the two families to meet and discuss the date for the wedding
dance, which was, until later when the Jesuits insisted on the
additional solemnization of Christian service, the final and
binding ceremony.

In the meantime the two principals were denied any associa-
tion with one another. The wedding dance, to which the whole
village was invited, was a festive occasion that would begin
with feasting and go on far into the night. Then, once again,
the pair, now officially wed, were separated, going to their
respective homes. And for at least a week strict watch was kept
upon the groom to prevent any clandestine meetings with his
bride.

Then at the end of this trial period of continence came the
ceremony known as "the carrying of the bed." The groom,
accompanied by his friends, bore his bedding to the home of
the bride. Together, and alone for the first time, they were left
to themselves. The wedding was over, the marriage begun.

But the trials, the testings, were not over. In the ancient
tradition of the Penobscot tribe it was the rule that the brave,
after a few brief weeks with his new bride, set out alone into
the wilderness to hunt and trap, and prove his manhood. This
lonely odyssey consumed a year or more and took him far into

unknown places. He was expected to bring back a bounty of pelts, thereby proving his responsibility as well as his fortitude and continence. Should he return with a girdle laden with Mohawk scalps, his standing was further elevated in the eyes of his tribe and young wife.

He could take not more than his frail birch could carry: his weapons, his crooked knife—the tool of a hundred uses—blanket, snowshoes, fish spear, a few awls and needles of bone, his precious fire-making kit, together with tinder held in a skin bag. The ordeal was dictated by a thousand years of tradition. Hardships were to be endured, cunning, self-reliance and courage to be honed. He would leave as a boy and return as a man.

It is logical to accept that it was one such Ulysses of the Penobscot tribe who first explored the wilderness fastness of the Allagash. There was a first and then there were others who set out west, taking the rivers they knew by name, making the carries marked by their precursors, moving on across a necklace of lakes until each in turn came to a new frontier, a place unknown and unmarked.

In the Penobscot legends it was a family whose totem was the raven that first claimed the Allagash as its hunting grounds, and it was the greatest territory of all the families of the tribe, extending from Katahdin north to the St. John and east to the Little Madawaska.

It was the river that gave this place its name. There were few things in life or nature more important to the Indian than a river. It was his orientation, his personal identification. The sea was always there, impressive and eternal. The mountains stood fixed against the sky, awesome and constant. But the river flowed, beckoned, and along its curling course it was never the same. It was a friend, for it went from here to there and carried a burden; it was a challenge, for it possessed a mind and will of its own; angry, placid, amenable or fractious in turn, it could never be taken for granted. It would reflect the great trees at one point in its journey, and, at the next, go brawling into a gorge in a froth of spume.

Without the river there were only the trees. The river that flowed through this wilderness made it a place and gave it its history.

PART TWO

THE CURTAIN RISES 6

To the first who came to hew out settlements at the fringe of the Maine wilderness the trees were daunting. The forest was black, black as death, black as sin. Those who journeyed first from the coast to be swallowed up by the trees were in the eyes of their home-loving brothers no better than savages. Bearded, Indian garbed, they followed the ancient tribal trails seeking furs. They came upon the bright string of lakes and streams that is called the Allagash.

They found unending forest. They found the wilderness of the North Country much as it had been for those uncounted ages; wild, disordered, unkempt.

The savage and ceaseless struggle for natural survival had been going on across those same ages of unrecorded time. Young seedlings sprang from the black mold of decay, crowding, choking, killing, persisting by their very abundance. The plan within the anarchy was that a few should survive and reach for the sun.

Victory was hard bought and against fantastic odds. And there was no immortality, for all that. Storm and wind and lightning took its toll upon the giants. And when the giants fell, there were no human ears to hear. When lightning sundered a lofty tree, there were no eyes to see the fire that spread havoc until the rains came to still the terror.

Far from the Allagash fastness, a struggle of a human sort was shaping the future of the Maine wilderness. Along the ragged coast and up the big rivers those few meager settlements—clearings gnawed out in the forest—were tentative footholds. From the vantage of the slowly advancing settle-

ments on the River Piscataquis, this Allagash wilderness lay to
the north. The French had penetrated along the River St.
Lawrence; from this life line of French colonial power, the
Allagash lay to the south.

The French and the English held stubbornly to their separate points of view on all fundamental matters. Neither had
more than fragmentary knowledge of this no man's land of
trees, yet each wanted it simply because it was there. Unex-
plored, unmapped and, as are all places on the dark side of
knowledge, it was a region of dread. No one truly wanted it, of
course; but to relinquish claim upon it was unthinkable to
kings and commoners alike.

There it was, a blank area on the map. A vacancy on a map
was an anomaly, an abhorrence. More realistically, it was a
bastion between two contending powers. There were the trees,
and the beginning and the end of the long struggle for domi-
nation of the New World was a matter of trees few white men
had ever seen.

The rival colonies were governed by widely divergent laws
of growth. The English expanded by slow extension on a broad
front, rooting firmly as they spread. The French, like wind-
borne seeds, spread themselves out over the vast wilderness,
establishing tenuous and isolated footholds. It was the nature
of French colonization to seize strategic points and attempt to
hold them by bayonet, forming no agricultural base upon
which to consolidate. Instead, their efforts were directed toward establishing Indian trade and to hold their commerce by
conversation and conversion. Muskets, rosaries and beaver
skins were the bonds of their dominion.

The French were not essentially an emigrating people; or,
more accurately, any such tendency was blocked by royal fiat.
From the moment the Edict of Nantes was revoked, hundreds
of thousands of the persecuted Huguenots looked to the New
World as a haven of freedom: they were denied even a refuge
in a wilderness.

British America, on the other hand, was from the outset an

asylum for the oppressed. Trained in adversity and possessing the essential qualities of self-government, they came to find a new life rather than to transplant the old to virgin soil. Louis XIV, for his part, was determined that New France be Bourbon-ordained and bound inseparably to the Papacy.

For the French a mighty opportunity was lost. For the English the door was opened wide. It was soon clear to those who crossed the sea that not even kings could make an old world of the new. When General Wolfe took Quebec in 1763, the French ambition for supremacy fell with it. A few years later France surrendered her possessions in the north and the Maritimes.

On paper, at least, the English Crown held undivided sway over the wildland of Eastern North America. The decimated, war-weary Abnakis made a grudging and uneasy peace. In an effort to consolidate their mastery, the English built a few forts at strategic points to command the rivers which were the sole means of communication and expansion into dark regions of the interior.

The region of the Allagash remained Indian country. The treaties had not dissolved tribal bitterness. Only a few years earlier, Indian scalps had brought handsome bounties, the white man's forked tongue had cheated them, his rum had debased their manhood. The Maine Indian was not an easy forgetter.

To the English colonists the victories at Quebec and Louisburg were a spur to expansion. So great was the uplift of their hearts after the signing of the treaty that they were eager and ready to push out into the wilderness and conquer the whole great span of forestland from the coast to Quebec by peaceful penetration. There was talk of a great road through the wilderness, a four-hundred-mile artery that would knife through regions where no Englishmen but lonely captives, fur hunters and solitary scouts had passed.

It was this expansionist fever that prompted Francis Bernard, His Majesty's Provincial Governor of Massachusetts, to

dispatch a surveyor, Joseph Chadwick, to map out this territory for the first time. True, there had been a few crude attempts to map the region which antedate Chadwick's 1764
survey. The great-scale map of Franquelin-DeMeulles appeared as early as 1686; the Bellin map in 1744, and the English army engineer Colonel James Montrésor had rendered a
credible map of the southwest section of Maine wilderness in
1761. (It was the Montrésor map which fell into the hands of
Benedict Arnold and prompted his ill-fated wilderness march
to Quebec during the American Revolution.)

Montrésor started his trek from Quebec. Proceeding up the
Chaudière to the fork of the Rivière-du-Loup, he crossed to
the West Branch Penobscot, descended it to Northwest Carry,
where he went down Moosehead Lake to the Kennebec and on
down that river to Fort Halifax (Waterville).

Chadwick took the course in reverse. He went up the main
Penobscot to the Piscataquis branch, up that river by the so-
called "Piscataquis-ahwagan" or Indian route to Moosehead
Lake; up Moosehead Lake to Northwest Carry; thence up the
West Branch Penobscot and down the Rivière-du-Loup and
Chaudière to Quebec. Returning, he repeated the route as far
as Northwest Carry; but from that point on he followed the
West Branch Penobscot its whole length to the main Penob-
scot.

Chadwick stated in an annotation to his journal that he
made two maps, a small one on the scale twenty-five miles to
an inch, which is now in the Massachusetts Archives, and a
large one on the scale of two miles to an inch. Long assumed
to have been lost, this map turned up in the State Paper Office
in London in the early 1920s. In addition, a third and smaller
map was discovered in the Crown Collection which added
some confusion and cast some mystery upon the Chadwick
exploration. All three maps appeared to have been made on
the same survey; but the elegant calligraphy on this third map
suggested that it was executed by some person other than
Chadwick.

The mystery in no way diminished the fact that these crude maps, along with Chadwick's curious journal, constitute the first solid documentation of this wilderness region. It was an expedition that very nearly failed to take off.

The party started out early in May to avoid the plague of black flies and mosquitoes—of this hazard, at least, Chadwick had some preknowledge. Chadwick lists his complement of men which was led by John Preble, the celebrated Indian interpreter. The party was made up of four white men and eight Penobscot Indians, a fact that was to have a definite bearing on the story.

Understandably, the Penobscots were not happy about this expedition into their ancient hunting grounds, despite the fact that they had been given assurances by the Provincial Governor that the English would make no settlements beyond Treat's Fall on the Penobscot. Actually, Chadwick had been instructed to lay out a line at this spot, acquaint the settlers of the proscription, and present a copy of the sketch to the tribal leaders.

The Penobscots had every reason to be skeptical of such good intentions. When several stalwart young braves were hired on to shepherd the expedition, certain of the wiser elders of the tribe decided to join the party. The pay was good; but the elders had something more important in mind: They were determined to learn the nature of the expedition and Chadwick's intentions.

Chadwick's journal records the confrontation that came to pass almost immediately. Clearly, Chadwick was both a forceful and resourceful man. The ingenuity of his spelling suggests an ignorant man, but certainly "unschooled" is a better word. In part, a "Memorandem" read:

The Indeins are so jealous of their country being Exposed to this survay: as made it impracable for ous to preform the work with Acqurice. Altho they waer Ingaged in the service by the Large wages . . . three of the party Refused to go forward. And the disput between our party & the other Indeins was so great as to com to a fray. Which after two days dispute the Result was that I should make no Draughts of an Lands but only wrightings. And saying that when they were among English Men thay Obayed their Commands & best way you do obay Indeins Orders.

In short, Chadwick was told bluntly that the white men were outnumbered and that the Indians were giving the orders. And most particularly, the Indians were going to see to it that Chadwick made no map, although Chadwick did gain permission to take notes.

It appears that Chadwick, although irritated by the delay and restrictions placed upon him, was not without sympathy for the tribal position. He noted:

> That there hunting Grounds & Streames were all paseled out to certen famelys, time out of mind. That it was there Rule to hunt every third year & kill ⅔ of the Beviers Leving the other third part to breed and that their Beviers ware as much their stock for a Leving as Englishmens Cattel was his liveing. That sence the late War English hunters kill all the Bevier thay find on said Streames. Which had not only Empoveished many Indine famelys but Destroyed the bred of Bevier &c.

Precious above all to the Penobscots was the region of the Allagash. Particularly stubborn in his restriction of Chadwick was an Indian leader Chadwick called Joseph Aspegueunt who had been described earlier by the commander at Fort Pownal as "sullen and snappish." The chief resisted all efforts on the part of the explorer to penetrate deep into the region of the river. Nonetheless Chadwick did manage to wangle enough information to enable him to include the area on one of his maps. In the Massachusetts Archives map this ancient Indian route to the St. John was indicated with reasonable accuracy. A series of four S's placed Umbazookskus, Mud Pond, Eagle and Churchill lakes, and a crude, curved line showed the general sweep of the St. John River. There was a note in his journal stating that this route was said to be the "most navigable to the sea."

Of special historical interest is Chadwick's description of Chesuncook Lake, not only because his was the earliest description, but also because the lake he saw is no more.(3)

Gesoncook Lake [was] Very shole water & a mud bottom. In most parts of this Lake our conos could not pass within a hundred rods of the Shore by which we had not a very good View of the Shore & Land . . . but the ground appears to be ded leval. Large tracts of Grass Land and at sum distance backwards riseing with esey asent Grows a thick Growth of young Trees.

Chadwick's account of his view of Katahdin—which he called Satinhungemoss—was remarkably vivid despite his strange spelling and awkward syntax.

The Indines say that this Hill is the highest in the Country. That they can ascent so high as any Greens Grow & no higher. That One Indine attempted to go higher but never returned. The hight of vegitation is as a Horizontal Line about Halfe the perpendiciler hight on the Hill & intersects the tops of Sundry other mountines. The hight of this Hill was very apperent to ous as we had a sight of it at Sundre places Easterly [and] Westerly at 60 or 70 Miles Distence. It is curious to see . . . Elevated above a rude mass of Rocke large Mountins . . . So Lofty a Pyramid.

It seems incredible that Chadwick achieved even marginal "acqurice" considering his primitive methods of surveying. His wary Indian guides must have been somewhat perplexed by the modus operandi. Wrote Chadwick:

The Commete did not order a measure by chain. but to be preformed in the most expeditious methard. Which was preformed Computing Courses & Distances as the usal methard in plain Sailing . . . as we passed in Birch Conoes: The distence is found . . . from a fishing Rod Suspend a fine Silk cord of eight feet & 3 inches in lenght to a Smal pece of brass Latten of the bigness of a 6 pence being properly ballenced shews the noumber of Rods Run in one menut &c but in Rapid water and land by Estamation . . .

The expedition was gone six weeks. Eight Indians and four white men probably called for four canoes which left little space for gear and food. The white contingent was made up of good woodsmen—or at least durable and seasoned men—for hardship or discomforts they may have endured were not a part of Chadwick's record.

Joseph Chadwick was not an adventurer in any sense of the word. Nor were the trappers, hunters, timber explorers who penetrated the Allagash region before him. Alike, they were professionals with a job to do or a living to wrest from the wilds. There was a difference, of course: the hunters and trappers were as disinclined as the Indians to share their knowledge with the world. They wanted neither company nor competition. Theirs was a loner's life and the less that was known about the wild interior, the better they liked it. Temperamentally and practically, loneliness was a banner and secrets a stock in trade.

Moses Greenleaf was a man obsessed with another sort of dream. For him a wilderness was a place to fill up with people. The deep woods were a resource to be utilized, the lakes and rivers meant carrying trade and arteries of communication.

The biblical Moses led his people out of the wilderness. Moses Greenleaf's passion was to lead his people into it. He never quite succeeded. The obsession was to kill him in the end. But not before he had placed his mark upon his times and the Allagash as well.

DREAMER
AND MAP MAKER

I T S E E M E D that Moses Greenleaf would never amount to much. He was born in Newburyport, Massachusetts, in 1777, eldest of five children. His brother Simon became an illustrious professor of law at Harvard; Jonathan, a noted divine; Ebenezer, a bluewater sea captain at a time when Yankee sea captains were men of the world and first citizens of any town in which they chose to live.

When Moses was thirteen his father moved his family to a farm in New Gloucester in the District of Maine. As Moses grew to manhood, it became clear that he was not cut out to be a farmer. A smattering of education in the frontier schools qualified him to preside over a country store. He was not very good at that either. Moses was a good talker and he commanded respect, ideal talents for a young man in trade. The trouble was his talk was confined to what interested *him* and he had little business sense. He went bankrupt twice before he realized that keeping accounts and shoveling dried beans were getting him nowhere.

Moses Greenleaf was a frontier man with all the virtues and limitations, the tough resilience and the prejudices of the vanguard breed. His frustrations and restlessness kept him moving ever nearer to the raw and brawling brink of the Maine wild lands. At the age of twenty-seven he found himself in Bangor, already being referred to by optimists as the "Lumber Capital of the World."

Bangor, by Boston standards, was not much of a town in the dawning years of the nineteenth century, but, for a man with a mind to the future, it was where the action was. Sawmills were humming and the talk on the mud streets and in the groggeries was of ships and of pine that stood unaxed up the rivers to the west and the north.

No one in Bangor yet knew where the Yankee pine left off and the Canadian pine began, but that didn't matter, for, after all, the Canucks didn't either. It was there, sure enough, first come, first served and devil take the hindmost.

It was in Bangor that young Greenleaf, in 1805, met up with William Dodd, a Boston gentleman of means. The fever of land speculation, which was to reach a peak several decades later, was already beginning to stir. Mr. Dodd had made a small investment in the Eastern Lands, as they were termed, and under the usual conditions set down by the Commonwealth of Massachusetts that the land be settled with twenty families in four years and twenty more in eight.

Dodd had no intention whatever of renouncing his Boston comforts. What he sought was an agent, ideally one unspoiled by the delights of civilization who would not only move into the wilderness but induce others to follow his coattails. He could not have found a better man than Moses Greenleaf. Young Moses gratefully shed his mercantile affiliations and entered into a partnership agreement with the gentleman from Boston.

This marked the turning point in Greenleaf's life. From that moment forward his eyes were to the trees and never once did he turn to look back.

Greenleaf was a frontier man, but more specifically, a Maine frontiersman for whom special privilege was anathema and absentee ownership and authority insufferable. Since 1653 Puritan Massachusetts had held jurisdiction of Maine. Although this had been agreed to by "popular" vote, few in the outlying settlements had been given the opportunity to express their blunt opinions. The Maine settlers held no love for their Commonwealth neighbors. The Puritans returned the suspicion: they had long disapproved of the royalist colonies in Maine with their more liberal attitudes toward religious freedom, a fact that had strengthened the Commonwealth's determination to take over the royal grants after the Revolution.

This dependency upon Massachusetts was a constant irritation to the Maine settlers. The citizens of what became the District of Maine suffered the situation only because they needed the help of their Puritan cousins. The Indian wars had thinned the population and checked the region's growth; hardships and submarginal living had left them a half-wild race of men, hard-working, hard-drinking and semiliterate. Scandal, wenching and brawling was a way of life; and, to the despair of the guardian Commonwealth, churches were as scarce as schools.

Concerning the wilderness of trees, the settlers held an attitude of ambivalence. The big trees were enemies for they had to be got out of the way for farmland so desperately needed, and it didn't take a long memory to recall when the trees hid howling savages. Yet there was a sense that these big trees were their salvation: if there was ever to be any hard money, it was from these trees that it must come.

The demand for pine was already outstripping the supply. More and more trees were needed for the building of ships and for trade around the world. They were cutting the big pine up the navigable rivers, the Piscataquis, the Kennebec, and the Penobscot. In a matter of a few decades the accessible pine was ravished and the end in sight. Already, men of vision and a love of profits were looking to the north and west. They had heard tales of this wilderness from the Indians and white trappers. There to be taken were vast forests of mighty trees and the greatest and loftiest stands were hard by the lakes and rivers.

Little was known of this wilderness except that it was there and the big pine was there and enough of it to stir the minds of pine-obsessed men. They gathered that there were but two rivers down which pine could be driven to seaports. One was the Aroostook which flowed through a shallow valley to enter the St. John in Canada and go on to the Bay of Fundy. The other was the St. John which, somewhere in the western region of the district, flowed northward through unsurveyed lands, fed by the St. Francis and the Allagash, and thence eastward into Canada and on to the Atlantic. Rivers and only rivers could bring logs to market and money into the pocket.

Moses Greenleaf was soon caught up in this wilderness fever. But his dream was not of a bonanza of pine timber and lumber baronies: water power was for turning mills, and land was for freeholders to take up and improve—for churches, schools and social organization.

At the brink of his new adventure he wrote to his seafaring brother, Ebenezer, "However improbable it may appear to you . . . a society will in a few years be found north of the Piscataquis which will approach near to your own ideas of the useful & agreeable than any with which I am acquainted in any of the country towns of Maine. . . . And what difficulties are insuperable to those determined to conquer them. I am persuaded that when the subject is accurately & closely examined the 'obstacles' you mentioned will dissolve into thin air & the bugbear terms 'wilderness', 'savages' . . . be remanded to the place from whence they came . . ."

Moses Greenleaf was, indeed, a determined man. Much more than a mere dreamer, he was a man who implemented his vision with action. In the summer of 1810 he took his family into the wilds and began a settlement at Williamsburg, clearing land and building a farmhouse. But his mind continued to outrun his prodigious energy. He had to know what lay beyond the clearings.

Greenleaf discovered quickly that there was no reliable source of information on the Maine interior. Neither books nor dogged inquiries produced much more than folklore and conflicting hearsay.

Previous to 1800 there had been published four or five maps of the region that made some pretense of accuracy. Osgood Carleton had prepared a small map prior to 1795; but it was little more than a sketch. In 1795 he published a larger map under the direction of the General Court of Massachusetts that purported to be an accurate map of the entire district of Maine taken from "actual" surveys which were, Greenleaf soon discovered, neither actual nor accurate.

He had no better luck with D. F. Sotzmann's map published in 1798 and compiled by C. E. Bohn. In 1795 a small map was published bearing the inscription: The Province of Maine from the Best Authorities. The map bore no publisher's imprint, but it appeared to be from the same plate as the map in Carey's American Edition of *Guthrie's Geography*, compiled by Samuel Lewis and engraved by W. Barker.

Whoever were these "Best Authorities," Greenleaf was convinced that not one of them had ever set foot upon the wilds of Maine. It was even clearer to this unsinkable Maine pioneer that he could get nowhere in his plan to fill up the wilderness with people until he could present some facts and figures.

To make an actual survey was out of the question: he had no training either in drafting or surveying and he had no private means to support such an undertaking even had he had such qualifications. The governing authorities in Massachusetts were interested, quite naturally; but not interested enough to subsidize such a monumental effort.

There was never any hope that sales of his work would cover even the bare expenses. A labor of love it needs must be and, once committed to the task, he set about gathering all the available data: maps, plans of surveys, field notes of surveyors. Winnowing the good from the bad, the truth from the myths, he began the long and painstaking effort to bring some light into the darkness.

Early in his investigation he found that there had been no actual surveys ever made of the North Woods region of the Allagash. He attempted to build up a body of reliable information by correspondence and contact with hunters, trappers, timber cruisers and adventurers with personal knowledge of the region. For three years he applied himself to the task,

finding time somehow to stand at the forefront in the fight for
Maine's separation from Massachusetts, a matter that was stirring up some fervid controversy in those years just before
1820.

Some idea of how partisan he was in this matter of Maine
autonomy may be gathered from a letter written to a friend
during the heat of the debate. He wrote from Boston where he
was attending a hearing at the General Court: "Massachusetts
will be restored to correct principles! . . . The 'squatters' are
about to manage their affairs in their own way. A caucus was
held yesterday morning on the subject of separation. . . . The
Demos are decidedly in favor & many of the Federalists.
—Who knows amid the revolutions that are coming what may
await us. . . ?"

His consuming passion, however, was to chart the wild lands
of Maine and open them up to settlement. To this same friend
he wrote exhorting him with apostolic fervor to come north
and join him in his dream. "You may judge by appearances
whether our 'Siberia' may change to an *Utopia* & whether you
had better become one of the 'household of faith.'"

At this time the passionate partisan was making innumerable
personal forays into the wilds. Just how far into the lower
reaches of the Allagash this indomitable map maker penetrated on these treks is not clear. There is no doubt that he
explored the lakes of the river's headwaters for the observations he set down in the book that accompanied his first map
indicate a firsthand knowledge of the region. He used variations of the early Indian designations for Eagle and Chamberlain lakes, but the lakes and waterways were delineated with
reasonable accuracy and in correct relationships, and his geographical notes cannot be faulted.

From a pond at the source of the Allagash the river descends in some places rapid, but in general moderate, about
2½ miles to Lake Baameheenungamook which is about 18
miles long and from one to four miles wide. Leaving the

lake at about 10 miles from its inlet, the river descends with a rapid current 2 miles farther to the Lake Pongokwahem which is about 14 miles long and 2 to three miles broad. The river issues from the lake broad and deep, with a current hardly perceptible for about three miles to the Lake Wahlahgasquegamook. From this lake the river, considerably augmented, proceeds with a somewhat rapid current about 10 miles to a long narrow lake, or chain of lakes, called Umsaskis, 10 or 12 miles in length. From this it runs with a rather uniform gentle current to the falls; on its course expanding distances into two small lakes, called upper and lower Pataquongamis. At the falls the river is suddenly precipitated about 20 feet, below this are rapids for a short distance, in the course of which it descends from 10 to 15 feet more, and from this 12 miles to the mouth of the river, the current is in some places smooth and gentle, in others rapid . . . The whole length of the Allagash is variously estimated at 77—90 miles.

Greenleaf's map appeared in 1815 after five years of strenuous and unstinting efforts. And it was an astonishing performance, most particularly astonishing in view of his complete lack of professional training in surveying and drafting. The value of Greenleaf's map was immediately recognized. Massachusetts subscribed for one thousand copies at three dollars each, a matter of critical importance to the cartographer, for hard cash was urgently needed if he was to continue his work.

The book and map made their appearance at the time the separation question was reaching a heated climax and there is little doubt that the work presenting Maine's untapped resources weighed heavily in the balance and influenced the decision that made Maine a state in 1820.

Little noted at the time was Moses Greenleaf's passing mention of the need and practicality of a waterway communication between the Allagash and Bangor by way of the Penobscot. In fact, he laid out the route in minute detail, suggesting dams and locks which could make operative a water link to hook the undeveloped interior to the industrial towns on the main Penobscot. It was an audacious Yankee idea that was, two decades later, to stir up a heady brew.

By the time his final book, *A Survey of the State of Maine, In Reference to its Geographical Features, Statistics and Political Economy,* was issued in 1829, Moses Greenleaf had come to the end of his useful life. While the work was still in progress he had journeyed into the wilderness with a companion, William Cushing Hammatt. Fifty miles from civilization he was struck down by typhoid fever. Too weak to move, he insisted he could care for himself while his friend went for help. He lay alone in the deep woods in a delirium for a week before help arrived. He never fully recovered from the harrowing experience. Moses Greenleaf died in 1834 at the age of fifty-six. The dream that led to his early death was never realized. The wilderness he hoped to conquer was never to be conquered in the context of his vision.

Some decades later a French priest speaking of his people who moved into homestead in the St. Lawrence valley west of the Allagash said: "The Good Lord made this country for trees and we poor fools are trying to farm it."

The French priest was right. The region of the North Woods was made for trees. Moses Greenleaf had opened the door for another sort of penetration. The red-shirted, axe-wielding army of exploiters was on its way.

WHITE PINE AND THE NORTH WOODS 8

JOHN SPRINGER, in his memoirs of the early lumbering days in Maine, *Forest Life and Forest Trees,* referred to the pines of the North Woods as "whales of the sea." The figure was apt. The pine was the quarry in the awesome sea of spruce and, much like the whaling mariners peering out from the vantage of the masthead, the early timber cruisers climbed aloft to mark their prizes down.

The unending spruce forest was a wasteland that must be traversed and searched for the fortunes lying hidden in its vastness. In this dark sea of trees the white pine was ever the treasure.

Technically, the North Woods extend westward from the shores of the North Atlantic, across the snow belt of the Great Lakes, then northwestward to the Yukon. Dominated by spruce, this immensity of forestland constitutes the largest continuous conifer forest on earth.

The conifers are of ancient lineage. They emerged from the mists of the ages, relics of the swamp forest spore trees that preceded them. The tree ferns, the club moss of the Coal Age were their ancestors. North America may have cradled the conifer forests on the planet.

The evolution of the conifers represents one of the greatest triumphs of plant life on earth. The conditions that brought to fruition this highly successful tree type were the same as those that caused the downfall of the dinosaurs. The rise of mountain chains restricted the distribution of rain. Lakes evaporated, leaving immense areas of dry sand and rock. Changing patterns of prevailing winds refrigerated a region where a

benevolent climate had reigned. While the reptiles were losing
their battle for survival, the conifers responded to the pressures
of bitter weather. Environmental changes are the spurs of evolution. The conifer adapted to the marginal conditions, evolving roots, bark, wind-blown pollen, seeds and cones—the tools
it needed to prevail against unfertile soil and cold, drying
winds. Only by developing its needle leaves, resinous insula-
tion, and rigid form could the conifer resist the frigid drying
gales and long bitter winters.

The spruce is the mainstay of the North Woods. The spruce
—red, white and black—along with balsam fir, larch and
northern cedar constitute the sea of trees that make up the
forest cover of the northern forest. The pyramidal spruce cone
is the miniature image of its parent tree and the secret of its
success. Tough, durable, built to resist cold, it snugly nests two
naked seeds at the lower end of each hard, woody scale,
curved upward like a scoop to snare wind-blown pollen. There
are no soft parts to rot away, no flesh to tempt predators. In
this tightly clamped vault the seeds have one to two years to
ripen in darkness before the gluey resin dries and the seeds are
sprung. The spruce with its needle-cone equipment succeeds
by its very simplicity.

This dense, continuous conifer forest has been termed a
biological desert, and in many ways it is just that. Unlike the
deciduous forest, with its pantry of berries, tender shoots and
mast crop of nuts and acorns, the conifer woods offer little for
bird or beast. The great stag, standing in a glade in an evergreen forest, is an artist's myth. There is little for him there,
nor for any living creature. Early explorers were awed and
immensely disturbed by the ghostly silence through which they
would travel for mile upon mile, hearing nothing to relieve the
stillness except the rapping of the woodpecker or the scolding
of an occasional squirrel.

Yet there were others who responded to the very loneliness
and vastness, much as the sailor is drawn to the sea. In the

integrity and simplicity of the indomitable spruce they found its majesty.

Although it is the white spruce with its soft milk-white wood and sugar-coated needles that dominated the far northern landscape, it is the red spruce that most truly represents the Maine North Woods. The black spruce thrives in the lowlands and the cold, damp bogs. The fragrant balsam fir, the Christmas tree of all New England, and the tamarack (hakmatak to the woodsman) favor the more sunlit exposures, while the northern white cedar crowds the swamps.

Maine's northern conifer forest was a gift of the ice age. The ice withdrew to leave an inheritance of lakes and streams and dowered the region of the Allagash with its replenishing vitality. The rains and melting snows are stored in clear, deep lakes, delivering water when and where it is needed. This glowing health is reflected in the gleam of resin, the conifer's antiseptic coat of mail, which repels bacterial growth, fungi or decay, and keeps the hordes of preying insects at bay. Without its water supply the North Woods would be a sorry place, a true desert of wind-twisted, stunted trees. The Allagash and its waterways, far from being an adjunct to the Maine wilderness, are its godhead.

In this great sea of spruce, the first explorers had eyes for only the pine, Springer's "whales." The big pine was there in the region of the Allagash in numbers to stir the hearts of poets and the greed of lesser men.

The New England white pine belt of Colonial times struck east and north, roughly paralleling the coast, from New Hampshire to the lower Penobscot, with fingers extending up the major rivers. The pines stood intermediate between the deciduous forests and the North Woods, invading beyond its optimum range where conditions favored its growth. The big pines required sandy, well-drained soil and less extreme temperatures than their more hardy cousins, the spruce. The white pine leapfrogged up the waterways into the Allagash region, finding here and there favorable situations along the lakes and watercourses. It was said that early timber cruisers could, from a height, mark the course of a river by their presence.

Those first explorers found the stands of pine not only along the waterways but in the old burns as well. Fires, spawned by lightning strikes, made favorable situations by eating away the debris and pine-needle duff and exposing the mineral soil.

The great pines were vulnerable to man from the beginning for they towered above the sea of spruce forming a second story canopy of greenery. They stood in groves, conclaves of giants, to be descried from any high vantage. Like the whales they were much too large to hide from searching eyes.

John Springer noted that the early timber cruisers frequently chose a pine to ascend, first lodging a spruce against its trunk in order to reach its lower branches. Such a lookout would place an explorer at a height twice that of the surrounding forest, from which he could mark the clumps and veins of pine. "Such views," Springer wrote, "fill the bosom of the timber-hunters with *intense interest*. They are the object of his search, his treasure, his *El Dorado*, and they are held with peculiar and thrilling emotion."

Springer explained, in some detail, the methods used to survey pine timber in those early days. "The man in the tree-top points out the direction in which the pines are seen; or, if hid from view of those below by the surrounding foliage, he breaks a small limb, and throws it in the direction in which they appear, while a man at the base marks the direction indicated by the fallen limb by a compass which he holds in his hand."

The islands of pine were oases in that dark wilderness of spruce. The spruce forest was suffocating and forbidding to those first Europeans accustomed to parklike groves of oak. And except in the deep of winter when the trees crackled like rifle shots, the ambience was awesome silence.

The congeries of pine, underlaid with a carpet of needles and soft yielding earth, were a restful relief to the eye and spirit. The giants, some six feet through at the butt and reaching one hundred and fifty feet to the sky, had a somber grandeur. Mere men, walking under the green canopy down the uncluttered aisles in the cathedral hush, could only have been diminished by their awe. Here it was cool even in the heat of summer, for the high green ceiling gave off vast quantities of moisture and the thick carpet of humus stored like a sponge the cooling shade. Among the pine there were vistas, space and room for the mind to reach and legs to stretch, unhindered.

Hardwoods had their place in this primeval forest. Monarch beeches, maples, and yellow birch stood in open groves on the high, well-drained ridges, shielding a light growth of viburnum, hobblebush, moosewood or hazel in the dappled half-shade. And they were to stand for another century, inviolate, for hardwoods were inaccessible and unmerchantable in those first decades of man's invasion when one fabulous pine could fetch up to one thousand hard dollars at the boom.

Fires, ancient and recorded, left their scars upon this North Woods silva. The great Katahdin fire of 1795 consumed two hundred square miles of wilderness, denuding both banks of the West Branch Penobscot, reaching up into the headwater region of the Allagash.

The great pines that survived the ordeal by fire appeared all but immortal; but it took mere decades to cancel out a thousand years of growing once the axes began to flash. The virgin pine stands were venerable, of course, and while much was prime timber, age was already betraying its advance in thousands of heart-rotted stumps. Some few in those first days saw the cutting of the overmature trees as a timely harvest. Too many saw only the dollars and cents. For them any standing pine was a waste, when, as boards, there was nothing on earth to match it. The great pines made lofty masts without piecing and wide boards that were strong, yet easily worked: they were straight-grained, knot-free and sweet and white as milk.

Yet, not even the plunderer with dreams of money in the

bank was immune to aesthetic response and a moment of reverential pause before his axe struck deep. John Springer wrote poetically of the greatest pine he ever felled in his long years in the Maine woods of the early nineteenth century. The monarch measured 144 feet, 60 feet of which was limb free.

> The afternoon was beautiful; everything was calm. After chopping an hour or two, the mighty giant, the growth of centuries, which had withstood, and raised itself in peerless majesty above all around, began to tremble under the strokes of a mere insect, as I might appear in comparison with it. My heart palpitated as I occasionally raised my eyes to its pinnacle to catch the first indication of its fall. It came down at length with a crash that seemed to shake a hundred acres, while the loud echo rang through the forest, dying away among the distant hills. . . . It made five logs and loaded a six-ox team three times. The butt log was so large that the stream did not float it in the spring, and when the drive was taken down we were obliged to leave it behind, much to our regret and loss. At the boom that log would have been worth fifty dollars.

Several decades later, Thoreau was to make a bitter and telling commentary upon the pine lumberman's "trophy" mentality. "When a chopper would praise a pine, he will commonly tell you that the one he cut was so big that a yoke of oxen stood on its stump; as if that were what the pine had grown for, to become the footstool of oxen. . . . Why, my dear sir, the tree might have stood on its own stump, and a great deal more comfortably and firmly than a yoke of oxen can, if you had not cut it down."

The virgin pine came big, right enough, and what but a breed of unaweable and bragging men could have been gathered to tackle them with nothing but a puny axe? One pine cut at Telos Lake in 1842 measured seven feet at the butt, four feet from the ground. Commonly a giant scaled 6,000 feet board measure and many references are made to monsters

White Pine

which scaled up to 8,000 board feet.(4) All too many were so
large that the first log from the butt could not be hauled to
water or, once borne to a landing, was left to rot for want of
sufficient water to float it downriver to market.

Thoreau, in his Maine Woods Journal, contributed, with his
own special irony, a footnote on the matter.

One connected with lumbering operations at Bangor told
me that one of the largest pine belonging to his firm, cut the
previous winter, "scaled" in the woods four thousand five
hundred feet. . . . They cut a road three and a half miles
long for this tree alone. He thought the principal locality for
the white pine that came down the Penobscot River now
was the head of the East Branch and the Allagash, about
Webster Stream, and Eagle and Chamberlain Lakes. Much
timber has been stolen from the public lands (pray what
kind of forest warden is the Public itself?). I heard of one
man, who, having discovered some particularly fine trees
just within the boundaries of the public lands, and not dar-
ing to employ an accomplice, cut them down, tumbled them
into a stream, and so succeeded in getting off with them
without the least assistance. Surely, stealing pine-trees in
this way is not so mean as robbing hen-roosts.

Long after the great pine had gone down the rivers, Fannie
Hardy Eckstorm wrote, "It was wasted in every way, wasted in
cutting, wasted in driving, wasted in sawing, wasted in sorting.
. . . Most of all it was wasted because no one believed there
could ever be an end to it."

It was a time in new America when no one was in a mood to
consider the end of anything. The virgin land was a gift of
God and the Good Lord's largesse was limitless. Maine's logging pioneers had little time for poetry. The job was to cut
down the pine forest and drive it to market. When one pocket
of pine was cut and the drive was in, they would drink hearty
in town, break a few skulls in playful exuberance and set out in

the fall to cut another pocket. There was no end to the pine. They could chop away forever or so long as the rum lasted.

White pine is white pine; but not to the early loggers: there was a difference in white pine and one axe blow into the heartwood would tell them a story. When the chips came out in chunks, soft, dry, pumpkinlike, this was the "punkin pine," the virgin growth, a tree that had been growing slowly over the centuries. Belknap, an early writer on the lumbering scene, differentiated between the pumpkin pine and "sapling" pine. "The sapling pine," he wrote, "is not so firm, and is more sensibly affected by the weather."

John Springer also offered an opinion on this subject, expressing, one assumes, a consensus of the loggers of his day.

Of the white pine there are varieties, which by some are attributed to the particular characteristics of the various locations in which they grow. That variety called sapling pine, bull sapling &c usually grows on high, hard-wood land, or a mixture of evergreen and deciduous trees; particularly on the boundaries that mark damp, low forests and the lower borders of ridges. The pumpkin pine is generally found on flatland and in ravines; also on abrupt ridges, called horsebacks, where the forest is dense.

Springer goes on to say that the sapwood, or the first layer under the bark, was thicker on the sapling pine than on the pumpkin variety, and he attributes this difference to the rapidity with which the sapling pine grew. But, sapling or pumpkin, the big pines fell under the axes of the red-shirted invaders with no appreciable discrimination. "Squared" pines brought the standard price of forty dollars a ton for heart logs. The standard ton-weight "square" of pine was a sawn log forty feet long and one foot square.

Square timber was intended for export and was rafted via rivers to seaports, chiefly in Canada in the early logging days before the mills on the Penobscot began spewing forth pine boards and filling the river with mountains of sawdust. Square timber stowed economically in the holds of ships and the manpower required to handle it was dirt cheap and in over-supply.

It is interesting to note that the sawmill was developed in Colonial America and its utilization resisted in England for decades. In 1767, an English mob destroyed a sawmill, fearful that its proliferation would take the bread from the mouths of the poor.

In 1816, a mere one million board feet of pine timber was sawn in the Bangor area; but, by 1831, the figure had rocketed to thirty million. Six hundred feet a day was a big day's work for the early single saw. Better saws were coming. The gang saw, which arrived on the scene in 1850, could manage 40,000 board feet in a single working day and, by 1860, the rotary saw set a one-day's record of 132,917 board feet.

Allagash pine came last to the axe, for vast organization, capital, hard-nosed, rugged individualism and Yankee in-genuity were required to tackle that last wilderness fastness. Early land-agent records indicate that cutting was first autho-rized in the Allagash headwaters in 1835. By 1840 the two-bitted axes were ringing to a fare-thee-well. The limitless sup-ply of big pine was more apparent than real.

The great stands were assaulted and all that were spared were the twin-crotched trees—"schoolmarms" to the loggers—and those in which a testing axe betrayed a hollow heart. Only the huge stumps remained to commemorate the behemoths. These stumps remained sweet and sound for decades after-ward. The saying was that no man who cut a pine would live to see the stump rotted away. The great pines resisted to the very end.

Scattered across the region of the Allagash a few of these lordly old-growth pines remain. They can be seen from a great distance for they stand alone for the most part reaching high above the surrounding spruce forest. These overmature giants betray their years. Many are dying back from their crowns. Others are scarred or split asunder by lightning strikes, the price they pay for standing alone and reaching for the sky.

The great pine had their day and now their day is past. It took some thousands of years to grow them, a mere fifty years to cut them down.

THE RIVER IS HOME 9

A WILDERNESS river is a precious place. The early lumber baron who upon purchasing a tract of Allagash wilderness insisted that his rights to it in no whit differed from his private rights to his own living room seemed to forget that the wild land he had usurped had been the living room for an astonishing variety of life since the northern landscape recovered from havoc wrought by the retreating glacial ice.

Without water a wilderness is a desert. The Allagash, flowing north from its headwater lakes, carries the life blood of the wild lands through which it flows. In this fluvial world the dragonfly and skater bug, no less than the mink, the otter and muskrat, the moose and hunting cat, serve in the chain of life. Despite man's intrusive presence, the habitat has remained essentially pure. The desperate struggle to survive against awesome odds persists.

Unlike modern man, the aboriginal Indian was very much a part of this natural struggle. Depending as he did upon fish and game, he, like those other living things, lived eternally in the shadow and fear of hunger. And in common with those other living things, he seldom hunted far from the river. It was to the water that the moose, the bear and caribou came to forage. It was to water that the meat-seeking predators came to cut them down. Beyond the margins of the river the dark canopy of a mature conifer forest closed out the sun and nature's cupboards were all but bare.

The chain of life is a magic circle in which life has no meaning except in terms of death. The Allagash has ever been a

stern and competitive environment. Along the waterway in
summer and fall nature serves up a bountiful spread. It is the
long, harsh winters that impose a regimen of scarcity, dictate
the terms for survival and place a strict limit on populations.
The Allagash as a habitat is only as sustaining as its winter
range. The river, once the early snows come, can be a hungry
place.

The Indian, because this was his home, accepted the terms.
There were winters when even along the river game was
scarce and he was forced to fall back on his caches of dried
corn and beans. There were winters when both game and
crops failed him and neither magic nor appeal to his gods
brought salvation. The weak died before spring.

And winters there were when the predators themselves went
hungry and were forced to hunt day and night. John Springer
offered a vivid account of the early loggers' encounters with
wolf packs. The teller of the tale heard a distant howling
which reminded him of the screeching of forty pairs of old cart
wheels.

> Presently, there came dashing from the forest upon the
> ice, a short distance from me, a timid deer, closely pursued
> by a pack of hungry wolves. The order of the pursuit was in
> single file, until they came quite near their prey, when they
> suddenly branched off to the right and left, forming two
> lines; the foremost gradually closed in on the poor deer,
> until he was completely surrounded when, springing upon
> their victim, they instantly bore him to the ice, and in an
> incredibly short space of time devoured him, leaving the
> bones only. . . .

In this harsh environment there were many winters when
the prod of hunger overcame the wolf's fear of man and logging teamsters traveled ice-slicked haul roads in fear of their
lives. John Springer relates once such unnerving experience
with hunger-emboldened wolves.

They were of unusually large size, manifesting a most singular boldness, and even familiarity. . . . Sometimes one, and in another instance three, volunteered their attendance, accompanying the teamster a long distance on his way. They would even jump on the log and ride, and approach very near the oxen. One of them actually jumped on the sled, and down between the bars, while the sled was in motion.

Some of the teamsters were much alarmed, keeping close to the oxen, and driving as fast as possible. Others, more courageous, would run towards them and strike them with their goad-sticks; but the wolves sprang out of the way in an instant. . . . There was something so cool and impudent in their conduct that it was trying to the nerves.

The settlers and the lumbermen of the Allagash were not ones to have their nerves tried by a plague of wolves so long as their powder was dry. Poison of both the arsenic and molded variety decimated the hunting packs. The last Allagash wolf was brought in for bounty around the time of the Civil War.

The howl of hunting wolf packs was certainly unnerving in the depth of an Allagash winter. But this was a reasonable fear. The presence of a big cat was something else again. The Eastern mountain lion, the catamount of early legends, ranged the deep woods of Maine, favoring the lonely high country. In the hungry years the big cat, too, came down to the river to strike dread into the hearts of the Indian and settler alike.

The Indian had a deep unreasoning fear of the big cat. These great tawny felines were seldom encountered except in hard winters. Understandably, they appeared as harbingers of harsh times and symbols of evil. So shy were these big cats that not even John Springer, well acquainted with the North Woods of the early nineteenth century, was quite certain of how to classify the beast.

"There is an animal," wrote Springer, "in the deep recesses of our forests, evidently belonging to the feline race, which, on account of its ferocity, is significantly called 'Indian Devil'—in the Indian language, 'the Lunk Soos': a terror to the Indian, and the only animal in New England of which they stand in dread. You speak of the moose, the bear, and the wolf even, and the red man is ready for an encounter. But name the object of his dread, and he will significantly shake his head, while he exclaims, 'He all one debil!' "

Springer then proceeded to relate a hearsay account of one lumberman's confrontation with one of these Indian devils. The logger, identified only as Smith, was on the way through the woods to join his lumbering crew when he came face to face with the animal. He was unarmed, and, with no chance to retreat, prudently took to a small tree only to have the beast clamp its teeth on his heel before he could scramble out of its reach. Smith freed his badly mangled foot by dispensing with his shoe, and climbed to a more secure position in the tree. Not to be thwarted, the cat immediately sprang into a neighboring tree and leaped across ten feet of intervening space and fixed its fangs into the leg of the hapless logger.

Hanging suspended thus until the flesh, insufficient to sustain the weight, gave way, he dropped again to the ground, carrying a portion of the flesh in his mouth. Having greedily devoured this morsel, he bounded again up the opposite tree, and from thence upon Smith, in this manner renewing his attacks, and tearing way the flesh in mouthfuls from his legs. During the agonizing operation, Smith contrived to cut a limb from the tree, to which he managed to bind his jackknife, with which he could now assail his enemy at every leap. He succeeded thus in wounding him so badly that at length his attacks were discontinued, and he finally disappeared into the deep forest.

Let it be added that Smith escaped with his life and recovered from his frightful experience. This story was put down as a "true relation," and who is to question that something of the sort occurred in that bygone day? Springer admits that such desperate encounters with big cats were rare and, in his per-

Mountain Lion

sonal experience, he appears to have had but one view of the Eastern panther in all his many years in the Maine North Woods.

This is not to suggest that the panther was uncommon in the region of the Allagash in Colonial and post-Colonial times. More pertinent is the fact that there were few human eyes to see him and those few the big cat took particular pains to avoid. Panthers, historically, have taken a dim view of people, both as friends and items of diet. The big cat's prime virtue is his habit of minding his own business.

Actually, there is reason to believe that the Eastern panther (*felis concolor couguar*) was well entrenched in Maine in that early period. But the big cat's days were numbered once the white settler claimed the wild range as his own. The white man's fear of the cat was no less unreasoning than the Indian's. There was no vision to see that the big cat's predation upon the weak and maimed of other four-footed species kept these species strong and fit for survival and helped to maintain populations at levels the range could sustain. Man, the only wanton predator on earth, killed the big cats whenever and wherever they were found.

The panther ceased appearing in the lists of Maine fauna after 1891. Presumably, the Eastern mountain lion had joined the swelling roll of extinct species of the world. Or had he?

In the fall of 1947, a woods boss of an operation near Churchill Lake on the Allagash was walking a woods road when one of his loggers came flying out of the brush.

"A lion's chasing me!" the fellow shouted.

"Now, Joe," the woods boss soothed, "there ain't been a lion in the Maine woods for a hundred years."

"That's what you think!" Joe said. "I just saw one!"

Pressed, the lumberman described a mountain lion down to the three-foot tail.

Since that time sightings of a "thing" that fits the description of the Eastern mountain lion have increased. Many were discounted as stimulated by suggestion or something stronger. Less easily dismissed were reports by seasoned woodsmen and qualified observers. A state game warden, whose district abuts the Allagash region, submitted this unemotional account in his official report in the early 1950s:

> I noticed a large buck running towards me. . . . About seventy yards in the rear appeared this cat bounding along. As it saw my car it stopped in the road broadside, paused a few seconds, then walked into the thick bushes. I stopped and walked in where the cat had disappeared.
>
> About fifty yards into the swamp I saw this reddish-brown animal which looked to be six-feet long, overall, and at least twenty-four inches high. It seemed to be making a whispering noise and moving its long tail. . . . For two days I searched the woods along the stream for a good track. However I did make a cast of the track on the roadside. It measured four inches by three and one-quarter.

It is not strange that there is more folklore than knowledge about the big Maine cat. The Eastern panther was something to be slaughtered rather than examined. It has been assumed that this Eastern cat, like his cousin the Western cougar, ranged great distances, in circles as large as two hundred miles. Unlike the bobcat, the mountain lion has a keen nose, a further aid in keeping out of sight of his prime enemy, man. The hope that this distrust of man has saved him from total extinction and that a few remnants of these lonely hunters still range the Allagash wilderness has been buttressed in recent years by sightings of seasoned Allagash woodsmen. Several of the big cats were seen near the village of St. Francis in 1966. In the early fall of that year, Sam Jalbert, old-time Allagash guide, got a glimpse of a loping mountain lion near the thoroughfare that connects Umsaskis and Long lakes on the Allagash waterway.

Unlike the big cat which managed to mind his own business in the Colonial period, the Maine black bear, though every bit as wary, adapted to man from the very beginning. It was not so much that he liked man more; he feared civilization less, and what fear he had was overcome by the temptations a campsite afforded.

John Springer wrote: ". . . there is no animal among us with whom encounters are so frequent as the common black bear. Their superior strength, the skill with which they ward off blows, and even wrench an instrument from the hands of an assailant, and their tenacity of life, render them a formidable antagonist. We have sometimes been diverted, as well as severely annoyed, by their thievish tricks."

There is little doubt that the black bear amused less than he annoyed those first trespassers upon the region of the Allagash. Smashed canoes, pillaged camps, violated pack baskets and larders tended to lower the wilderness man's threshold of tolerance. Bruin was a "black critter" and a "varmint" and nothing good could be said of him. He was shot down, trapped and remorselessly cudgeled to death in his winter den. A good bear was a dead bear, a bearslayer, a benefactor.

An Indian, on the other hand, held the bear in high regard. To him the bear was near-human, a brother, and even as he was hunted down and killed for meat, fur and decoration, he was revered for his strength, cunning and sagacity. The bear was an honored totem and borne by one of the most respected families in the Penobscot tribe.

The Indian held the wolverine in no such high regard. This largest of the weasel family was prized for its fur since the long hair would not frost and could be fashioned into trimmings and fringes for winter garments; his person, however, was viewed with distaste.

This rapacious animal was the archcriminal of nature's underworld, a triple-threat beast that could swim, climb and run fast enough to further its own dark ends. John Gyles, in his account of his captivity by the Indians in the late seventeenth century, placed the wolverine among the animals commonly taken by the aborigines. He reflected his captor's antipathy in describing the "wolverene" as "a very fierce and mischievous animal."

They will climb trees and wait for moose and other animals which feed below, and when the opportunity presents, jump upon and strike their claws in them so fast that they will hang on them till they have gnawed the main nerve in their neck asunder, which causes their death. I have known many moose killed thus.

The wolverenes go into wigwams which have been left for a time, and scatter things about, and most filthily polute them with ordure. I have heard Indians say that this animal has sometimes pulled their guns from under their heads while they were asleep, and left them so defiled.

The early Allagash trappers had even less affection for this cunning marauder. Many instances were reported of the

wolverine operating on a trapper's line and systematically re-
lieving the traps of their bounty. The wolverine was already
rare at the close of the pine-lumbering days. The great weasel
retreated northward and is seen only occasionally today in the
isolated reaches of the Canadian North Woods.

Deer were rare to nonexistent in the deep woods of the
Allagash region in the early lumbering days. It wasn't until the
early 1890s that their range extended into the northwest section of the state in the wake of the axe. The moose was liege
lord of this lake and river kingdom. What the virgin pine was
to the timber cruiser, the moose was to the first Allagash hunters, red and white alike: the treasure and trophy prized above
all other game.

When Caesar and his legions invaded Albion they found
royal sport in hunting the Irish elk, of which the General
wrote upon his return, "It is nearly the equal of the elephant in
bulk." The forest monarch is now known only by fossil remains
found in the subsoil of English bogs. A mighty beast he was.
One set of antlers of the great Irish elk, preserved in a London
museum, spread eleven feet, and assembled skeletons show the
beast to have stood ten feet high to his antler tips.

The moose is the descendant of the great Irish elk and heir
to the realm of the wild lakes and bogs. A specialist in his
feeding habits, stubborn in his refusal to adapt to the advent
of mere man, the moose has for a century been on the list of
species on the way to extinction. In the 1850s, Thoreau proph-
esied that the moose would be gone in his century. But the
animal still persists to roam his ancient dominion, an anachro-
nism and as defiant of the natural law of selection as he is of
man himself.

The favorite moose-hunting time for the Indian was in September when the meat was prime and the bulls were in rut and
could be called into range by a horn that simulated the yearning bellow of a cow moose. Moose calling was developed to a
high art by the Abnakis who passed on to the white hunters of
the Allagash the techniques of this hunting lore.

When the voice of the tree frog was heard in the cool of the evening it was "moose-calling time." A camp was made in a region where the moose were known to be ranging and a strict silence was maintained beside a small, glowing fire until after midnight. At a signal from the leader, the moose caller raised his horn—a sheet of birch bark rolled into the shape of a megaphone—and sent forth several long, tremulous calls. If the bull was within hearing, an immediate response could be expected. If the answer came, the luring call was given once again, briefly. Then the waiting began.

The great bull could be several miles away. His approach, though devious, was frequently noisy, designed to frighten away his rivals or to challenge them for a mate. The timing was critical for the dawn light was necessary to see to aim. At the first crack of dawn, another call was offered. As the light strengthened, the final efforts were made to bring the bull within range. These final calls represented the highest degree of artistry, for one false note and the long night was wasted. The moose caller cleared the leaves from a patch of earth and held the mouth of his horn to within a few inches of the ground and a seductive squealing was incorporated into the call to inflame the bull's passion and bring him quickly into range.

If all went well the trampling of brush was heard close at hand. Perhaps one final call was required to bring the great antlered beast bursting into full view to meet the lead or feathered arrows of the crouched hunters.

There was a rush to the spot where the moose had stood. If the blood was dark the beast had been fatally wounded and was not far off. If the color was light, the wound was superficial and there was a long blood trail to follow, a trail the braves were often forced to abandon before the day was over.

On the rivers and lakes of the Allagash country the canoe was employed to good advantage by the Indian. The birch, one hunter in the bow with the horn and the other in the stern with paddle, was eased noiselessly close to the shore. The chosen time was dusk or gray dawn. The bow man's call was directed at frequent intervals toward the wooded shore. If there was an answer, a seductive note was added, delicately and with prudence. The stern man ceased his paddling while the bow man dipped up water with his bark horn and poured it back into the water to approximate the sound of a cow moose feeding or urinating.

The bull might appear suddenly on the shore, quietly or with a crackling of brush. The shadowy shape of the canoe and hunters to the bull moose's poor eyes was a feeding cow. The stern man backed the canoe away and the bow man prepared to fire. The moose, enraged at seeing his prospective mate retreat, advanced into the water, presenting himself for sacrifice.

Moose

The moose also was hunted later in the season when the snows were deep and the moose herds had migrated from the bogs to their winter quarters on the hardwood ridges. The yarded moose—yards are winter herding places—were easy prey for the braves on snowshoes. It was not so easy on the light early snows. In this situation the hunter would take a track and dog it day and night with little rest. The early white hunters learned from the Indian that a moose would neither rest nor feed when pursued. A tough Indian hunter could walk down a moose in three days and three nights if conditions were right; but there were times when it required as much as seven days on the snowshoe trail before the moose would drop from exhaustion.

At the end of the trail there was that moment of truth when the great beast would turn, legs trembling, eyes red with hate, to face his unrelenting enemy. Too weak to charge, there was yet enough defiance for one last bellow of rage before submitting to the hunter's *coup de grace.*

Next to the moose, the caribou was the most prized of the Allagash creatures by the Indian hunters. The writers on the early scene were unanimous in their agreement that the supply of woodland caribou was plentiful in the deep woods during the first centuries after the white man's advent. In the United States, the range of this native reindeer included all the border states from Maine to Washington. There were few who saw the end of these great herds which seemed such an enduring part of the American wilderness landscape.

The very fact that the Indian found the caribou a relatively easy source of food should have been sufficient warning that the herds could not long stand up against European weapons. The fleet animal could usually outdistance his chief enemies, the wolf and bear; but against firearms the caribou had no defense. Alarmed by a shot, a feeding herd seldom fled but instead stood motionless, permitting time for a leisurely aim and a second and even a third barrage. Only then did the great dark creatures run for cover leaving their dead and wounded behind.

Nor did the caribou have any defense against another relentless enemy, the deer botfly. These noxious insects stung through the caribou's hide and the developing maggots brought suffering and frequently death.

Thoreau saw no caribou on his Allagash trip in the 1850s, but he did record that fifteen had been killed by a single hunter around Moosehead the year before. Thoreau's guide, Joe Polis, remarked that the caribou was "a very great runner" and that there had been great herds around the Allagash headwaters in times past. Joe attributed the decline to the dry-ki(5) caused by flooded lakes. "No likum stump," Joe said, "when he sees that he scared."

In 1892 a herd of eighteen caribou was seen near Katahdin. This was the last sighting of any sizable group of woodland caribou in Maine.

One wintry afternoon in October of 1899, Willy Jalbert was working around his place on the old Michaud Farm on the lower Allagash when he spotted a single caribou on the far shore. Willy took up his rifle and canoed across the river. A fresh snow lay on the ground. He took up the track. There just a few rods from the river stood the lonely animal waiting for him. This was possibly the last caribou killed on the Allagash. The last recorded killing in Maine occurred in 1908. That was it. The woodland caribou, *Rangifer caribou,* incapable of adapting to man's invasion, went the way of the heath hen.

In recent years, a belated effort was made to restore the woodland caribou to his native habitat. A few pair were airlifted from Canada to Katahdin. Sightings have been made of the transplanted herd, but the status in Maine of the gentle reindeer that once ranged the region of the Allagash is uncertain and at best but a sorry reminder.

The hunt enjoyed a pre-eminent place in the life of the Maine Indian. No other activity occupied his mind, spirit and body so completely. In their moose and caribou hunts in the

Allagash woods the early native hunters frequently employed "pure men" or runners. These specialists were carefully picked and trained from boyhood to run down game. An elite corps, the chosen few were zealously guarded by the old men of the tribe lest defiling influences undermine their endurance and reduce their fleetness.

The Pure Men could not marry and all sexual dalliance was denied them. Their unsleeping custodians kept a vigil by night to see to it that they did not sleep with legs outstretched thereby tiring their leg muscles. Chewing spruce gum was taboo for it was suspected that indulgence in this common Indian habit would impair breathing and cause the testicles to clack while on the game trail.

In the order of their importance as game to the native Indian were moose, deer and caribou, followed by beaver, bear, muskrat, hare, porcupine and partridge. Beaver and muskrat were taken both for fur and food and, indeed, there were few delicacies, unless it was the lips and tongue of the moose, that were so highly prized. (The muskrat was the "musquash" to both the red man and the white until comparatively recent years, and it is reasonable to believe that its flesh would still be eaten with relish had the early name been retained.)

The beaver, important as it was as an item of food, was perhaps even more important to the Indian for fur and as a medium of exchange in the tribal dealings with the white man, French and English alike. Only beaverskins could buy the guns, lead, powder and rum that the aborigines came to regard as necessities.

Precious above all other skins, however, were the pelts of the fisher and pine marten, both identified with the deep conifer forests. The silken coat of the female fisher was the prize among prizes, a single pelt bringing a premium of barter goods and to the settlers up to three hundred and fifty dollars for a single fur, as much hard cash as a pioneer trapper was likely to see in a year.

The fisher, no fisheater as the name might imply, preyed on

the squirrels and porcupines of the conifer forests. No re-
specter of family relationships, he preyed on his cousin the
pine marten as well, a habit which accounted, even more than
trapping pressures, for the virtual extinction of this small
arboreal weasel. With depressed prices on furs and the conse-
quent relaxing of trapping pressures, the pine marten—sable to
trappers—appears to be recovering in the Allagash and is seen
frequently once again in the deep conifer woods.

Also prized was the skin of the winter weasel, or ermine,
pure white except for his ink-dipped tail, whose baffling speed
of motion the Indian saw as legerdemain. In residence, too,
was the frolicsome otter whose speed and agility, both on land
and in the water, made him more than a match for any
predator large enough to challenge him.

The shy Canada lynx was another common and highly
regarded denizen of the Allagash fastness. Curiously, the
bobcat was of relatively rare occurrence in the North Woods in
those early days, or so it would appear from the evidence of
the day. As late as 1862 there appeared in Hitchcock's *Second
Annual Report upon the Natural History and Geology of the
State of Maine* a section on mammals, written by J. C. Rich.
Presumably a qualified observer, Rich was nonetheless curiously naive. To the lynx was ascribed all the aspects of villainy.
Of the common bobcat he seemed to have had nothing but
hearsay knowledge. Wrote Rich:

> The lynx is one of those animals of which the ancients
> told so many fables. That they could see through opaque
> bodies and even through stone walls, and that their urine
> often contained a valuable stone called "lapis lincurius" . . .
> Our lynx has a very sharp, large, round eye, and is capable
> of staring at you for a great length of time. Such is however
> the natural ferocity of this animal that it is believed to be
> impossible to perfectly subdue it. . . . Doctor Richardson
> states that the early French writers, who ascribe to this
> animal the habit of dropping from limbs of trees on the
> backs of deer and destroying them by tearing their throats

and drinking their blood, gave them the name *loup cervier*
or wolf stag. . . . I have been informed of another kind of
lynx in this state, but have never seen one of that kind. It is
said they live in open cultivated regions, and have no fur on
the bottom of their feet. . . ."

The North Woods was ever a place for the strong alone. The
long northern winter has no tolerance for the weak. There is a
glow of health upon the conifer forest dwellers, for when the
deep snows slump with the first spring rains only the strong
have survived to mate with the strong and perpetuate their
species.

If one were to seek a symbol of wintry woods—one single
wilderness creature that would express the white, blue-shad-
owed silences of the North Woods—the first animal to come to
mind would most surely be the snowshoe rabbit.

Blessed with fecundity, snowshoes for feet, and a coat he
changes from brown to matching white in the winter, he is as
much a part of the wintry woods as the Canada jay and the
cheerful chickadee. Accurately, this bounding courser is the
varying or snowshoe hare, but to the Maine woodsman he was,
and will probably always remain, the snowshoe rabbit.

The Indian knew this long-eared turncoat as *Wabasso* and
made him a central figure in many of his legends. The bread
and butter of the wilderness, he counts among his enemies: the
fox, cat, hawk, owl, weasel, mink. His only defenses are his
speed and coloration. In the ruthless economy of selection the
Northern hare survives by sheer numbers. Through many bitter Northern winters it was the hare that kept Indian villages
alive when all other sources of food and warm fur failed.

The Indian believed that *Wabasso* changed his coat as winter approached. In truth, the snowshoe hare has two coats and
the change is a molt. Each autumn white hairs come into the
brown. The brown falls out and in about ten weeks the trans-
formation to pure white is effected and the hare becomes a
ghost in a white landscape.

The snowshoe hare lives out his brief life within a few hundred yards of where he was dropped, open-eyed and full-furred, by his mother. His end, inevitably violent, comes in silence on velvet wings or flashing talons. There is a certain fitness that this symbol of the North Woods should be linked in nature's scheme with the chickadee. An emblem in feathers of the Northern winter, the chickadee seeks out the carcass of the snowshoe for the soft fur with which he likes to line his nest.

Understandably, the loon, too, figured prominently in Indian legends for there is a humanness about its lonely night cry. Thoreau wrote in his Maine Woods Journal: "In the middle of the night, as indeed each time we lay on the shore of a lake, we heard the voice of the loon, loud and distinct from across the lake. It is a very wild sound, quite in keeping with the place. . . . I could lie awake for hours listening to it, it is so thrilling."

And, as have so many other wilderness lovers before and since, the Concord naturalist attempted to find the words to describe the loon's unforgettable cry—"This of the loon—I do not mean its laugh, but its looning,—is a long-drawn call, as if it were sometimes singularly human to my ear,—*hoo-hoo-ooooo*, like the hallooing of a man on a very high key, having thrown his voice into his head. I have heard a sound exactly like it when breathing heavily through my own nostrils, half awake at ten at night, suggesting my affinity to the loon; as if its language were but a dialect of my own, after all."

Lucius Hubbard, some decades later, hearing loons calling at Eagle Lake, was moved to explore the bird's expressive versatility. "Subjectively the loon seems to have been little studied, but its different notes surprise us with abundant material to interpret its varying moods. Its cry of alarm, and its shrill note when on the wing, are probably by many persons supposed to be the only ones it utters, the expressions of joy and affection being entirely overlooked. Its notes are more significant than those of many other birds, at times merry, tender, dreary, or full of fear. . . ."

Hubbard noted the variations of the common looning, then added: "These dreary cries are startling, and sound like those of a child in distress. . . . Again at night there comes softly over the water a single note, full of tenderness, like the cooing of a mother to its young, a short gentle 'Hu!' or sometimes the longer 'Hu-whu'-oo!' in low plaintive tones . . . the sounds seemed too full and mature to come from other than the old birds."

This assiduous student of Maine woodsways proceeded to make musical notations of the loon's spring song. He oberved: "By far the most interesting manifestation of the loon's feelings, however, is the cry, sometimes heard late in the summer, but oftener in the springtime, in that joyous season when all nature is bright, and our bird, happy in his old haunts perhaps, or with his mate or new-born offspring, rings forth with a merry swing his 'Oh-oo-whi-oo-hoo-wi, whi-oo-hoo-wi, whi-oo-hoo-wi!' "

The "howling" wilderness that daunted those first white invaders of the Allagash was in truth an immensity of stillness. Except for the brief vernal choruses it was the ineffable quietude that characterized the deep conifer forest, stillness broken only occasionally by night looning, the bark of a fox, the whistle of an alarmed otter, the beeping of a nuthatch, or chattering of a squirrel.

It was no more than a legend that the big cat screamed to

Loon

freeze his prey in fear: the big cat was a silent hunter, his prey a silent quarry.

In the depth of winter the silence is all but complete in the Allagash woods. The surf-roar of high wind in the spires of the trees, the pistol-shot *pang* of ice making on a lonely lake are the small, brief voices in an ambience of silence.

THE ROYAL ROAD   10

B^{Y THE} early decades of the nineteenth century man was becoming increasingly capable of modifying the physical world he inhabited. The creatures of the forest, the very forests themselves, far from being imperishable, were becoming more and more dependent upon the tolerance of the human invaders they once had balked and threatened.

The lesson was implicit in the status of the forests of England across the sea. Once heavily wooded and teeming with game, less than 10 percent of English land remained with forest cover.

There were those in authority in the Plymouth colony who deplored the waste of timber and made zealous efforts to control it. Penalties were imposed upon the settlers who were inclined to clear lands the easy way. Fines, damages, and even whippings were imposed upon the miscreants who employed fire to gain a clearing in the trees. As early as 1660, Portsmouth, in New Hampshire, exacted a penalty of five shillings for every tree cut except for personal use for building, firewood or fencing.

"Conservation" in its modern context had small bearing on these early restrictive measures. The laws were directed primarily to control outlawry and trespass upon property rights. It soon appeared to the ruling hierarchy that the worst offenders lived on the wilderness frontiers of Maine.

And so they did. In Maine, there was a basic resentment of the polished and worldly city men who came with money in their pockets to buy up great tracts of Maine lands they never intended to occupy. It was antipathetic to the frontier spirit

85

that a man should own more than he could himself use and improve. The usufruct tenure principle was as much a part of the fabric of frontier thinking as it had been for the Indian.

These "conservation" laws, framed as they were to protect privilege, found little favor among the backwoodsmen who flouted them with free-swinging gusto. No more popular was the law passed in 1783 designed to check illicit cutting of pine on public lands. Whose public lands? the settlers were inclined to ask. But by 1794, when the rights of large property owners were further buttressed by laws that protected floating timber, the timberland investors were firmly in the saddle.

After all, timberland *was* an investment. Timberland meant pine and pine was merchantable. What other possible reason was there for buying up a wilderness if not for realizing a profit on the investment? And there was no such thing as a good law that did not strengthen the security of such investments. This position, in the context of the times, was unassailable.

The concept of public lands held in the public interest was unknown and undreamed of in early America. Since the middle ages all lands were the king's lands. The English kings certainly never questioned their right to parcel them out freely for money, whims, or in return for favors.

It was an old English custom and one that was to have a profound influence on the development of the Maine wilderness. In the loose social organization of the Middle Ages, a man held property only if he could defend it. The small landowner, if he was to survive, placed himself under the protection of a neighbor powerful enough to resist attack. These great land barons in turn sought protection from their king, placing their holdings in the monarch's hands and pledging him eternal fealty.

When James I and Charles I of England made grants in the New World to friends, relatives and corporate groups, centuries of custom had firmly established their right to do so. The time for questioning was still in the future.

For a century before the American Revolution, the territory east of the Penobscot River had been constantly changing hands. Charles II of England had given a part of it to his brother, the Duke of York. The French refused to acknowledge the title, claiming much of it in the name of their own monarch, and they continued to claim it until the Treaty of Utrecht settled the matter in the English favor. As for the land west of the Penobscot and north of the Piscataquis, no one gave it too much thought and few made a fuss when, as early as 1658, Massachusetts announced its claim to all the vaguely defined region referred to as the Province of Maine.

The righteous and expansion-hungry Puritans were serious, as it turned out. When all land claims in Maine reverted to the early English grants after the Treaty of Utrecht, Massachusetts strengthened her Maine position by purchase, occupation and litigation. She did not succeed, however, in enjoining the King's Agent from cutting mast pine. The Crown's advocates insisted that such rights were inalienable. The Revolution settled that matter, as it did a number of things.

It failed to settle, however, the title to the region of the Allagash. The Indian claim was solidly based, of course. Ancient Indian law made *use* the decisive factor in ownership. The Indians used the territory as their hunting grounds and they had never relinquished their claim by sale or treaty. Unfortunately for the Indians, there were, by 1790, very nearly 100,000 white settlers in Maine and scarcely 600 Indians. It was no contest.

Massachusetts, now a sovereign state and bankrupt by the recent war, needed money desperately. She could call no further upon her already overburdened citizenry for financial help. All she had in the way of resources to fall back on were her wild lands in the District of Maine. With the idea of legalizing her shadowy claim once and for all, commissioners were appointed to preside over the partition of the Indian lands. Agreements were imposed and hard bargains exacted and sealed with blankets, guns and gunpowder.

The agreement provided that certain reserved lands be set aside for the impoverished tribes. But almost immediately the Indian lands up the tidal rivers proved too valuable and the terms of the "Old Indian Purchase" were hastily superseded by the "New Indian Purchase" which stripped the Indians of all but a few tracts of land considered "unsuitable for white settlement."

With that matter tidily settled, Massachusetts embarked upon the royal road. The wild lands of Maine went on the block. A land office was opened. Preliminary surveys were made so a buyer could see, on paper at least, what he was getting for his money. Grants were made to colleges, academies, and even literary societies. The long-unpaid Revolutionary soldiery was paid off in undeveloped Maine real estate. Any offer that would bring in a little hard cash was entertained.

Sales went slowly nonetheless. Nor did lotteries stimulate buying to anywhere near boom proportions, disposing of a mere 165,000 acres. Not that timbered land was considered worthless; but what good was pine you couldn't get to? Allagash pine was too remote and inaccessible. It was like buying lots on the moon.

Public sentiment in Maine went along with Moses Greenleaf's dream. The citizens favored any policy that would encourage settlement. After generations of frontier loneliness it was towns they wanted—farms, industry, trade and, most of all, hard money that would bring them and their families some of the good things of life.

But the buying and granting went on. William Bingham, a wealthy Philadelphian, sent a timber cruiser into the woods of northeastern Maine and, getting a glowing report, bought up for $12\frac{1}{2}$ cents an acre over two million acres of virgin pine and spruce. Investment began taking on the color of speculation, with hunger not so much for land as for a quick dollar. Even college grants were tossed into the pot for a quick profit. Finally, the bubble burst.

When the district of Maine became a state in 1820, an act provided that the public lands in Maine be divided equally between Maine and Massachusetts. Each was to hold its share in severalty, with Maine holding jurisdiction over the territory.

The virgin State of Maine immediately found itself hard pressed for money. Maine, too, took the royal road. Once more, land brokers set up shop, hawking their wares in the groggeries and along Exchange Street in Bangor. The fever once again infected the multitudes with dreams of easy money. Timberland that had been bought for ten cents an acre one day sold for as many dollars the next. Fly-by-night promoters staged Roman holidays for wealthy Easterners, which featured entertainment banquets and auctions, with champagne served from bathtubs thrown in. Loggers, who were already beginning to develop a thirst and a taste for exuberant living, were nothing loath to join in the fun.

Moses Greenleaf's dream of settlements advancing into the wilderness along a broad front was finding little nourishment. Even before Greenleaf's time, there were clear indications that such a direction was not in the stars for the Maine wilderness. Almost from the beginning, the structure of investment worked against homesteader ownership of the wild lands. The vision fetched up against the realities of a one-crop resource. The pine resource of the Allagash region was too large and too remote for small, undercapitalized landowners to exploit.

The logistic and economic realities were such that for exploitation to be practical at all, it had to be big. And men, if they were to tackle the harvesting of that roadless and hostile territory, had to think big.

The typical eighteenth century lumberman had been a farmer with some strong sons and a few pair of oxen. He worked in the woods clearing land and making a little side money on the timber he salvaged in the process. He cut trees close at hand and perhaps ran a small sawmill. In many cases timber became his money crop and farming a side line. He

would run winter-cut logs he had ponded in the spring
through his saws, and when the water got too low to turn his
wheels, he shut down the gates and turned logger again.

These were family men, frugal, hardworking, independent.
They might hire out to go into the woods as teamsters and
hewers so long as they could get home at night to their fire-
sides.

This was not good enough for the job that had to be done
once the wilderness townships began falling into the hands of
the outlanders and risk capital was on the line. A new breed of
man had to be developed and conditioned to a new way of
life, men for whom a town was merely a place to let off steam
after the drive was in, professionals who knew nothing else
and cared for nothing else but the job of cutting timber and
letting sunlight into the swamps.

And once the lumber baronies began to take shape, homesteading, more and more, became something to resist rather
than encourage. Later, Thoreau was to ask "Uncle George"
McCauslin, at whose outlying dwelling he stopped on his trip
up the West Branch Penobscot, why more settlers did not
come into the wilderness. McCauslin answered that the one
very good reason was that they could not buy the land; it
belonged to companies who were afraid that their wild lands
would be settled and incorporated into towns, inevitably causing taxes to rise. Personally, "Uncle George" wanted no neighbors. He was quite happy with things as they were.

Nor was the state much interested in unloading the public
lands on a paltry, piecemeal basis. The wilderness was something to be got rid of, the larger the pieces the better. Besides,
there were irritations and complications. It had been proposed
at the time of the separation that Maine buy out the Massachusetts holdings. Collisions were foreseen in the arrangement
of two states holding these lands in severalty. Neither state,
however, would ratify the proposal with the consequence that
the whole period of dual ownership was characterized by
bickering.

Maine did eventually purchase the remnants of the Massachusetts holdings in 1854, for $362,000. Maine's Governor Hubbard, who was largely instrumental in effecting the purchase, remarked at the time that he deemed "the value of said lands to Maine far greater than it can be to Massachusetts or any private speculator."

The Governor's thoughts notwithstanding, the state pursued its policy of unburdening itself of its public lands. In 1868, there was a mere one million acres of wild land remaining in public domain when the State Legislature voted to sell—and finally to give—to the European and North American Railway 700,000 acres to build a railroad from Bangor to the New Brunswick border.

A few years later, a sale took place in Bangor and the last of Maine public lands was gone. In 1878, the Land Agent wrote this terse statement in his report, "All the public lands having been disposed of, no further favors are now in the power of the state to grant for homestead to settlers."

So it was pine hunger that shaped the course of the development of the Allagash country and fixed upon it the unique ownership pattern that persists to this day. From the beginning, when the first timber explorers cruised the river and marked upon their maps the lofty stands of pine and the survey crews ran those first lines, making neat, geometric boxes of a wilderness few but the hardy had ever seen, scarcely more than a dozen families were involved in the partition and management of the Allagash.

And a shrewd and prudent lot they were, those first Yankees who ventured their capital in Maine timberlands. Bred for the most part in shipping and allied mercantile fields, they were cognizant of the risks entailed in putting all their bets on one horse. It had long been their custom to spread risks among a number of investors by employing the expedient of each buying a fraction of a vessel or cargo.

This practice made good sense once the acquisition of Maine timberlands drew their interest. Uncut pine in the Allagash presented every bit as much of a risk as a vessel embarked upon stormy seas. It was all but impossible to police trespass cutting, particularly by Canadians, or to control squatters from the St. Lawrence valley to the north and west; and settlement sharply increased the fire hazard that could wipe out whole townships. To this was added the additional uncertainty of where Maine ended and Canada began. American surveyors frequently were running into nasty little squabbles with their opposite numbers across the border over this very matter.

Such uncertainties dictated the prudent course. Why not, they reasoned, get together and each buy a "piece of the ship"? They did just that. As many as a half-dozen individuals or groups were frequently involved in the purchase of a single wilderness township. No division lines were drawn. Each interest held an undivided share. The management was usually placed in the hands of the major owner or conducted under some joint management plan, each sharing in the profits according to the percentage of the acreage owned.

In laying out these wilderness areas so that a prospective investor would know what he was buying, there was some natural confusion until a standard survey method was adopted. The range and number system, used by the Federal Government in laying out the public lands in the western territories, appeared to have its merits and its fundamental points were made standard practice in Maine during the last decades of the eighteenth century.

The system is based on townships six miles square, subdivided into sections one mile square, and these further divided into half sections and quarter sections. In the wilderness of the Allagash, needless to say, no one was interested in thinking in any terms smaller than a thirty-six-square-mile township.

In running out or surveying this wilderness, an initial starting point was chosen, more or less arbitrarily. From this point a meridian line, called the Principal Meridian, or simply P.M., was laid out on the face of the earth in a true northerly direction. This line was measured and appropriate markers placed to show the township and section corners. Starting also from this initial point, a due east and west line was run, called the Base Line, with points marked in the same manner as on the meridian.

At the Base Line, at a point twenty-four miles from the Principal Meridian, another guide meridian was run connecting this last point with the twenty-four-mile point on the P.M. When this block was divided off into townships, there were then within its bounds, sixteen townships each containing thirty-six sections, one square mile each.

Once this job was done, each township received a number that defined its location with respect to the initial point of the survey (for instance: the WELS designation in the Allagash region means: WEST OF THE EAST LINE OF THE STATE). The township numbers represented its position north of the east and west Base Line; the range number its position east or west of the Principal Meridian.

Although these lines run by early practitioners were amazingly accurate, errors did occur simply because the earth was a sphere. The surveys were made on magnetic courses with no allowances made for the curvature of the earth. A surveyor and his party armed with instructions from the state or the "proprietors," as the large owners were called, took to the woods and with simple staff or hand-held compasses blocked out a series of townships; upon returning to civilization he drew up a map from field notes and presented it to his employer.

A few years later another surveyor might run some lines and block out adjoining territory, using the same methods. The second surveyor seldom followed the same true course as the first, primarily because of the variance of the magnetic compass from year to year. Later, when more sophisticated tools were employed and errors discovered, corrections were made. A common corrective expedient was to set off a "gore," a little orphaned wedge of territory that did not belong. These odd little testaments to venial human error, which spoiled the neat geometry here and there, persist on our maps today.

Thoreau referred to these timber cruisers and surveyors as mere "hirelings," using the word in its usual pejorative sense. So they were; but they were a doughty tribe and many were true explorers, endowed with a venturesome spirit and a quota of natural curiosity. There was Silas Barnard, who in 1831 went into the Allagash region for the purpose of surveying and proceeded to go far beyond the letter of his instructions and above and beyond the call of duty.

The crude Barnard map in the Land Office of the State of Maine covers the whole wilderness route from Moosehead Lake to the St. John, by way of the Allagash, and on it were meticulously notated the various portages. There was no mention of the obstacles he met and overcame in this wild bailiwick, but that they were considerable no one can doubt. His map indicated six carries in all, with distances of each recorded:

N.E. Moosehead to West Branch Penobscot—2 miles, 2½ chains.
Portage on Umbasookskus Stream—17 chains
Umbasookskus—Mud Pond—125½ chains
Portage of 29 chains at beginning of Mud Pond Stream to Pomogine Cammoe Lake [Chamberlain Lake].
Portage of 57 chains—Allagash Rapids
Portage of 12½ chains—Allagash Grand Falls

Another explorer-surveyor, William P. Parrott of Boston, went into the Allagash wilderness at the behest of the proprietors, charged with more specific duties. He was instructed "to examine the river Allagash from Chamberlain Lake, down to the portage as marked on Greenleaf's map." This was in 1843 when the Telos Cut controversy was heating up and Parrott was directed "to ascertain whether a dam can be constructed at any place below the dam built by Messrs. Stickland & Roberts so that timber may be brought from below said dam into the Penobscot."

Parrott went into the woods and came out with plans, costing $16,500 and $18,303 respectively, for getting Allagash logs to Bangor. In his report he told his lumbermen employers exactly what they were waiting to hear:

> A large number of streams large enough for driving logs flow into the Allagash below Chamberlain Lake, and although these have not yet been explored sufficiently to determine with exactness how large a territory they flow through, still enough is known to prove that a tract of country containing eight to ten townships is watered by these streams, and that the timber can by them be brought into the Allagash River, and from thence by means of the contemplated improvement to the Penobscot . . . The land in this region appears to be heavily timbered, and I do not doubt as much so as any other tract of land of the same extent in the State. The amount of timber in the ten townships will probably exceed eleven millions average to a township, and the timber is worth at least double to come into the Penobscot than it would be to go into the Provinces to market.

This was music to the ears of one David Pingree of Salem, Massachusetts, who had begun to look to the wild lands of Maine for investment of his considerable capital. If there was pine to be cut and profits to realize, it was time for him to make his move, not with a few niggling dollars but on a massive scale.

There were no inhibiting moral issues involved. For Pingree and the others who moved with him to assault the North Woods of Maine, the forested wilderness was there to be subdued, an impersonal enemy and a physical barrier to be exploited. It was there to be used up to the very limits of existing knowledge and technology.

For them and to all who lived in its shadow, nature in the raw was potentially evil. It was to be another hundred years before man, the user, acquired guilt and was to be confronted with the accusations of sin against the same wild lands that were so long his deathless adversary.

THE BATTLE
OF THE DITCH

11

D AVID PINGREE had no intention of getting himself involved in Maine timberlands. He was pushed into it. It
was a twist of fate that would change the face of the Allagash
and contribute some lusty footnotes to its history.

Born in Bridgeton, Maine, in 1795, young David had some
early exposure to the lumbering business, a form of endeavor
that apparently fell short of generating any great enthusiasm
in him. At least he jumped at the chance to chuck the job and
get off on his own. He was still in his teens when a maternal
uncle, one of the leading merchants in the salty town of Salem,
Massachusetts, offered him the opportunity to manage his farm
in Georgetown. David hesitated not a moment.

He was a likely lad, as the saying went, a young fellow with
his eye on the main chance. At twenty-three there he was in
Salem, head over heels in business and being carefully
groomed to assume his uncle's mercantile and shipping enterprises. When his uncle died a few years later, this Yankee Dick
Whittington was established as a young man of means and
position.

It was in the decade after Maine had become a state in 1820
that a wealthy friend by the name of Fisk dropped by at
Pingree's office and in the course of the conversation unbur-
dened his personal problems. His sons were taking the prim-
rose path and refusing to engage themselves in gainful labor.
With the idea of diverting these profligates, he had invested in
a large tract of Maine timberland in some out-of-the-way region called the Allagash.

The gentleman was disgusted, to say the least. The boys

97

simply refused to go near the place, stating that canoeing with a bunch of Indian savages just wasn't for them. So there was Mr. Fisk with a large tract of wilderness land he didn't know what to do with.

Actually, Pingree was at the time thinking seriously about reinvesting his capital. Shipping was moving away from Salem, and he suspected that the golden age of this old coastal town was already on the wane; but as for investing in timberland in a place no one had ever heard of, David Pingree saw nothing but folly.

And there the matter might have been left except for the pitcher ears of an office clerk. The young employee persuaded his boss to loan *him* money to buy the tract of land, the loan to be secured by a mortgage.

The young clerk took directly to the woods. It appears that he was successful beyond his dreams in his first timber dealings. He did not, however, stick to timber, dabbling instead in all sorts of highly speculative ventures. He awoke one morning to find himself wiped out. Back in Salem, David Pingree found himself with Mr. Fisk's Maine timberland on his hands.

Searching his brain for a way out of his dilemma, Pingree recalled a young man in town who had attracted his attention. Ebenezer Coe was an engineer, a genius of sorts. Moreover, he was enterprising, shrewd and extremely reliable. Straightway, Coe was signed up and dispatched to Maine to investigate the property and evaluate it as an investment.

David Pingree's judgment in his choice of a surrogate was quickly vindicated. Eben Coe was not a man to do things by halves. He hired guides and boats and proceeded personally to explore not only the Pingree lands but a considerable section of the Allagash headwaters. What he saw astonished him: great islands of virgin pine that extended, so his guides informed him, far to the north and downriver all the way to the St. John. And the fact that the greatest stands of pine timber stood hard by the waterways impressed his practical mind.

Coe returned to Salem with a report. It was his considered

opinion that David Pingree should not only hold onto his Maine land but proceed at once to acquire more. Pingree, having hired the man for his acumen, could not in good conscience ignore his advice. Promptly, he made Coe a full partner in the timber enterprise, the young engineer to invest his time, brains and energy, and Pingree, the money.

Coe did not underestimate the problems that confronted him. Churchill Lake lay in the center of the largest tract of pine timber in the state, perhaps in the world. But all the lakes of the Allagash headwaters were in the St. John watershed. Logs cut on the lakes had only one way to go—north into Canada, to Canadian mills and Canadian ports, a long journey that would certainly reduce profits by half. Clearly, the Good Lord had not had the interest of Maine lumbermen in mind when He had arranged the topography of the Allagash.

A few of the early operators had attempted to correct this iniquitous situation by turning the logs into Eagle and Churchill lakes, booming them down the lake in the summer, then taking them out of the lakes and, the following winter, laboriously hauling them cross-country on the snow and landing them in East Branch Penobscot waters where finally they arrived at the mills on the main Penobscot where American logs belonged. The cost had proved prohibitive.

There was another possibility, an idea that boggled the imagination. Of course, the sly suggestion that, according to the original plan, the Lord had meant those headwater lakes to flow water south instead of north had been bruited about for a number of years. There were some adroit interpreters who found support for their contention in Indian legends which hinted that in ancient times these waters had in fact flowed south.

The reasoning was sound enough. The true head of Chamberlain Lake was a small body of water called Telos Lake which was connected by a thoroughfare with the main body. Between Telos Lake and Webster Lake on the East Branch watershed was a gorge a scant mile long that had in prehistoric times most surely been incised by the agency of fast-flowing water. Ebenezer Coe's engineering eye saw immediately that with very little help the Allagash headwaters could be encouraged to flow south to the accommodation of the Bangor lumber interests.

To begin with, Webster Lake was some 45 feet lower than Telos. Say a dam were to be built at the foot of Telos Lake and another at the outlet of Chamberlain. The formation of the terrain at the lake's outlet suited the purpose admirably, for the stream ran for some distance between steep banks. Perhaps a third and fourth dam below this Chamberlain installation could be constructed to complete the plan of raising the water of the headwater lakes, at which time natural laws would force the lake to flow into the Penobscot watershed and cause 270 square miles of Allagash River waters to become tributary to the Penobscot River.

At the heart of this elaborate plot was the shrewd hunch that waters once released at Telos Dam would have sufficient force to scour out the canal, eliminating the necessity to devote more than a minimal amount of manpower to making the cut to Webster Lake.

It was indeed an audacious idea. But this was a time of canal fever, a period when imagination and enterprise was demanded if New England was to survive. The Erie Canal, dedicated in 1830, had opened Eastern markets to the great farmlands of the West, rendering obsolescent the Yankee hand-labor agricultural economy. In tackling the exploitation of the new resource, Maine lumbermen were forced to think big.

Actually, Kennebec lumbermen for some years had been regarding that same Allagash pine with hungry eyes. They, too, had been toying with the idea of implementing their dreams of timber riches by revising the Lord's arrangements.

Understandably, their idea was to drive the pine into the Kennebec. The Kennebec cabal envisioned cutting Allagash pine and driving it south by way of the West Branch Penobscot and Moosehead Lake where it could be sluiced into the Kennebec River. There was no connection between the West Branch and Moosehead Lake, of course; but that, they figured, could be arranged.

A pair of enterprising Kennebeckers, William Boyd and William Moulton, in 1839, petitioned the legislature for an act to incorporate the Seboomook Sluiceway Company. In their appeal they represented that "they were interested in timberlands lying on the upper waters of the Penobscot River, northwesterly of Moosehead Lake." They suggested that running logs down the West Branch to market was much too unfavorable and circuitous and prevented all lumbering operations on those lands. "These evils may be remedied . . ." the petition continued, "by opening and constructing a sluiceway for the passage of logs, from the waters of the west branch of the Penobscot into the head of Moosehead Lake . . ."

William Anson, surveyor and civil engineer, was commissioned by the Board of Internal Improvements under the instructions of the legislature to explore and survey this suggested route for a canal.

Anson discovered no serious obstacles to the plan. His report stated: "The different localities, features and character of this section are highly favorable to the object in view." Indeed the situation was ideal. The land between the West Branch and Moosehead at Northwest Carry was low and marshy and the lake itself was appreciably lower than the river.

Needless to say, the Bangor lumbermen found it anything but ideal. Once the Penobscot men got wind of the proposal they set up a howl that could be heard all the way to Augusta.

The Good Lord, they cried out in righteous outrage, would have sent the Penobscot into Moosehead if *He* had wanted it to go that way! No good would ever come of such a sacrilege! A strong remonstrance was framed by James Crosby and twenty other Bangor partisans and presented to the legislature. This opposition clique maintained "there was a great danger if such a connection is made as the petitioners ask for, that it would divert the waters in such quantities as would be highly injurious to those interested on the Penobscot." Why such a digging might start a water route that would be disastrous should a freshet enlarge it and a permanent and irremediable diversion of water result!

What made the controversy even more heated was the natural rivalry that had existed for some time between the Kennebeckers and the Penobscot men. The feelings of the inhabitants of these two lumber rivers about each other were strong and bitter. The Kennebeckers, having an older lumbering tradition, were apt to feel a bit superior and their condescension irked the Penobscot rivermen. Kennebeckers were, to the Penobscot man's jaundiced eye, "Fancy Dans," dudes and any number of other things, mostly unspeakable. After all, Bangor was still a rough, backwoods town, ungiven to such effete niceties as mustache cups and table napkins. The Kennebeckers, when they deigned to come to Bangor, were wont to carry, of all things, flowered carpetbags when an old meal sack was plenty good enough for a Bangor Tiger to take into the woods. For decades afterwards almost anything in the way of a fancy knapsack or carrying bag acquired the derisive name of "Kennebecker."

It was never quite clear how much trading and dealing was required behind the scenes at Augusta to thwart the Kennebeckers' sound and reasonable plan. In any event the petition was turned down and the plot to divert Penobscot water into Moosehead Lake abandoned. The Bangor lumbermen, and presumably the Lord, breathed easier.

The tumult and the shouting had scarcely died away when it became quite clear that the Penobscot men were intent upon proceeding with their own plan to steal water from the St. John drainage system. The original plan of Pingree's partner Ebenezer Coe was to dig a canal from Mud Pond to Umbazookskus Lake and drive Allagash pine into the West Branch. The Telos Dam idea seemed sound enough to him, but that would mean driving the East Branch and there were few wilder and more twisting rivers in the state.

Events were moving too fast and, as it turned out, Coe and Pingree moved too slowly. A pair of Bangor lumbermen, Hastings Strickland and Amos Roberts, purchased from the state Township 6R11, paying a premium price of $35,500 for it, with the specific idea of making the cut between Telos and Webster lakes and building dams at Telos and Chamberlain. The first dams were built in March of 1841 and a small crew was put to work for several months grubbing out a rough channel between Webster and Telos.

Troubles arose at once. The first dam at Chamberlain was carried away and with it went a portion of the shore. The second dam was, in consequence, more costly and no more successful, being too low. It was at this juncture that David Pingree and Ebenezer Coe came back into the picture. By this time Pingree had acquired six or seven Allagash townships none of which had much value unless he could buy his way into this Telos Canal setup and be assured of getting his logs through. Pingree promptly offered to build a third dam at Chamberlain. This dam, with Coe's engineering experience brought to bear upon the problem, worked admirably.

It was at this point that Amos Roberts began to get nervous. To him, the whole risky business seemed fraught with intangibles. He saw trouble ahead because of the manner in which tolls were to be charged, and there was, indeed, a question about the legality of this sweet little monopoly. And what about the St. John interests? The undeclared Aroostook War over the border issue was in its critical phase and American-Canadian relations were brittle. Would the Canadians stand meekly by while St. John watershed waters were bled south? What was to prevent them from blowing up the dams?

Amos Roberts decided to dicker with David Pingree. Why not let Pingree take part of the risk? With the idea of unloading his interest, Roberts went to see Pingree at Salem. What happened at the meeting was revealed a few years later at the hearing in Augusta, called to settle the whole complicated affair. Roberts testified:

I went to Salem and staid in his [Pingree's] counting house
till midnight; I asked him for $30,000 for the town; he said
he wanted me to keep it and not sell it; I told him I would
always keep it and sell the other half for $15,000 and would
establish the tolls at two shillings [per thousand feet of
lumber]; he thought it was too high; I undertook to con-
vince him it was not. . . . After talking till twelve we could
not agree and I went away. Saw Smith(6) in Boston the next
day; he said Pingree, after sleeping on it, thought he had
better buy; wanted I should go down to Salem and see him.
Went down an hour before the mail train in which I was to
return home . . . We talked until the cars came along and
could not agree. I told him I could not talk about selling
unless we fixed the toll at two shillings. He thought thirty
cents enough. . . . He asked me if I saw a young man in his
counting house. I told him I did. He told me he was going
to send him down to make another cut (Mud Pond to
Umbazookskus); his name is Coe, our engineer. I replied
that I did not think he could do it; that if we could it would
be fifty to $100,000. . . . Considered it a threat if I did not
sell. I asked him what would become of his cut if he should
make one, and I should dig mine deeper. He said he would
get an injunction. . . .

Quite obviously, Roberts' canal was worthless without
Pingree's Chamberlain Dam and Pingree's dam was useless
without Roberts' canal. Pingree would have preferred that
Roberts hold onto the dam and cut at Telos if a reasonable rate
could be established for running logs through it. When they
failed to agree on this point, Pingree, after some horse trading,
offered $9,000 for half the key township 6R11 with agreement
to make up the difference to $15,000 when and if he realized it
from the timberland. When the two stubborn traders parted, it
was only the matter of the interest on $2,000 that kept them
apart.

Too late, Pingree realized he had made a big mistake in not
meeting Roberts' terms. Amos Roberts turned around and sold,

for $15,000, the Telos Canal rights to Rufus Dwinel, a Bangor lumberman with his fingers in many pies.

Then, the trouble really began. The squabble between Kennebeckers and Penobscot men was a love fest compared to the fight that broke out when the Bangor men fell out among themselves.

Once Dwinel had the little monopoly in his hands he became a passionate defender of property rights, insisting that his canal was every bit as sacred as his own living room and trespass upon it was exactly as culpable. In short, no one was driving any logs through his cut until they paid his price. The toll was set at two shillings (34 cents) at first. But when Pingree and others cried "robbery," the price went to fifty cents per thousand feet of lumber. It was Dwinel's contention that in this refusal there was an implied threat to drive logs through by force which necessitated the hiring of a force to defend his property. Now the users, he declared, must share the police expense.

The exchanges between Pingree and Dwinel, at first moderate and reasonably conciliatory, descended quickly to acrimony. In insisting on levying a part of the expense incurred in defending his property, Dwinel accused Pingree of cupidity and avarice and attempting to violate "my just and assured rights." In his later appeal before the legislature Dwinel let himself go with excoriating sarcasm.

"This poor man Pingree, worth only twenty-five townships of the best timberland in the state of Maine, on which his agents think he will make half a million dollars or more, is afraid I shall make or receive half a dollar per thousand on timber growing on five townships of his land."

David Pingree refused to be put down by Dwinel's righteous anger. In a letter to Dwinel he said: "I wrote you last hoping we might come to some arrangement, and in case we do not agree, proposed to have the toll fixed by three good disinterested men . . . for them to say what percent of it should

belong to me, for my dam, which is my part of the improvement. I well know you are capable of managing your own
business, as you say, and thought we might settle the whole
matter between ourselves. . . . I am sorry the offer should have
offended you . . . I do not agree with you that an improvement
for use of the public is like your dwelling house, the door of
which you can shut and keep closed as long as you please."

The matter was coming to a head—and fast. Throughout the
battle it was Dwinel's contention that there was a conspiracy
to defraud him on the part of the Allagash timberland owners
and a threat to run logs through by force. This charge was
firmly denied by Pingree and his cohorts. There can be little
doubt, though, that Pingree and others brought logs into the
thoroughfare with the idea of making some sort of test of
legality, if not of strength, the thinking being that whatever
the damages incurred by driving through would amount to
considerably less than Dwinel's asking price.

Dwinel's resolution that the trespassers were not going to
have the chance to make any such test was clearly indicated at
the outset. Henry Cotton, for one, had cut some pine under a
permit from Pingree. When he arrived at the dam he was met
by Henry Head, Dwinel's chief deputy. When Cotton offered
to pay two shillings toll he was told that the price was fifty
cents and that there were 100 armed men standing by to back
up the price.

Cotton reported later that it was more like fifty to seventy-
five men but that was quite enough as far as he was concerned.
It was a piratical crew armed with villainous knives and, to a
man, they appeared ready and eager to use them.

Samuel Hunt, who also had cut logs under a Pingree permit,
agreed with Cotton at the subsequent hearing that the force
was formidable and sufficient to give him pause. Hunt testified: "When we got to the cut we found some men there; they
boasted there were 100; think there were not so many; saw
some with large size butcher knives. I had rather face a piked
hand-spike than such knives . . . Mr. Head was the principal

man with the posse. He said we couldn't pass unless we agreed to pay certain expenses that had been incurred to get men there, and I signed an agreement to pay half the expenses of getting the posse, and two shillings toll besides."

Some of the crew of persuaders insisted they came from Bangor, but the consensus was that the last address of the majority of the ruffians had been the State penitentiary. But Dwinel had made his point. The loggers with pine in the thoroughfare paid up almost to a man. The one holdout was Leadbetter, of Bangor. He steadfastly refused to pay the toll. His logs remained in the thoroughfare.

Dwinel had won the first round. But it was a Pyrrhic victory. Pingree and his followers forced the matter before the Maine State Legislature. This august body listened for a number of days to testimony on both sides of the issue and in due course passed down Solomon judgment. Two acts were passed: one act permitted Dwinel to incorporate under a state charter and set the toll at twenty cents a thousand feet. A deadline was set for his acceptance. If Dwinel refused to agree by the deadline date, a second act empowered Dwinel's opponents to organize and incorporate the Lake Telos & Webster Pond Sluicing Company which would open the canal to free access.

Rufus Dwinel, caught between the devil and the deep blue sea, capitulated. The Telos War was over. There were other disputes and heated arguments in the course of the ensuing decades, but the waters of the Allagash, diverted by the hands of man, continued to work for the Bangor loggers until all the big pine had gone downriver.

THE
BLOODLESS WAR

12

IT WASN'T much of a war, as wars go. A cow was killed by a stray shot, a militiaman caught cold and died of pneumonia. It was hot enough while it lasted and it lasted quite a spell; at least, the argument about where Canada ended and Maine began had been blowing up a storm for over half a century.

Essentially, it was Maine's private little war with pine timber the stake. Maine was proud of her new status as a sovereign state and her feisty citizenry made it quite clear that it was nothing loath to take on the whole British Empire single-handed rather than give an inch of the state's timbered land to the King's men.

History has put it down as the Aroostook War. The detractors of Maine's Governor John Fairfield termed it "Fairfield's Farce" and were quite outspoken in the opinion that Maine's wilderness wasteland was scarcely worth a parlor discussion let alone a shooting war.

It was never anything more nor less than a lumberman's war, and the fact that it very nearly developed into a test of arms between Britain and the United States was a measure of the conviction on the part of Maine lumbermen that this was no joke and the threat to the integrity of Maine's territory and millions of board feet of standing pine no comic opera matter.

Of course, the Canadian lumbermen were every bit as exercised over the ambiguity of the title to certain sections of eastern and northern Maine. Northern Maine? It was their sturdy contention that much of the timbered lands so identified

108

by the Yankees were in fact southern Canada. It was the very height of audacity to accuse them of "trespass cutting" on their own Crown Lands.

The trouble had begun some two hundred years earlier with overlapping grants of European kings who knew little and cared less about the geography of eastern North America. In 1621, James I of England granted to Sir William Alexander territory designated as Nova Scotia, mentioning the St. Croix River as the boundary between New England and these lands. Several decades later, Sir Ferdinando Gorges received from Charles I a tract called "Province of Mayne" whose northeastern boundary was only vaguely defined in relation to the Alexander grant. In 1674, the Gorges grant was purchased by the Massachusetts Bay Colony. Then, to compound the confusion, the Treaty of Utrecht in 1713 dictated that the French cede the whole territory of Nova Scotia to England "according to its ancient boundaries." Here again the "River St. Croix" was mentioned as a natural boundary line.

For a number of decades more, the French settlers and the scattered inhabitants of Maine's eastern lands were in constant dispute over who owned what and why. When Quebec fell in 1759 and all of New France became English soil, the exact definition of the bounds was rendered academic. The American Revolution changed that. When the United States became an independent nation, that question of just where the British Crown's jurisdiction ceased and that of the new nation began became once again a matter of moment.

The problem should have been put to rest when the negotiators got together in Paris after the Revolution. It was not. The velvet-gloved hands of diplomacy, far from settling the matter, further confused the issue. Both parties to the treaty accepted the fuzzy term "traditional" or "ancient" boundary. Using as a basis for discussion the map drawn by John Mitchell of Massachusetts in 1744, an agreement was reached that designated the northeast line as "that angle formed by a line drawn due north from the source of the St. Croix River to the highlands which divide those rivers that empty themselves into the St. Lawrence from those which fall into the Atlantic Ocean."

That should have been simple enough, even for a diplomat. It might have been conclusive except that the diplomats were in such a rush to get the treaty signed and head for home that, although they defined this northeast border, they failed to identify it.

Just where were these mysterious "highlands"? And, for that matter, which river was the "true St. Croix" so frequently mentioned as the "traditional boundary"?

Earlier treaties were of little help. Three rivers that flowed into Passamaquoddy Bay had been called in turn, or interchangeably, the "St. Croix." There was the Magaguadavic, the most easterly; the Schoodic (the present St. Croix) in the middle; and the Cobscook, the most westerly.

When asked to give an opinion, the Indians just shrugged. They used the Indian names for their rivers and had never heard of the St. Croix. The stew began simmering. It would have gone on at a low boil for years except that, suddenly, the Crown at the sharp prodding of Canadian lumbermen decided that the "true St. Croix" might very well be the Penobscot River and that the mysterious "highlands" could be found by drawing a line due west from a point a mere forty miles north of the St. Croix.

The British Government needed no great amount of prodding, for the Royal Navy was running out of sources for mast pine which it needed desperately. The last great stands of white pine stood in the region of the Allagash. They reasoned that any boundary line drawn that would give them that mast pine was the right line.

The Tories who had fled across the border during the Revolution had their eyes on that pine, too. Some had private claims in these wild lands; others hoped for royal grants to compensate them for their losses, or to reward them for their loyalty to the king.

Understandably, Maine lumbermen were in no mood to accept such thinking, particularly when it became clear that their opposite numbers across the nebulous border were not so much interested in clearing up the legalistic aspect of the long dispute as clearing up those last stands of virgin pine in Maine's North Woods.

The Treaty of Ghent which ended the War of 1812 recognized the dispute as a serious problem requiring settlement. It was agreed that commissioners should meet and arrive at some resolution of the perennial dispute. The commissioners did meet at St. Andrews in New Brunswick and continued to meet over a period of five years without coming to any amicable solution. Finally, the King of the Netherlands was asked to arbitrate the issue. After four more years he did come up with a reasonable compromise. The Yankees, traditionally suspicious of kings and all their works, refused to accept his recommendations on the rather shaky grounds that "the King of the Netherlands has ceased to occupy that independent station among the sovereigns of Europe contemplated by the convention of 1827." In historical perspective this was a mistake, for Maine would have gained more territory under this compromise plan than she eventually settled for.

So the border troubles continued. In the Madawaska region along the St. John, the New Brunswick magistrate began issuing warrants against Maine settlers, insisting they pay taxes as aliens. There were harassments and property confiscations. One John Baker, who had settled himself on land granted him by the Commonwealth of Massachusetts, carried on a private war of his own. His home became a meeting place for the Yankee minority group. Wishing to make his sympathies clear, he erected a "Liberty Pole" in front of his home and raised the flag of the United States. The Canadian magistrate promptly replied to this overt act by dragging Baker from his bed and carrying him off in irons to the Provincial capital at Fredericton where he was arraigned and convicted on the charges of conspiracy and treason.

Repeatedly, the harassed settlers appealed to the Federal

Government for redress. Washington tried valiantly to assume the position that the border trouble didn't exist, or, if it did, that it would go away if painstakingly ignored.

This Federal insouciance served further to arouse the ire of the proud Maine citizenry, particularly the lumbermen who saw the virgin pine they considered their own being systematically plundered. The State of Mainers were fighting mad and it was quite clear that the settlers were ready to precipitate a shooting war, with or without a federal blessing.

Dr. C. T. Jackson, Maine's first official geologist, fresh from the North Woods on a resource exploration, raised his respected voice in 1838 in the foreword of the *Second Annual Report on the Geology of the Public Lands.*

The claim set up by Great Britain to more than *ten thousand square miles* of the territory of Maine, on the plea that the St. John does not empty into the Atlantic, but pours its waters into the Bay of Fundy, and that the chain of highlands designated in the Treaty of 1783, is the range which divides the Penobscot and Kennebec waters from the Allagash and Walloostook, is certainly too absurd for serious refutation, and shows only an earnest and grasping desire of that country to extend its territory into lands belonging justly to this country. . . .

I will ask you if we are prepared to make a sacrifice of one of the most valuable timber and agricultural districts in the State of Maine, or if we shall willingly give to Great Britain military power over our territory which she would be able to possess, should we relinquish to her, in any degree, our boundary line. . . . Although war is a great evil, yet exigencies arise by which we may be forced into such a contest.

A decade later, Thoreau, certainly no hothead, had some wry afterthoughts on the matter as he stood ankle-deep in water at Mud Pond Carry, en route to the Allagash.

I remember hearing a good deal about the "highland" dividing the waters of the Penobscot from those of the St. John, as well as the St. Lawrence, at the time of the northeast boundary dispute, and I observed by my map, that the line claimed by Great Britain as the boundary prior to 1842 passed between Umbazookskus Lake and Mud Pond, so that we either had crossed or were then on it. These, then, according to her interpretation of the treaty of '83, were the "highlands which divide those rivers that empty themselves into the St. Lawrence from those which fall into the Atlantic Ocean" . . . I thought that if the commissioners themselves, and the King of Holland with them, had spent a few days here, with their packs upon their backs, looking for that "highland" they would have had an interesting time, and perhaps it would have modified their views of the question somewhat.

Thoreau was exactly right about the British claim. The King's men saw no point, so long as they were making a claim, not to make it a good one. The extreme British claim did indeed move the "St. Croix" to the Penobscot, and from there they drew that due north line a mere forty miles, thence west to the "Highlands." Due west, that is, except for a little southerly dip that gathered in Chamberlain and Eagle lakes. They not only wanted the Allagash, they dearly coveted the Allagash headwaters where stood perhaps the greatest treasure trove of virgin white pine remaining in the continent.

The Americans took another extreme position, although much more firmly supported by antecedent maps and treaties: The American line went due north from the "True St. Croix" one hundred and forty miles, all the way to the St. Lawrence. The Americans put the "Highlands" just south of the St. Lawrence.

The New Brunswickers wanted, above all, to hold the St. John. This was their trade line: it was also their access to the Allagash pine. They wanted that pine to flow their way, north and east to their seaports. The Maine lumbermen were already doing some serious thinking about the Telos Canal which would realize their dream of kiting Allagash logs south and east to Bangor and obviate the necessity of driving them north to the St. John and into Canadian territory.

As more and more reports began drifting into the lumber capital of Bangor of Canadian trespass cutting and incidents of Maine loggers being arrested by provincial authorities and timber seized, the demands for formal action reached a crisis pitch. John Fairfield, long a passionate champion of the Maine cause, rose before the assembled legislative body in Augusta and delivered a ringing philippic.

"Maine, sirs," he said, "feels that she has suffered deep and enduring wrongs at the hands of the British government. She has been unjustly and illegally deprived of her property and her jurisdiction in a portion of her territory which has been flaunted and violated. Her valuable timber has been the object of plunder and waste. Her citizens have been seized and imprisoned, without the semblance of lawful right. The nation guilty of these gross offenses not only denies redress, but arrogantly refuses to let her acts be tried before an impartial tribunal. What is worse, Maine feels that her distress has been ignored by the Federal Government. The mother abandons the daughter in the latter's hour of need. . . . To endure this insult silently and supinely would be the last measure of disgrace. We do not advocate war. But if resistance to all forcible attempts to take our property from us be war, then war it must be. . . ."

Fairfield's fiery words failed to intimidate the Canadian lumbermen. Incidents continued and relations between Maine and Canada rapidly deteriorated. Fairfield ran as a Democratic candidate for governor making his aggressive attitude a prime issue. He won handily and one of his first actions upon assuming office was to send a message to the Maine Legislature making categorical charges against the trespass cutters and estimating that a hundred thousand dollars' worth of pine would be plundered in the course of that winter unless prompt and firm action was taken. He asked that the State Land Agent be dispatched to the troubled area on the Aroostook and Fish rivers with a sufficient force to seize teams and equipment, destroy Canadian lumber camps and send the rascals running.

The legislators gave their governor a rousing cheer and promptly authorized Land Agent Rufus McIntire and Major Hastings Strickland, Sheriff of Penobscot Country, to go into action. With firm resolve and a body of two hundred militiamen and volunteers to back it up, the posse leaders proceeded to the Aroostook.

That this action on the part of the State of Maine constituted an act of war, no one doubted for an instant, least of all the new commander of the small Federal garrison at Houlton. Major Reynold Kirby, upon getting wind of this punitive force and its intent, dispatched a frantic note to Washington in which he said, "From the state of feeling existing in the Province of New Brunswick there can be no doubt that this demonstration on the part of Maine will be viewed as an overt act of hostility, and I am apprehensive it will lead to retaliatory measures . . ."

That was a fair statement. The Maine posse was looking for trouble and promptly found it. The New Brunswickers, not about to give ground without a fight, supplied themselves with arms from the provincial arsenal at Woodstock and met the invaders head on.

The two forces were fairly even in manpower. The Yankees, however, had a slight edge in firepower, having brought in a six-pound cannon. The provincials judged discretion the better part of valor and retreated with McIntire at their heels.

The American force camped that winter night near the mouth of the Little Madawaska River while McIntire and four companions found more comfortable quarters at a farm four miles upriver. McIntire had arranged to meet with the provincial warden of the disputed territory and talk things over.

The Canadians were in no conciliatory mood. Learning of McIntire's whereabouts, a party of forty surrounded the farmhouse in the dead of night. The Americans were ushered from their cozy beds and carried by ox team to Woodstock and turned over to the civil authorities who in turn took them to Fredericton where they were summarily clapped into jail.

There was a question of whether or not McIntire's host had been the betrayer. If he was, he had second thoughts, or a change of mind, for he hurried forth in the darkness to warn Strickland and the encamped posse, an act that inspired a snatch of doggerel.

Run, Strickland, Run!
Fire, Stover, Fire!
Were the last words of McIntire!

Sheriff Strickland, a man of action, ordered his men to hold their ground and set out for Augusta as fast as a relay of horses could carry him to inform the governor of this crowning outrage.

Coincident with the arrival of this unremembered Paul Revere, Governor Fairfield received the tidings from another source. The uneasy Federal commander at the Houlton garrison had this to say:

Sir: An express is about to be sent by the inhabitants of this place, and I avail myself of it to inform your exc'y of the fact that Land Agent of Maine, Mr. McIntire, Gustavus G. Cushman, and Thomas Bartlett, Esquires, Magistrates of Penobscot County, were on yesterday made prisoners by a party of armed men within the claimed limits of the State of Maine, under the Treaty of 1783.

. . . My object in making this communication is that you may be early apprised of these events, and especially that your Excellency may believe, upon such assurance as is in my power to give, that the acts of outrage upon the persons named . . . are, in my opinion, totally without any legal authority from the Provincial Government.

Whatever may be the results of the operations of the

party sent to the disputed territory under the authority of the State of Maine, I take the liberty to represent to your Excellency, with all deference to you, and a full sense of my own humble position in regard to the important question of Sovereignty, that any hasty measure of retaliation for the outrage committed would compromise the interest of the State, and complicate those matters which are now subjects of negotiation between the two General Governments . . .

A few days later, Major Kirby dispatched to his superior in Washington a report on the incident in which he further firmed up his fence-sitting position and stated his fears that Maine was going too far and too fast. In conclusion he wrote:

A Regiment of the West Indies landed about 7th inst. at Halifax and may be momentarily expected at Fredericton . . . I presume it will be moved to the Aroostook within the bounds of the disputed territory. This I understand would be a violation between the two Governments. . . . In the meantime I feel it my duty, in no way to compromise the General government, either by furnishing supplies to the militia, or making any movement in concert with them, but the command will be held in readiness to meet any violation on the part of our neighbors of the *acknowledged* territory of the State of Maine.

Governor Fairfield wasn't waiting for Federal support. At the Governor's insistence the legislature appropriated $800,000 and authorized a draft of 10,343 men from the rolls of the State Militia. Such action was scarcely necessary, for volunteers were pouring into Bangor from all over the state.

The sound of drumfire and the tramp of marching men was, at long last, heard in Washington. The very thought of a single state embarking on an independent war with a major power sent shudders down the backs of the mighty. The House of Representatives in Washington took hasty cognizance of the demands of Provincial Governor Sir John Harvey that the Maine forces be withdrawn and the stern announcement that he had been empowered by his government to move in and hold exclusive jurisdiction over the disputed territory. President Van Buren was authorized to raise 50,000 volunteers in the event that England made good her threat forcibly to maintain control over the region in contention. General Winfield Scott was dispatched in haste to investigate the situation.

Apparently, the general was not at all sure of what his function should be. To the President he said, "If you want war, I need only to look on in silence. The Maine people will make it for you fast and hot enough. I know them. But if peace be your wish, I can give you no assurance of success. The difficulties in my way will be formidable." To this the President replied, "Let us have peace with honor."

Nor were the Maine settlers at all sure they wanted General Scott to calm down the situation. They had seen quite enough of Washington's vacillation and pusillanimity and envisioned another sellout. General Scott was dubbed, with ironic implications, "The Great Pacifier."

Governor Fairfield, although he gave the general assurances that Maine had no desire to plunge the two nations into another war, stuck to his guns. He would withdraw Maine troops from the troubled area if New Brunswick's Governor Harvey retracted his threat to move into it with military force. Harvey did back down. The British Government agreed to refer the dispute to a boundary commission.

It was at this point that the wily Daniel Webster was called in to contribute his good and shrewd offices. Webster had become Secretary of State under William Henry Harrison and was beginning his negotiation for a final settlement of the prickly problem when Harrison died. John Tyler assumed office and, not wishing to disturb the delicate situation, kept Webster on to deal with the newly appointed special envoy, Alexander Baring, the first Lord Ashburton.

The bargaining and dealing began in the spring of 1842 and a treaty was signed in the fall of that year.

The Webster-Ashburton Treaty didn't please everyone. Particularly disgruntled were the Maine lumbermen who had never been in a mood to compromise in the first place. There was one compromise that seemed reasonable to all concerned. Of the three "St. Croix" rivers, the middle one, the Schoodic, was pinned down finally and forever as the "True St. Croix." The due north line proceeded from that point to the St. John and thence up the middle of the river to the St. Francis. The United States was awarded something more than half of the 12,000 square miles of disputed territory. The British were happy to retain control of a good part of the St. John, their vital lumber river, and to hold the military road that linked New Brunswick and Quebec.

After the fact, many in the upper echelons of British diplomacy admitted they got more than they had ever expected out of the deal. The Yankees, on the other hand, were awarded the whole region of the Allagash with its pine riches virtually unexploited. To compensate Maine for the loss of public land the Federal Government settled for damages to the amount of $150,000; Massachusetts received a like amount for her loss.

No one has explained satisfactorily why the line was carried up the St. Francis River rather than continuing up the St. John, a happenstance that gave Maine a sizable piece of territory *she* possibly never expected to get. Folklore and romantic fancy have a way of filling the gaps of knowledge. It was much too simple to accept that the arbiters recognized the St. Francis as a part of the American watershed and clearly not tributary to the St. Lawrence. More appealing was the waggish notion which had currency at the time that the American loggers plied Webster and Ashburton with black rum and sent them up the wrong river.

It was part of frontier pride to insist that Dan'l Webster, whatever his failings as horse trader, could certainly outdrink the British delegate on any given day and had knowingly fallen in with the loggers' plot.

There is another romantic footnote to the history of the Northeast Boundary Dispute which concerns William Bingham, one of the largest investors in Maine wild lands, some of which were involved in the controversy.

William Bingham, for all his wealth, was land poor. The several millions of acres he purchased east of the Penobscot were to be paid for in installments to the Commonwealth of Massachusetts. Unable to meet the installments, he had tried unsuccessfully to borrow money from American banks. He finally appealed to the English banking house of Baring. Sir Francis Baring, head of the firm, dispatched his son, Alexander, to America to inspect the land and in the course of this duty he journeyed into Maine with William Bingham and his wife and two daughters. Alexander reported favorably to his father on the loan and on a Bingham daughter, Anne, as well.

Moreover, he married the girl and the two families were further bound together when Alexander's young brother married Anne's younger sister, Maria. It was Alexander Baring, by then elevated to the peerage, who was sent to America as Lord Ashburton to attempt to settle the Northeast Boundary Dispute.

A conflict of interest? Clearly, he was involved in the arbitration of a matter of deep and personal interest, for his wife was a major heir to the vast Bingham tract. It can only be said that the final treaty left the Bingham lands intact and American.

Although the boundary lines between Maine and Canada were fixed forever, troubles continued for years and generations to plague the lumbering community. Daniel Webster had worked diligently to plug every loophole by which the Canadians might seek to close the St. John River to American lumbermen. Under the quite specific conditions of the treaty of 1842, "All timber situated on land ceded to the United States, which, from its position must pass down the St. John, *shall be dealt with as if it were the produce of the said province.*"

In other words, the St. John was declared the line of boundary and the river was declared open to both parties to the agreement and "all the produce of the forest in logs, lumber, boards, staves, shingles, or of agriculture, not being manufactured, grown on any of those parts of the State of Maine watered by the River St. John or by its tributaries . . . shall have free access into and through the said river. . . ."

Treaties between nations do not always resolve the rankling problems between men, particularly men bred to solve their own problems. The treaty ink was scarcely dry when the Canadians began slapping a provincial tax on lumber run down the St. John. Nor had the opening of the Telos Canal, which the Canadians contended was bleeding water from the St. John watershed sorely needed for their own log drives, designed to soothe Canadian feelings.

For almost a hundred years Maine-Canadian relations were to be marked by sporadic bickering, legal actions, incidents of blown dams and attempts to dynamite dams. Nor were the American Allagash lumbermen, downriver from the dams that diverted Allagash water south, reluctant to employ vigilante tactics when their drives were threatened by a low head of water. Frontier law was all the law there was and no law that could not be backed up by strength was worth a crotched "schoolmarm" pine.

There was the day Joe Michaud had his logs hung up between Chamberlain Dam and Allagash Falls for lack of water. Joe, called "One Eye" behind his back, saw only one way to get the water he needed to drive his logs to the St. John. He arrived at the dam with a forty-five on his hip and a box of dynamite in his hands. Backing up his play was a determined crew that counted in its numbers such indestructibles as Willy Jalbert, Nazaire Pelkey and Nazaire St. John.

Some insisted that Joe had time to toss but one stick of dynamite into the works before the watchman drove him off with several rounds from his thirty-thirty rifle. Others relate that the watchman was disarmed and hog-tied and that the boys accomplished a more leisurely job, with Joe exhorting the crew with a spate of purple oaths that withered the spring buds for miles around.

All agreed that the efforts were unavailing. Water broke through, but not enough to float Joe Michaud's logs and he was forced to wait for rain and a rise of water. Later, a concrete dam was built at the spot which discouraged further attempts to relieve water shortages on the Allagash.

Perhaps he failed to get the water he needed to float his drive, but, as Joe Michaud remarked, he sure enough showed those so-and-sos from the Penobscot how he felt about their blankety-blank dam.

From the beginning, Maine loggers were a special breed with a special and explicit manner of communicating.

DAYLIGHT IN THE SWAMP

13

FOR A good hundred years there were lumbermen, lumberers, woodsmen, loggers, hewers of timber. Then, along
about the time when spruce replaced pine timbering, the saw,
the axe, woods horses took over the hauling burden from oxen
and the logger himself became a professional, the designation
"lumberjack" made its mysterious appearance in the lexicon of
Maine lumbering.

According to Mitford Matthews' *Dictionary of American-
isms*, the term first appeared in print in April of 1849 in an
issue of *Spirit of the Times*. There was no general acceptance
of the word for some decades. As late as 1884, Lucius Hubbard, in his *Woods and Lakes of Maine*, seemed satisfied with
"logger" and "woodsman." Thoreau, clearly, had never heard
of the term "lumberjack." He relied primarily on the term
"lumberer."

Fannie Eckstorm, one of the most knowledgeable chroni-
clers of the Maine logging scene in the latter half of the last
century, spurned to use the term, which suggests that it never
was in common usage among the loggers themselves and was
essentially a literary hybrid popularized by such writers as
Holman Day whose *King Spruce* and other works glorified the
last-century Maine logger.

It is doubtful that the Maine logger in any period including
the present thought of himself as a lumberjack. The word seldom appeared in authentic logging minstrelsy. The man who
went to work in the woods thought of himself in terms of his
specialty: he was a chopper or teamster, sled-tender, swamper,
barker, topper, scaler, clerk. The cook, of course, was simply

123

"the cook" and would not have taken kindly to any less lordly designation.

The river drivers, although frequently a mixed bag of mavericks, specialists, and unholy terrors, were equally select. The men who took the logs downriver in the spring were handpicked from the winter crew for the exacting and hazardous job of driving the winter harvest to the boom. A man stayed on, or came in for the drive, on invitation only, and the prime requisites were knowledge of the river, agility on the running logs, and the stamina to take a bruising dawn-to-dark day. Only "catty" men got the call and a man who couldn't sleep on the ground in wet clothes, with his boots on, didn't last long.

The river driver got a premium wage which could account for Pierre Blanchette's insistence that spring on the Allagash that he could work like a horse. The walking boss hired Pierre only to find before the drive got past the first pitch that Pierre hung back whenever the situation required men on the running logs. The boss pointed this out in no uncertain terms, reminding Pierre of his boast that he could work like a horse.

Pierre's rejoinder became a classic Allagash riposte.

"You bet," Pierre replied, "you ever see horse out on log?"

Typically, the first Maine loggers were no more than casual woods workers and logging was a seasonal job taken up in the winter to eke out a slim frontier living. This was to change dramatically as the lumber industry expanded. By 1850 the Maine logger was evolving a personal style and a way of life that would make him unique, an American archetype. And, like the bluewater sailor for whom the sea was home, mistress, and master, the Maine logger carved out for himself an all-consuming calling. The woods became his only true home, his dedication to assault the forest with axe and saw, to lay the trees low, to let daylight into the swamp.

The new breed, *logger americanus,* whether in sorrow or glory, was recognized as a distinct species. More accurately, perhaps, he was a mutant, an animal with inheritable characteristics that differed from the parent stock. Certainly the Maine logger, who came strutting and roaring upon the scene with the opening of the spruce era, was as different from the common man as a cow from a feathered bird.

Not even Thoreau who castigated him as a "plunderer" and a mere "hireling" was immune from his spell. A meeting with a party of timber cruisers in the Allagash in the mid-1850s moved him to write: "I have often wished since that I was with them. They search for timber over a given section, climbing hills and often high trees to look off,—explore the streams by which it is to be driven, and the life,—spending five or six weeks in the woods, they two, alone, a hundred miles or more from any town,—roaming about, and sleeping on the ground where night overtakes them,—depending chiefly on the provisions they carry with them, though they do not decline what game they come across. . . . It is a solitary and adventurous life, and comes nearest to the trapper of the West, perhaps. They work ever with a gun as well as an axe, let their beards grow, and live without neighbors, not on an open plain, but far within a wilderness."

Thoreau was one of the first to note that the logger's garb was as special and characteristic as his behavior. Writing of his predilection for red, Thoreau remarked, "This is the favorite color with the lumbermen; and red flannel is reputed to possess some mysterious virtues, to be most healthful and convenient in respect to perspiration."

The Concord naturalist commented also on the headgear which had become standard at the time. He referred to the article as a "Kossuth hat," using the name of a similar headpiece popularized by Kossuth, the Hungarian patriot, during his visit to America in the early 1850s. It was of dark soft material with a rolled brim and guaranteed, according to the local advertisements of the period, to "shed water like a duck."

These forest rovers were strictly Maine men in the beginning, second and third generation settlers whose fathers and grandfathers had beat back the trees to make a patch of growing earth. As the lumbering industry expanded, more and more men were needed to harvest the trees. Outlanders and outright "furriners" joined the ranks to the muttering of the natives who saw such recruitment as a plot to lower wages, already less than princely. The first wave of Irish arrived in the mid-1830s and in such numbers as to call forth the suspicion "that the Pope was planning to establish a new principality in North America."

In the north the first settlers moved up the St. John from the Canadian provinces to the region of the Allagash. English, Scotch-Irish, Irish, some settled at the confluence of the Allagash and the St. John, some pushed on up the river above Allagash Falls to clear patches of land and become a part of the lusty logging annals.

"Moosetowners" they were called; but first, if they hailed from the provinces, they were "Bluenoses" or "Herring chokers." Distinctions were apt to be crude and they grew even more gross when the northern and middle Europeans piled in to take up the axes and saws. A man may never have been within a thousand miles of Warsaw; he may have been a Lithuanian, Austrian, Hungarian or Serb; but, to the landed woodsman, he was simply a "Polack" or perhaps a "Bohunk." The appellation could be affectionate or opprobrious, depending on the mood or situation. Finns, Swedes and Norwegians were faced with much the same problem of preserving their national integrity: they were simply lumped as "Swedes" or "squareheads."

These new Americans, once they proved they could stick it out—"go the route"—were given their due, if grudgingly. There was no faulting the Polack in the winter woods; his massive frame, strength and endurance made him a match for the best. On the spring drive, though, he was judged less than catty. There was the myth that the Polack who could walk a running log was yet to be born. His saving grace was his good humor under stress and chivying. The Finn, on the other hand, was apt to be quiet and moody, a good and tidy workman, but emotionally unpredictable.

The French, of course, were there from the beginning. They were "Canucks" or "Frenchies" who could not, in all fairness, be disparaged as loggers or woodsmen, but were nonetheless reproved for their stubborn refusal to learn to speak English.

But whatever the roots, the tongue, or special traits, the great melting pot of the woods made them loggers and many of the differences were lost in the larger alikeness. They were rough, tough, excessive; they were rammed into a mold that the job demanded. Lusty, hard-drinking, hard-working, brawling, they acquired the stamp that made them, to a man, unique and recognizable.

The late Stewart Holbrook suggested in his *Yankee Loggers* that the breed evolved by natural selection. He wrote: ". . . of say, a crew of fifty green loggers, going into the woods in October, about half would find the life too rigorous. They would soon quit and leave. Of those remaining, the less alert or sure-footed would be struck by fallen timber or crushed flat on the log landing. The spring drive downriver, most dangerous of woods work, would surely remove a few more. Once the drive was in, two or three would die of acute alcoholism or in saloon brawls . . . as for the survivors, they were immune to disease and you couldn't kill them with a pole ax."

It took no more than a generation to evolve this awesome race of men under the dynamics of such a ruthless culling process. An early observer, exposed to the breed for the first time, was moved to write, "They are a young and powerfully built race of men, mostly New Englanders, generally unmarried, and though rude in their manners and intemperate, are quite intelligent. They seem to have a passion for their wild and toilsome life, and judging from their dress, I should think possess a fine eye for the comic and fantastic. The entire apparel of an individual consists of a pair of gray pantaloons and *two* red flannel shirts, a pair of long boots and a woolen covering for the head, and *all* these things are worn at one and the same time."

If only ten out of fifty proved physically and temperamentally fitted for the woods that was quite enough. An endless supply of raw material was piling across the Atlantic from Europe, willing and eager to test strong backs against the standing timber.

There were still a sturdy few in the last half of the nineteenth century with farms, families and a stake in society, but, for the most part, the trees were cut by a breed of rootless men who saw the future no further than the day the drive would be in. Six, eight months in the woods meant a settlement of three to four hundred dollars, depending on what a man owed to the company store. Whatever it was, Bangor was waiting for it, and Fort Kent, or the wide open bar at Connors just across the Canadian border.

The towns got it a little at a time, or all at once in one glorious explosion. After all, it was only money. For those Allagash men who got by Connors and Fort Kent with their stake still reasonably intact, there was Bangor a mere five hour ride on the B&A. The downriver Allagash men were inclined to rate themselves a cut above the "Bangor Tigers" and "Mooseheaders" as loggers and watermen. Whoever heard of a lake man who could snub down a batteau in white water? And was there a man anywhere above Long Lake Dam who could stand up to the likes of Dunc Stewart, Joe Savage, or Bob Nobles?

Yes, there was liquor to be drunk and there were points to be made in Bangor Town, and if any lop-eared, bandy-legged, jumped-up so-and-so begged to differ there was a lively time to be had. The logger's standard circumlocution when he had an itch to get to town was "I need to get my teeth fixed." The best "dentist" could be found in Bangor's "Devil's Half Acre" and the price was likely to depend on the degree of drunkenness and the fatness of the poke of the customer. There was Dolly Jack and there was Fan Jones,(7) both ladies to whom

a house was not a home. In the great Bangor fire the flames
raged all about the emporium known as Fan's and left her
unscathed and still in business. The lady, it appeared, was not
for burning.

The logger who went back to camp in the fall with jingling
money in his pocket was a rare one indeed and considered less
than human and not to be trusted. By and large, it was an
uncommon one who got by the first few weeks after the logs
were at the boom. It was a long hard summer for the logger
without money in his pocket.

The woods had a deadly attraction for the maverick, the
reject from society, the man who could not adapt to the stric-
tures of normal life with its attending responsibilities and
complications. For him the winter lumber camp offered a sort
of protective custody; there he was taken care of, life was
simple and, if he could handle a man's job, he was respected
by his fellows. After a spell of being broke and unwanted in a
heartless town he needed the woods to regain his pride and
manhood.

The Maine logger was variously damned and apotheosized
by his contemporaries as well as later observers of the scene.
Of the Maine logger, one early critic wrote: "His habits in the
forest, and his voyage for the sale of his lumber [the river
drive], all break up the system of persevering industry, and
substitute one of alternate toil, indolence, hardship and
debauch; and in the alternation, indolence and debauch will
inevitably be indulged in the greatest possible proportion. . . .
It is often amid cold and wet that all his labour is performed
. . . to ward off damps and chills he drinks spiritous liquors;
the liquors weaken his system . . . intermittents attack him and
his poverty reaches its last point."

James Russell Lowell met up with a group of loggers north
of Moosehead and remained for breakfast at their camp. Although he admitted his hosts might lack "external polish," the
urbane essayist paid the breed a glowing tribute in his *Moosehead Journey*.

"I have rarely sat at a table d'hote which might not have taken a lesson from them in essential courtesy. I have never seen a finer race of men . . . they appeared to me to have hewn out a northwest passage through wintry woods to those spice-lands of character."

The men of the cloth almost unanimously failed to see such virtues beneath the rough exterior, possibly for the simple reason that they seldom encountered loggers except in the towns and in the throes of a bout of "intermittents." One of the outraged wrote: "The younger men who followed the camp and the river had just two thoughts in mind and two topics of conversation—rum and women. You might hunt the world over and fail to find a breed to compare with them in sheer blasphemy, profanity, lechery and drunkenness."

One of the Maine loggers' staunchest defenders was Fannie Eckstorm. She freely admitted to the logger's frailties, yet found him larger than life, a man to remember.

"He is not concerned about himself, nor about his future in another world . . . for death he does not fear it. Sometimes he courts it, sometimes he scoffs it, sometimes he defies it; but always, always his work comes first. And however low he may seem, however crude, however inferior to that of a man of more culture, finer perceptions, larger opportunity, for emulation, for sport, for duty, for grim, stern, granite obstinacy, he risks his life and wills his will into achievement, or dies for his failure."

Of the Maine logger, Robert P. Tristram Coffin, an incorrigible eulogizer, was moved to write: "They filled the silence between the mountains with the sound of their axes and the sound of falling trees. They went at it with cant dogs and moustaches straining like the antennae of fierce insects. They flowered the virgin snow with sunflowers of tobacco juice. They shouted and sang. . . . They got down a lot of logs from sun to stars."

The truth often lies between the polarities of praise and damnation. They were something less than immortal and short of indestructible; but, as the saying went, if work, troubles and liquor didn't kill them, they lived a long time.

What they had in abundance was a hard-bitten pride and a hearty will to proclaim it.

On the lower Allagash and along the reaches of the St. John to Fort Kent and Edmundson, it was agreed there was no one to match the trio of Dunc Stewart, Joe Savage, and Bob Nobles in a knock-down-drag-out fight. The unholy three were in hearty agreement on this judgment. One small question remained, however: which of the three was the best man? The wondering went on for a number of years, each man in his secret heart slightly prejudiced in his own favor. Then came that day in June. The drive was in and the boys were relaxing at a bar in the little frontier town of Clair.

No one quite recalls which one of the three was the first to wonder out loud. Some say it was Dunc; others suggest that Joe, after tossing down a triple potion neat, hiked up his pants and aired the question in a manner that could not very well be misapprehended. There was no bad blood, mind you, no hard feelings; but, after all, a man couldn't spend the best years of his life in doubt about a matter of such moment.

It was a glorious fight, a classic that was regarded for years as a standard by which all others were measured. To call it a catch-as-catch-can would demean it: kicking, biting, gouging and stomping with calked boots were all a part of the indelicate art of mayhem. The fight consumed a half hour and just about everything in the bar that wasn't cast iron and bolted down. And when it was over it was Bob Nobles, and only Bob, who stood up and called for another round. The important matter had been settled amicably.

Not so amicable was the fight between Cut Chaisé and Pierre Charette. Bad blood had developed between them the year they picked up the rear on one of Will Cunliffe's last drives on the lower Allagash. They were held apart until the logs were at the boom and the delays served only to build up a powerful head of steam. It was Cut who came off top dog in

that rousing encounter, but it was at the cost of his right ear.
Pierre, who had chewed it off, averred a bit sullenly that
even with salt Cut Chaisé's ear would have been no delicacy.

Whether it was an escape to freedom or an escape into
custody, the lumbering life did call forth the best in a man
even if the best was no more than a demonstration of man's
infinite capacity to endure and survive. In the *Logger's Boast*,
the minstrel on the deacon seat of a winter camp would proclaim in song:

> Come, all ye sons of Freedom
> Throughout the State of Maine
> Come, all ye gallant lumbermen,
> And listen to my strain
> On the banks of the Penobscot
> Where the rapid waters flow
> O! we'll range the wild woods over
> And a lumbering we will go.

There was freedom of a sort. A man who didn't like his job,
the boss, or the food, or who simply had to "have his teeth
fixed," could pack up and "make 'er out." He usually got
docked if he failed to fulfill his contract to stay the route; but
if he was determined to go, there was no one to stop him.

There were as many reasons for quitting the job as there
were men, but Fred Madore's reason for departing from one of
Cunliffe's Allagash camps was one of the most curious. On a
diet that leaned heavily on beans, breaking wind was a recreation that was developed to a high art in logging camps. That
winter the camp was blessed with a particularly talented crew
of whom Fred was perhaps the most versatile. One night in the
cookshack the boss decided he had had enough of it. He announced that, as of that moment, any man who performed for
the sheer joy of it would be fined ten dollars and fired.

There was a deal of muttering and a few discreet violations

of the edict, but it was a fairly subdued night in the bunk-house. There were those who wondered how Fred Madore would take the cruel and arbitrary restriction, for Fred, two-hundred and fifty pounds of contrariness, was not a man to be told by a mere boss that he couldn't express himself in nature's innocent manner. Fred, as it turned out, was merely storing up and waiting for the moment when the boss appeared at dawn in the bunkhouse with his cry, "Turn out, you bastards! It's daylight in the swamp!"

Fred Madore's moment had arrived. They say nothing like it had been heard for years; it shook the beams and raised the field spread a good two feet. In the ensuing stillness Fred Madore spoke. "Now, if that ain't a ten dollar fart you never heard one," Fred proclaimed, "besides, I was figgerin' on makin' her out anyway."

The logger himself was the last to see the glamour in the life he led. That was left to the stray scribe who wandered in from the outside world. Charles Hallock, in 1860, offered a romantic account of the *Life Among the Loggers* to the wide-eyed read-ers of *Harper's New Monthly Magazine*. His account started with the "timber-hunter" and his tour of exploration "out from the abodes of men, out from the last new clearing of the pio-neer settler, deep into the recesses of the forest, where the feet of white men are unwont to tread."

About the logger himself, he wrote: "Even the rigorous vicissitudes of the logging camps have an inexplicable charm which the dwellers in cities can never rightly comprehend. The ringing echo of the axe, the merry 'wo-ha' of the teamsters, is exhilarating music, while the crash of falling pine, or the tumult of the logs borne on the spring freshet, thrill every nerve."

Hallock proceeded to go into the economics of the lumber-ing industry of the period. "The location of the pine having once been determined, the timber tract is either purchased or a

rate of stumpage agreed upon with the owner, usually $2.50 to
$3.00 per thousand feet for all timber cut, arrangements are at
once made for building the winter camp. First the supplies
must come in. What skill, what physical strength, what in-
trepidity, what self possession are requisite in transporting a
batteau loaded to the gunwales scores of miles over foaming
rapids, through dangerous rocks and intricate channels, and in
seasons when the fingers grow numb with cold . . ."

John Springer, a lumberman himself in those piney days,
offered a more complete and realistic picture of the early logging camps. As was true of all early American architecture, the
lumber camp was strictly functional, its form dictated by necessity and the materials at hand. The camp was a square
saltbox affair of notched logs, some eight feet high at the front
and pitching down to within two or three feet at the rear. The
double camp was built by placing two such squares face to
face with a fireplace in the center. The fireplace was built
directly under a hole in the roof, an arrangement that served
only casually to draw off the smoke.

The roof was covered with three or four foot shakes, rifted
on the spot from pine, spruce or cedar logs. These were not
fastened down, but merely secured by laying a heavy pole
across each tier.

There was a good and sufficient reason for this. Fires were
common occurrences and a fire, once it got started in such
combustible surroundings, took hold with a roar. Many a winter logging camp ended up as a death trap until the realization
dawned that, when retreat to the door was cut off by fire,
the roof was the quickest avenue of escape.

Once the logs were moss-calked and several layers of spruce
or fir boughs further insulated by several feet of snow were in
place, the camp was a reasonably snug habitation. A roaring
fire in the central fireplace furthered the end of keeping the
bitter winters at bay.

The first Allagash logging camps were primitive enough to
satisfy any champion of the Spartan life. Rooms were indi-

Lumber Camp Interior

cated by placing poles on the dirt floor, the bedstead was mother earth, cushioned by a layer of fir boughs; the bed-clothes consisted of quilts and blankets sewed together until they were long enough to cover the crew. Later, field beds were built off the ground, single- or double-deckers, and the stoutest of the crews were chosen to pin down the spread, one at each end of the long bed. Any freedom the early logger might have enjoyed was sharply curtailed at "lights out," for any movement in the bed was of necessity made in concert. Individualism, in a field bed at least, was not considered a prime virtue.

The beds were muzzle-loaders; a man rammed himself in from the foot. Along the lower tier ran the deacon seat; this standard installation was the split half of a giant log, supported by legs, its flat side up. It usually ran from one end of the camp to the other, along two sides.

Such niceties as oilcloth-covered tables, a separate section for the cook's domain and a dingle, where a chopper could hone his axe to a surgical edge on a grindstone, came later. Whence came the word "dingle" is another mystery, but it survives in parlance and utility to the present day as an area between the bunkhouse and the cookshack where saws can be filed of an evening for the next day in the woods.

The commissary or "wangan"(8) was another early camp fixture. Here a man could purchase—it went down on the books against his account—woods clothes, tobacco, salts and liniment. The best sellers were nostrums alleged to kill pain and whose formulae offered up to ninety-nine percent alcohol.

No doubt there was some muttering among the bosses when tables were first introduced. Godfrey mighty! They'd be asking for plates next!

Before the advent of the table, the crew used the deacon seat or stood around the central fire where a communal platter was set, each man putting his potato, saltfish or bread into the stew to mop up the salt fat. A shock of hair or a beard served well enough as a napkin, although the more fastidious used their wool pants.

The rigors of those early logging camps were softened somewhat by rum rations. So hard-dying was the conviction that timber could not be cut or the drive brought in without rum that it wasn't until well into the last half of the nineteenth century that spirits ceased to be considered a prerequisite to timber harvesting. It had magic power to grease the arm, exhort the will and ease all ills that cold-wracked bodies were heir to.

The conviction never fully disappeared, as evidenced by Stewart Holbrook's recollection of the indestructible Jigger Jones. The immortal Jigger, who lived his charmed life in the later spruce era, was wont to announce that he could run faster, spit farther, jump higher, squat lower and belch louder

Jigger Jones

than any ory-eyed so-and-so north of Boston, and there were few who took issue. Jigger was not exceptional in his personal conviction that a man did not live by bread alone. Wrote Holbrook:

The thermometer was down "two feet below zero" that morning. Jigger, sleeping in the bunk across from mine, sat up on the edge of the bed in his bright vermillion underwear and came up with a crock of Graves' Pure Grain Alcohol. He poured a draught into a tin dipper and drank it neat. Then, barefoot, and in his underwear, he strolled down to the brook through the deep snow and brought a pail of water back to the shack. He remarked that it was middling coolish. While putting on his pants and shoepacks he worked on half a cut of B & L, squirting the juice onto the sizzling stove—to kill the germs in the air, he always said. In a few minutes he took another shot of the grog. Then, just before the gut-hammer's *clong clong* broke through the cold silent darkness outside, he pawed again under the bunk and this time brought forth a bottle of milk of magnesia.

"I guess I better take a dose of this," he said, "you know, I got to be powerful careful of my stomach. . . . It ain't very strong."

Whatever the Maine logger was, glorious or disreputable, larger than life, or merely human, he was special and incomparable: he did the job that was to be done and the job in turn made the man and the legend. How good they were in the lights of the priest or the parson was a matter of opinion; but not a manjack in the crowd ever doubted he was good enough to do the job.

There were few drives on the Allagash that failed to take a toll of men who roared at the notion that a mere river, even at its downright ugliest, could ever take their measure. The river drivers remembered their own in song and legend. On the West Branch the boots the driver would never need again were hung from a pine pin-knot at the spot where the earthly remains were recovered from the river. There they remained until they rotted away. On the lower Allagash, crude crosses marked the tragic spots. These tokens of honor and sorrow are gone from the river but memories persist. And the memories must suffice, for it is unlikely there will again be men to fill those boots.

PART THREE

SCIENTISTS
AND SUFFERERS

I 4

" ALLOW ME, sir, in conclusion to say, that these observations were conducted under a degree of personal discomfort which prevented such an accurate and detailed examination of some of the more interesting and obscure points as I could have wished . . ."

Thus wrote Oliver White of Richmond, Indiana, to conclude his geological report that appeared in 1862 in the *Second Annual Report on the Natural History and Geology of the State of Maine*, prepared by Ezekiel Holmes and C. H. Hitchcock.

Professor Hitchcock, whose major scientific contribution on that trip was to confirm his hunch that the rock of the lower Allagash was trappean conglomerate and truly sedimentary, took pains to applaud his assistant's travail, stating by way of introduction that "so interested did he become in the geology of this part of the state, that at his own expense he undertook the exploration of the route from Chamberlain to Chesuncook Lake, by way of the Allequash and Caucomgomoc Lakes, a route never before traveled by any scientific man. His zeal was the more to be commended since the abundance of venomous insects rendered exposure to their attacks almost insufferable."

Under the same auspices, George L. Goodale was assigned to make a botanical report on the Allagash region. He was no happier about the physical discomforts he encountered in the interest of science.

After stating that the party of exploration consisted of Mr. Hitchcock, as geologist, Mr. White, of the Amherst Scientific School and himself, attended by two guides, James Bowley of Shirley and George O. Varney of Greenville, he recorded the

141

departure with gloomy prescience. "We arrived with our canoes and luggage at the northwest arm of Moosehead Lake, upon Monday, the 19th of May. The ice had broken up on the day previous, and we had every prospect of a cold, comfortless tour."

Comfortless or not, Mr. Goodale persisted and indeed took the Allagash Grand Tour of three hundred and one miles. The party ascended the West Branch Penobscot to the headwaters of the St. John and, passing down the river to the Allagash, pushed up the Allagash to Chamberlain Lake. Having visited the lower Allagash the year before, Mr. Goodale found nothing much new to add to the record except that he collected near Allagash Falls a number of specimens of *Calypso borealis* and at Churchill Lake found a forest fire raging that further contributed to his general malaise.

"It is the occurrence of such calamities as this that renders our immense tracts of woodlands so changeable, and it is this which causes proprietors of woodlands to shut out settlers and discourage the building of roads. This fire seemed to have had its origin at a point near the thoroughfare between Churchill and Eagle Lakes, and was slowly working round on the eastern shore. Finding that all exertions in our power would avail nothing in arresting its progress, we made a hurried examination of Spider Lake and pushed on to Chamberlain Farm. A single word will suffice concerning Spider Lake . . . The lake is about two miles in length, and on account of the absence of timber and the abundance of mosquitoes, was particularly uninviting to us all."

Upon reaching Chamberlain Farm on June 3, the party split up, Mr. White and the guide, George Varney, starting back to civilization by way of Caucomgomoc Lake and Chesuncook, while botanist Goodale and Mr. Hitchcock, attended by guide Bowley, struck out for Mud Pond Carry.

Mud Pond Carry, the bane of two centuries of Allagash adventurers, evoked a predictable response from Mr. Goodale. With examplary control, he stated merely that "it is not an easy task to carry on one's back a heavy load across a muddy mirey portage." He could not forego, however, the opportunity to preach a sermon and utter a caveat on the subject of his prime obsession.

The black flies have troubled us sadly ever since the first of June, or the day when the wild cherry trees blossomed. We have had them at all hours from the rising to the setting of the sun. The approach of the mosquito is sufficient warning of itself, but the black fly comes noiselessly and gives no intimation of his presence till he is ready to fly away. The insect, as figured in Harris' Insects of Massachusetts, is a little smaller than we have usually found them. Since they are common in the woods of Maine from June to August, it becomes the duty of one who urges settlers to take up the lands described in this report, to call attention to the remedy for this nuisance. At Chamberlain farm I was told that the workmen were not much annoyed by them after the first few days. In many cases the application of some unctuous substance to the skin is found to give an absolute exemption from the pest. But after a large clearing is made, when several houses are quite near together, the black fly becomes rare. So that this drawback which has kept so many from entering upon the occupation of new land, is really not so formidable as it first seems. It may be thought indiscreet in me to say anything about this discomfort to settlers, but I am sure that, although a survey may gain a temporary popularity by the exaggeration of certain facts and suppression of others, it is better to state all the facts, *pro contra*, as they really are found.

For a century or more, explorers, surveyors, and men of science, trekking into the Allagash country, had been recording a body of *pro contra* facts along with their pleasures and rewards. The tyranny of biting insects in spring and summer, the ordeals by snow and ice and perishing cold were not unnoted by the men of learning who were frequently ill equipped for the hardships that beset them.

Dr. C. T. Jackson, the State of Maine's first official geologist, became an old Allagash hand before he completed his illustrious tenure; but it was a rough road and his seasoning was bought by dint of stubborn effort. The doctor, in recounting his exploration of the East Branch Penobscot in 1837 in his *Second Annual Report on the Geology of the Public Lands Belonging to the Two States of Maine and Massachusetts*, made an admirable effort to explain that negotiating the wilderness waterways was no church picnic.

Those who have never been on such a journey, would be surprised at the dexterity of the Penobscot boatmen, as they drive their frail batteaux through rapids and among dangerous rocks. . . . When the waters rush swiftly down a rapid slope of smooth and round rocks, called gravel beds, the most strenuous exertions of the boatmen are required to stem the current, and, not infrequently, their setting poles are caught between rocks, so as to be jerked from their grasp. . . . One boatman stands in the bow, and braces his foot against the stem as he labors. The other stands in the stern, and they both pole on the same side, as they proceed up the margin of the stream.

For Jackson, misadventures were daily occurrences, the most notable a near-disaster at Grindstone Falls at the East Branch and main Penobscot.

While we were engaged in exploring rocks, our men tried to shove the boat up the falls, but the violence of the current prevented them effecting their object, the boat being instantly filled and sank in the attempt; while all our baggage and provisions were swept off and carried down stream. A scene of unwonted activity now ensued, in our endeavor to save our articles as they were rapidly bourne down the foaming waters . . . The bread barrel, although scuttled, was but half filled with bread, and floated down stream, with its opening uppermost so that but little of it was injured. Our bucket of rice burst open and was lost.

The teakettle, with other cooking apparatus sank in the river, and were fished out by hook and line. The tent was found about a mile down river, stretched across a rock. The maps and charts were all soaked with water. . . . Our spare boots and shoes were irrecoverably lost.

Much of Jackson's exploration of the lower Allagash was conducted in pouring rain. He found that Chamberlain Lake was incorrectly represented on his map and suggested an ideal site at the lake's outlet for a dam and sawmill. Jackson, like Greenleaf before him, consistently thought of the region in terms of settlement. His observations in the vicinity of Allagash Falls represent the first geological study of the area.

On the 28th, four miles above the Grand Falls on the Allagash, we met with argillaceous slate. This is succeeded by banks of clay and gravel, until a little above the falls we find micaceous and argillaceous slate; and at the falls the latter rock, forming the entire bed and shores of the stream. It dips 75° S.S.E., is of poor quality, and gullied full of deep pot-holes. At the falls the river is divided by a small island, on each side of which it pitches over rough slate rocks 25 feet, nearly perpendicularly. The banks just below are precipitous, and of about the same height. From the falls to the mouth of the Allagash, the water is shallow and quick; the immediate shores continue low, and are formed of gravel. Before we reach the mouth, the river makes a large bend or "ox-bow", after passing which we find it expands into a wide bay, at its confluence with the Walloostook. This bay is filled with small islands, and their banks are covered with a luxuriant growth of grass.

In the conclusion of his report the estimable Dr. Jackson made it quite clear that the wilds of Maine were not for everybody. It was with evangelic fervor that he pronounced that the wilderness was only for the brave, the strong, and the determined and that the weak and timorous had best stay at home.

"If you are already well situated—have a good farm—live in a pleasant neighbourhood, and are blessed with the common goods and chattels necessary for the well-being and happiness of your family, stay where you are—go neither east nor west. Are you a man of feeble health, with little capital, unable to undergo the severe toils of the subduing the forest, and unable to hire? It would not be advisable for you to go there. Are you idle—lazy—shiftless and vicious? Go not thither. Better stay where, (if you cannot reform) alms and houses and prisons are more abundant to administer to your necessities, or to ensure your safe keeping."

Jackson, like Dr. Hitchcock, was blessed with an "excellent assistant." James T. Hodge was delegated to investigate geologically sections of the Allagash from the Penobscot to the St. Lawrence. He left Boston on June 6, 1837. At Howland, Maine, he engaged two Indian guides and purchased a batteau. Hodge achieved the Allagash by way of the Ripogenus, Pemadumcook, Chesuncook and the West Branch Penobscot, stopping off to explore the region of the Moosehead Lake before heading north. Upon meeting up with Jackson in the fall, one of his first acts was to get himself lost, a fact that the more experienced Jackson took palpable delight in recording.

Night overtook the party as they returned from a day of exploration west of Katahdin. After they had spent some hours thrashing over blowdowns and getting tangled up in a peat bog, the moon came up. At this juncture all hands, with the exception of Mr. Hodge, agreed on the direction back to camp. Wrote Jackson:

"Mr. Hodge, choosing his own course, was soon lost, and wandered far up Shin Brook, mistaking the roar of the falls upon that stream for those of the Seboois. On reaching the river, we forded the stream and arrived safe at camp, from whence I sent out a party in search of Mr. Hodge, who was found encamped alone under the bark of a hemlock, the stump of which he had set afire, and had determined to remain until morning."

Posterity is offered another view of Dr. Jackson's Allagash expeditions in the account of William Clark Larrabee. A Maine educator and clergyman, Larrabee's great love of the out of doors led him, in 1837, to join up with the geologist's party on the wilderness tour. In Larrabee's treatment, *The Backwoods Expedition,* the party of ten set out from Old Town, September 13, in canoes and batteaux. He put down a minute description of that classic river boat and its handling.

> The batteau is about twenty feet long and three or four feet wide in the middle, while the extremities taper to a point and turn up, much like an old peaked shoe worn by our great-grandmothers. It is made of plank as light as possible, for it must often be carried by boatmen around the falls, which frequently occur in the river. It has a flat bottom, so as easily to slide over the rocks in shallow water . . . To manage the batteau requires two skillful, athletic men. One stands on the prow, and the other in the stern. Each has a long pole with a spike in the end. This is called a setting pole. Keeping time with their poles, they thrust them against the rocks, or on the bottom of the river, and pushing with great force, urge the boat rapidly up against the current.

What disturbed Larrabee was not so much the rigors of the journey as the uninhibited expressiveness of the boatmen who were not at all restrained by the presence of a man of the cloth in their midst.

"They were," Larrabee wrote, "addicted to the most horrid profanity of language. I did not know before that the English language could be tortured into such outrageous oaths. . . . Finding every means of correction ineffectual, I chose to go into the canoe managed by an Indian; for though he swore in Indian, it did not sound so bad as in English."

The surveyors, who had been in and out of the Allagash country ever since the Revolution and by the very nature of their profession a hardy breed, were much less inclined to stress the trials that attended their efforts. Field book notes of surveys in 1825 were studded with little gems of succinct understatement.

Last night about 2 o'clock we were alarmed by the falling of a large pine tree which fell within 10 feet of our camp and directly upon our tinware, which spoiled our camp kettle, 1 canteen, a teapot, and some other small articles which caused us some trouble.

Rainy morning. Stopped and caught 45 trout.

Out of provisions and have been allowed only a biscuit a day.

A small brook which is the first water we have had for 21 hours and having started this morning without breakfast we struck fire and cooked some dinner.

We met a supply of provisions. Having been on short allowance 3 days it was very acceptable.

This is the fifth snowy day and it is still stormy.

As Mr. Hodge of Jackson's party discovered, getting lost in the wilderness was no great problem. The Indian who upon occasion "got himself twisted around" had a simple answer: his camp got lost. He was, however, every bit as much at home when lost as he was at his own campfire. This was certainly not the case with John Way. John, who was eventually to become a first-rate map maker and a seasoned Maine woodsman, started out the hard way.

John Way was certainly something less than professional when the Maine Woods called him from the lap of luxury; but what he lacked in technical qualifications he made up for in determination and enthusiasm. A young man of good family and education, he was resolved that such a handicap should not disqualify him from a career in the wilds of Maine. He had read Thoreau's Maine Woods Journals and noted the naturalist's complaint that the current maps were a "labyrinth of errors." He set himself the task of correcting that situation.

According to Hiram Mansell, the Allagash guide who saved him from his folly, John was "one of them adventuresome splinters as are always flyin' around wantin' to see more and more and gets into wuss and wuss every step they go." Not having had enough of the Allagash in season, young John came back in the depth of winter to hunt. The party ran low on supplies at Haymock Brook near Eagle Lake and no amount of persuasiveness prevented the young adventurer from heading back alone to Chamberlain Farm to replenish the larder. He got turned around at Leadbetter Pond and that might well have been the Great Adventure for John Way had it not been for the perseverance of his guide.

When Way failed to return, Hiram Mansell set forth on his track. It took a grueling two days to unravel the circling snowshoe trail. And when Mansell finally found him, Way was still circling in a mindless daze. John Way insisted on lying down to sleep his last sleep; but Hiram, according to his account, "beat him like an old carpet" and somehow got him back to camp alive. Thus, John Way was saved to make his map of the Maine North Woods which appeared in 1874 and was the standard map until Lucius Hubbard produced a better one in 1879.

Edward Hoar, Thoreau's companion on his final Maine Woods excursion in 1857, got himself thoroughly lost in the region of Webster Stream. When Hoar was missed, Joe Polis, the Indian guide, went in search of him, calling like an owl. It did not occur to Joe, or, apparently, to Thoreau, that the lost man might accept the owl call as genuine and, expecting no help from a night bird, ignore it. Hoar did hear the "owl" and remained undiscovered until the next day.

Thoreau, although relieved, dismissed his friend's harrowing experience with a few words. He did, however, take pains to record that Hoar had seen one botanical rarity in the course of the adventure, a pure white great willow herb, *Epilobium angustifolium,* amidst the fields of pink ones in the burnt land.

One day Thoreau made a valiant attempt to get his guide, Joe Polis, to admit that he could get lost. He didn't succeed. When the Indian was asked how he managed to remain forever orientated in the woods, he slipped out of that one, too. "Oh, I can't tell *you,*" Joe said, "great difference between me and white man."

There is sufficient evidence to suggest even the most woods-wise of men, including Indians, mislaid themselves upon occasions. The difference, as many an early Maine woodsman enjoyed pointing out, was that the white ridge runner sometimes had to admit that he was lost. The Indian found face-saving solace in the mystic truth that he always knew where he was but sometimes his camp was lost.

A MAN TO REMEMBER

15

A LITTLE more than a century ago Henry David Thoreau died on a rattan bed in the "company parlor" of his mother's house in Concord, Massachusetts. At the very end his mother and his Aunt Louisa heard him whisper two words, "moose" and "Indian." He died with the Maine wilderness in his heart.

Thoreau's passing came in 1862 on the verge of his forty-fifth birthday. He had caught cold while counting rings on tree stumps one snowy day. For two years he fought a losing battle with tuberculosis. Finally, reconciled to his end, he settled down among his papers and notes and sought to complete his masterwork on the Maine Woods.

Aunt Louisa, a no-nonsense New Englander, refusing to indulge in the conventional deathbed attitude that her nephew would recover, asked him if he had made his peace with God and got the memorable reply that he was unaware that he and God had quarreled. A friend was to say to a fellow townsman, Emerson, that he "never saw a man die with so much pleasure and peace." For indeed he had made his peace with nature, if not with the world of men, years before.

He was a priest of the simple life, his church, the "big church," the woods. It was there that he found the order, the beauty and the wonder that made him whole. "One world at a time," he said with skeptical irony to a friend who probed his belief in immortality.

He was little known beyond his town and a small coterie of friends. At the time of his death, his printed works consisted of a few essays and two books. The first, *A Week on the Concord*

151

Thoreau

and Merrimack Rivers, had sold three hundred copies. The second, *Walden,* had been only slightly more successful. It was the opinion of Emerson that his friend Thoreau had somehow failed his early promise and ended up as a mere "captain of a huckleberry party."

Then, in 1864, two years after his death, the journal of his Maine Woods excursions appeared under the title *The Allegash and East Branch,* and with it the impact of his philosophy began to be felt throughout his New England and, finally, around the world.

The quintessential man never did quite emerge from the legend. Few of his friends saw him the same way. Was he a complex man, or a man so starkly simple as to baffle the minds of his fellow men? Some found him attractive in a rough-hewn way. To Hawthorne's mind he was "ugly as sin." He had a great beaked nose that jutted over full, unyielding lips. Sturdy, compact, he walked with a graceless purpose, overlong arms clasped behind his back, or swinging pendulously at his sides. A celibate bachelor, he looked it every inch. A prig? The more visceral of his friends insisted he was. Others called him monkish, principled, and incorruptible.

In common with Dante, his fire sprang from a certain vexation with the world of men; but unlike Dante he never attempted to conform to it. He made no compromises in the interest of being loved and in consequence the face he turned outward was unbeguiling. Henry James, Sr., decided Thoreau was the "most childlike, unconscious and unblushing egotist it has ever been my fortune to encounter."

Although humility was never one of Thoreau's prime virtues, this was palpably unfair. It was simply that Thoreau never doubted the truth of what he had to say. Unfair too, because it was a half-truth and was the generally accepted image of the man as a misanthrope and a recluse. He once said he would go into barrooms if he had business that would take him there. It would not be a questioning of his honesty to add that it would have had to be mighty pressing business.

Into the Maine woods he took companions; first his relative
George Thatcher and then Edward Hoar, a Concord neighbor.
Even at his hideaway at Walden Pond there were streams of
visitors, many of them invited. He was not a particularly good
listener, nor was he noticeably tolerant of fools, and only a
precious few failed to qualify for inclusion in this crowded
enclave.

Yet, to term Thoreau a fanatic is to miss the point of his
inward-directed thinking. No brash proselytizer, his central belief—an insistence upon individual responsibility to realize to
the fullest extent one's own self and potential—was essentially
a personal matter. Simplify, simplify, was his cry; but he
meant only that each man should refuse to pay the price for
what is not essential to *him*. No one has ever questioned that
he succeeded in living his beliefs as few men have before or
since.

"On the 31st of August, 1846, I left Concord Massachusetts
for Bangor and the backwoods of Maine." With that un-
adorned statement Thoreau opened his account of the first of
his three trips into the Maine woods. He had long cherished
the notion of a forest life. His friends in cozy Concord considered his dream a bit peculiar. They refused to accept at its face
value his remark that "cold and hunger seem more friendly to
my nature than those methods which men have adopted to
ward them off."

What manner of madman would set forth for the wilderness
expressly to starve and freeze? More likely, they charged, the
trip was an excuse to escape from gainful labor. Indeed,
Thoreau had stated that he found that six weeks' work a year
was all he needed to supply himself with his own necessities.

Clearly, Henry Thoreau needed no excuse to escape from
the drudgery of earning his daily bread. "Why," he asked,
"should anyone live by the sweat of his brow and bore his
fellow men by talking about it?" The mass of men led lives of
quiet desperation. Every law of the universe was controverted
by the effort to maintain a standard of living.

He simply believed and wished to prove, to his own satisfaction at least, that the more one simplified one's life the less complex the laws of life would seem.

Earlier, his friend, Isaac Hecker, had invited him to travel to Rome, all expenses paid. Henry Thoreau said, No. Europe would diminish Concord, his woods and streams. What culture of wealth could ever atone for the loss? To the Maine woods he would go, yes. There he would find space and air, a wilderness unrecorded. He would observe the ways of the woodland Indian who, like him, believed in owning no more than he could use.

On this first trip to Maine, Thoreau went from Bangor up the Penobscot. There an old Indian told him, "Up the river, one beautiful country." In the company of Thatcher, two Bangor friends and two native boatmen, he climbed Katahdin (it was always "Ktaadn" to Thoreau, as it was always "The Allegash").

The purpose of the next trip, in 1853, was to accompany his relative Thatcher "a-moose-hunting," although Thoreau himself had no true interest in hunting. The party went overland from Bangor to Moosehead Lake, thence to the West Branch to Chesuncook. The trip was made in a birch canoe, guided by the Indian, Joe Attien.(9)

Thoreau's final Maine woods journey was made in the midsummer of 1857. His original plan was to explore the St. John from its source to its mouth, returning by way of the Allagash to Moosehead. This would have entailed considerable upstream work; so the final decision was to reverse the order and go by the way of Moosehead and return by the East Branch.

This was Thoreau's most extensive and ambitious river trip, and his crowning adventure. It required negotiating the full length of Moosehead Lake in a birch, then crossing Northeast Carry into the West Branch, down to Chesuncook, up Umbazookskus stream, over Mud Pond Carry and into the Allagash waters—Chamberlain, Eagle and Telos lakes—and returning, finally, by Webster stream and the East Branch.

Edward Hoar was his companion and the Penobscot Indian, Joe Polis, his guide and, frequently reluctant, mentor.

Henry Thoreau was certainly not the first to explore this wild precinct north of Moosehead, but he was surely one of the first to journey into the region of the Allagash with no other motivation beyond pure curiosity and personal pleasure. In the course of his excursions he came in contact with timber cruisers, Indian moose hunters, white market hunters,(10) all with the purpose of material gain. Toward those others he recorded his ambivalence, a mixture of attraction to their wild and lonely way of life and distaste for their trades.

At an encampment he came upon a group of Indian moose hunters scraping moosehides. "They had killed twenty-two moose within two months, but, as they could use but very little of the meat, they left the carcasses on the ground. Altogether, it was about as savage a sight as was ever witnessed. . . ."

Thoreau referred to the killing of a moose by his party as "the afternoon's tragedy" yet he admitted that he could spend a year in the woods, fishing and hunting just enough to sustain himself. "This would be next to living like a philosopher on the fruits of the earth . . ."

It was the hunting of the moose merely for the satisfaction of killing that appalled Henry Thoreau. "This afternoon's experience suggested to me how base or coarse are the motives which carry men into the wilderness. The explorers and lumberers generally are all hirelings, paid so much a day for their labor, and as such they have not more love for wild nature than wood-sawyers have for forests. Other white hunters and Indians who come here are for the most part hunters, whose object is to slay as many moose and other wild animals as possible. But, pray, could not one spend some weeks or years in the solitude of this vast wilderness with other employments than those—employments perfectly sweet and innocent and ennobling . . . I already, and for weeks afterwards, felt my nature the coarser for this part of my woodland experience, and was reminded that the pure life should be lived as tenderly and daintily as one would pluck a flower."

All this notwithstanding, the subject of one of Thoreau's most sympathetic profiles was from the leader of an Allagash-bound hunting party he met on the stage en route to Moosehead Lake.

"Their leader was a handsome man about thirty years old, of good height, but not apparently robust, of gentlemanly address and faultless toilet; such a one as you might expect to meet on Broadway. . . . He had a fair white complexion as if he had always lived in the shade, and an intellectual face, and with his quiet manners might have passed for a divinity student who had seen something of the world. I was surprised to find, on talking with him in the course of the day's journey, that he was a hunter at all . . ."

Typically, Thoreau failed to recall the gentleman's name, if indeed he took the bother to ask it. Others have identified the man as Hiram L. Leonard,(11) noted sportsman and famed market hunter of the day who was destined to become even more famous as the inventor of the split bamboo fly rod.

The Concord naturalist, who was to inspire Gandhi's political technique of passive resistance which freed millions of subjected people, displayed little more than a passing interest in those who crossed his path. Even his daily companions on his wilderness treks remained in shadow and all but anonymous.

One of the avowed purposes of Thoreau's wilderness excursions was to study the primitive Indian. He did learn from Joe Polis the Indian names for certain birds and flowers and he carefully recorded such things as the Indian technique for carrying a canoe; yet, about Joe Polis the man, he demonstrated hardly any interest. Curiously, the readers of his journals learn more between the lines about Joe Polis and Joe Attien than Thoreau ever did.

Thoreau first came upon Joe Polis at his home on Indian Island on the Penobscot River. He described the Indian as stoutly built, slightly above average size and with perfect In-

dian features. He explained his plans and asked Joe if he knew
of a good man to go with him.

"Me like to go myself," Joe said, "me want to get some
moose." Joe had been scraping a deerskin, he went right on
scraping.

Joe was the only good man on the Island who wasn't off
hunting and Thoreau was afraid he would ask too much for his
services. He did ask too much to the Concord Yankee's way of
thinking—two dollars a day. After some dickering Joe agreed
to make the trip for one fifty a day plus fifty cents a week for
his canoe.

Understandably, the two never did hit it off too well.
Thoreau found Joe Polis sulky and at times even sullen. One
day he asked Joe the nature of the material he was using to
repair his canoe. Joe muttered that there were some things a
man didn't even tell his wife.

It is unlikely that Henry Thoreau was aware of the seat of
his dissatisfaction with Joe. Joe Polis failed as had his previous
guide, Joe Attien, to square with the naturalist's preconceived
notion of a child of the forest. (Thoreau records his amaze-
ment upon hearing Joe Attien whistling "O Susanna" as he
paddled, and his use of such un-Indian phrases as "yes-siree"
and "by George!" offended his ears. Something of a romantic
primitivist, Thoreau saw such manifestations as symptoms of
encroaching civilization.)

Joe Polis, for his part, found his charge frequently remiss in
his woods etiquette. Thoreau might dally to note a bird or a
flower, but felt no obligation to stop by and pass the time of
day with some lonely wilderness dweller. Joe considered such
behavior bad manners. Thoreau noted Joe's efforts to improve
this fault without truly understanding his guide's admirable
and human point of view.

"Polis had evidently more curiosity respecting the few settlers in those woods than we. If nothing was said, he took it for
granted we wanted to go straight to the next log hut. Having
observed that we came by the log-huts at Chesuncook, and the

blind Canadian's at Mud Pond Carry, without stopping to communicate with the inhabitants, he took occasion now to suggest that the usual way was, when you came near a house, to go to it, and tell the inhabitants what you had seen or heard, and then they tell you what they had seen; but we laughed, and said we had had enough of houses for the present, and had come here partly to avoid them."

On another occasion Joe reproached Thoreau for not observing the Sabbath.

"The Indian [Thoreau wrote] thought we should lie by on Sunday. He said, 'We come here lookum things, look all around; but come Sunday, lock up all that, then Monday, look again.'"

Once it was clear that his employer had no intention of resting on the Sabbath, Joe shrugged and began plying his paddle saying that he supposed that if he "not takem pay" it would be no harm. Thoreau records, a little wickedly, that Joe "did not forget to reckon in his Sunday at last."

Nor did Thoreau take Joe's suggestion that they continue on down the Allagash and return by the way of the St. John River. Joe's idea was to continue down the Allagash to the St. John, carry into Eel River to save the bend below Woodstock in New Brunswick, and so into Schoodic Lake and thence to Mattawamkeag.

Joe suggested, although it would take a bit longer, that it would be easier going than to return by the East Branch. This route made good sense to Joe since he was doing most of the river work. Thoreau, on the other hand, was determined to see as much of the Maine wilderness as possible. Joe admitted that much of the lower St. John was settled: so the East Branch it was.

Thus, the ancient Indian campground on Pillsbury Island on Eagle Lake was Thoreau's deepest penetration into the region of the Allagash. (12)

If Thoreau failed to appreciate Joe Polis, he succeeded even less in taking the true measure of Joe Attien, the Indian who

went with him on his second Maine trip in 1853. In his per-
functory description of the man he wrote, "Besides his under-
clothing, he wore a red flannel shirt, woolen pants, and a black
Kossuth hat, the ordinary dress of a lumberman. . . . He had
worked a good deal as a lumberman and appeared to identify
himself with that class."

Appeared, indeed! Joe Attien, even at the early age of
twenty-four when Thoreau first knew him, was renowned from
the Allagash to the Penobscot booms as a riverman no river at
its wildest could dismay. Joe was an aristocrat by birth and
nature. He was the son of the Governor of the Penobscot tribe
at the time Thoreau hired him and he was to be seven times
Governor himself before a river proved him to be a mortal
man by taking him to his death.

Fannie Hardy Eckstorm, in telling the story of Joe's death,
took the naturalist to task for his failure to see the man beneath his "ordinary dress." In her *The Penobscot Man,* she
wrote: ". . . all the cardinal virtues without aboriginality would
not have sufficed Thoreau for a text. He missed the opportunity to tell us what manner of man this was, and so Joe Attien's
best chance of being remembered lies, not in having been
Thoreau's guide on a brief excursion, but in being just brave,
honest, upright Joseph Attien."

Joe Attien in his simple probity refused to indulge his employer's primitivist bias. When Thoreau insisted that Joe
should, like his ancestors, enjoy living on what the woods
yielded and ask for no more, Joe agreed that perhaps his fathers had lived "wild as boars," but as for Joe he wasn't going
into the woods without provisions, hard bread and pork.

Into this Allagash country Henry David Thoreau took not
one man but four: Thoreau the naturalist; Thoreau the philosopher; Thoreau the poet and, finally, the reporter. He put
down his observations in clean, unvarnished prose. He took
pains in his descriptions of places and things and, being a
good handyman himself, his interest ranged into such detail as

the construction of an Indian canoe and the technique of utilizing the root of the black spruce for thread.

We learn from his journals that caribou was already scarce in the middle of the last century in the headwater region of the Allagash. On the other hand, moose were more plentiful than they had been thirty years earlier, and beaver, overtrapped when the price was high, were again on the increase. He took accurate measurements of the moose that was shot by his friend and identified and listed every bird and flower he came upon.(*13*)

In the course of his three Maine woods excursions, Thoreau found it necessary to remind himself that he truly was in the wilderness. He sought constant reassurance that he was indeed in a primitive world a hundred miles from nowhere. Lying at night by a fire in an Indian encampment, listening to the sounds of the strange aboriginal tongue, he was reassured.

"These were the sounds that issued from the wigwams before Columbus was born; they have not yet died away; and, with remarkably few exceptions, the language of their fathers is still copious enough for them. I felt that I stood, or rather lay, as near the primitive man of America, that night, as any of its discoverers ever did."

And time and again he attempted to atomize the nature of the wilderness. Is the wilderness all illusion, he wondered; or are the physical aspects of the wild lands distinct, unique and instantly recognizable? He made a stalwart effort to pin down the essence in the account of his second Maine trek.

"Humbolt has written an interesting chapter on the primitive forest, but no one has yet described to me the difference between that wild forest which once occupied our oldest townships, and the tame one which I find there today. It is a difference which would be worth attending to. The civilized man not only clears the land permanently to a great extent, and cultivates open fields, but he tames and cultivates to a certain extent the forest itself. By his very presence, almost, he changes the nature of the trees as no other creature does. The sun and air, and perhaps fire, have been introduced, and grain raised where it stands. It has lost its wild, damp, and shaggy look, the countless fallen and decaying trees are gone, and consequently that thick coat of moss which lived on them is gone too. The earth is comparatively bare and smooth and dry. The most primitive places left with us are the swamps, where the spruce still grows shaggy with usnea."

It was along the lake shores and waterways that the big pines went first; thus Thoreau never saw the great primeval stands of unaxed pine that he had dreamed of viewing, for his route hewed to the lakes and rivers as had the timber cruisers before him. But enough of the lofty first-growth pine remained to stir his heart and move him to write:

"Strange that so few ever come to the woods to see how the pine lives and grows and spires, lifting its evergreen arms to the light,—to see perfect success; but most are content to behold it in the shape of so many board feet brought to market, and deem *that* its true success. But pine is no more lumber than man is, and to be made into boards and houses is no more its true and highest use than the truest use of man is to be cut down and made into manure."

What he failed to understand was that the great pines were as mortal as he; they were even then overmature and their years, as his, were numbered.

Robert Frost was to say of him "he had a lover's quarrel with life." If Walden Pond was the rostrum for his running quarrel with life, the Allagash was the arena for his great adventure. He left his familiar green glades of Concord to test himself and his philosophy. The Maine woods supplied the needed challenge to that country boy who heard the beat of a different drummer.

"There is no sauntering(14) off to see the country," he wrote of his first experience in the deep woods, "and ten or fifteen rods seems a great way from your companions, and you come back with an air of a much-traveled man from a long journey with adventures to relate though you may have heard the crackling of the fire all the while."

It has been said that Thoreau was flawed by an incapacity to embrace his fellow man with an open heart. This he recognized without considering it a failing. In a time when man's prime battle was against nature, he sided with nature. "You cannot," he wrote, "have a deep sympathy with both man and nature," and admitted, "I love nature because she is not man but a retreat from man."

He was a lover for all of that. His heart, open to nature, was a full heart. Who could deny this of a man who wrote: "I felt a positive yearning towards one bush this afternoon. There was a match for me at last. I fell in love with a shrub oak."

BOATS, "BULLGINES" AND STAGES

16

ENRY THOREAU was one of a long procession of humble men who sought to learn from the Indian the tribal secrets of canoe making. The bark canoe of the woodland Indian was a classic example of an instrument evolved by time and use to fill a special need. The Maine Indian developed canoe making to the level of art and no white man ever learned to match his skill.

The bark canoe was already highly developed when the first European touched the shores of the continent. It was the product of prehistoric centuries during which it had been refined to meet the strict requirements dictated by the rivers which flowed through the tribal domain. What the woodland Indian required was a craft that could be propelled easily with a single-bladed paddle that permitted the paddler to face in the direction he was going and be in a position to avoid disaster which lay in wait at every twist of the river. He needed a light craft that could be portaged and yet was strong enough to bear heavy loads, at once a racehorse and a beast of burden. A certain stability was called for to take a chop in open water, along with the maneuverability necessary to avoid dangers of a narrow passage. And above all, the craft had to be simple enough to be built and repaired with simple tools.

The bark canoe was the transcendent answer to these special needs. Such a craft was an imperative, for it was only the canoe that made it possible for the woodland Indian to follow the seasons and reach far afield for the food he needed to sustain him.

164

In modern time, when the aboriginal art began to die out and the bark of necessary size was not readily available, canvas was substituted for bark and nails for lashings and stitching; but fundamentally the canoe has remained unaltered. The ancient craft that discovered and explored the Allagash continues to serve as the primary carrier and it is unlikely that it will ever be superseded.

When the loggers arrived and river work demanded a boat that would carry men and supplies, the batteau was the obvious choice. The flat-bottomed double-ender, its sides flared like a dory's, had been developed in the seventeenth century by the French to open up the interior of the New World to the fur trade. It was adopted by the English colonials and used extensively by them in military operations on the lakes and wilderness rivers. The Indians, and indeed many of the French themselves, doubted that a planked boat could be used successfully on white river water. They were proved wrong. Maine loggers found the batteau(15) ideal as the workhorse of the river. If the design had not existed, they would have been forced to invent it. Unlike the canoe, the batteau died with the close of the river-driving era and nothing but a few rotting bones of these old river boats remain.

Thoreau used a batteau for his trip up the West Branch Penobscot in 1846. There were six in the party including two expert native boatmen and, judging from his account, it was one of the most memorable episodes in all his wilderness adventures. "With Uncle George in the stern, and Tom in the bows, each using a spruce pole about twelve feet long, pointed with iron, and poling on the same side, we shot up the rapids like a salmon, the water rushing and roaring around, so that only a practiced eye could distinguish a safe course, or tell what was deep water and what rocks, frequently grazing the latter on one or both sides, with a hundred as narrow escapes as ever the Argo had in passing through the Symplegades. I, who had had some experience in boating, had never experienced an half so exhilarating before."

Later, Thoreau visited a batteau factory at Oldtown and recorded a minute description of these lumbermen's boats.

They are light and shapely vessels, calculated for rapid and rocky streams, and to be carried over long portages on men's shoulders, from twenty to thirty feet long, and only four or four and a half feet wide, sharp at both ends like a canoe, though broadest forward on the bottom, and reaching seven or eight feet over the water, in order that they may slip over rocks as gently as possible. They are made very slight, only two boards to a side, commonly secured to a few light maple or other hard-wood knees, but inward are of the clearest and widest white-pine stuff, of which there is a great waste on account of their form, for the bottom is left perfectly flat, not only from side to side, but from end to end. Sometimes they become "hogging" even, after long use, and the boatmen then turn them over and straighten them by a weight at each end. They told us that one wore out in two years, or often in a single trip, on the rocks, and sold for from fourteen to sixteen dollars. There was something refreshing and wildly musical to my ears in the very name of the white man's canoe, reminding me of Charlevoix and Canadian Voyageurs.

The Maine logger's batteau performed a multitude of jobs on the Allagash. Taking a workboat up a pitch or snubbing one downstream with setting poles was a test of fiber and skill. Only the best were assigned to the task and it was an honor to be chosen. There was one chore that had few volunteers, however. Perhaps the most grievous function these stout double-enders performed was "boating out the anchor" from the headworks when logs were boomed down the lakes.

The flow of water carried logs down the streams. On the open lakes and dead waters there was no such natural force. The logs were boomed; that is to say, the floating logs were enclosed in a corral made of logs linked end to end. To move the boom across a lake, sometimes against a contrary wind, required motive power. On some of the larger lakes steamboats towed the booms, saving sweat and imprecations. On the lower Allagash there was no such boon. There are venerable practitioners still alive who recall the anguish, the blisters and the sleepless nights, with no surcease from bone labor until the logs were secure at the dam.

The headworks to which the boom was attached was itself a rack of torture, and as medieval as the crossbow. This invention of the devil was a craft of a sort, for it was usually fixed upon a platform of logs, roughly one log long and fourteen logs wide. The headworks was essentially a windlass. It was sometimes turned by steam or horsepower, but on the lower Allagash River the old-time loggers will tell you men were less valuable than horses and a good deal more expendable.

The method by which the logs were moved was simple as kindergarten arithmetic. At least, Captain Bligh would have so judged it. The windlass, or capstan, on the raft was no more nor less than a great spool made of a single log and revolving around a shaft, pierced to take eight capstan bars. An anchor weighing two to three hundred pounds was placed aboard the batteau. Affixed to the anchor were 300 to 1,000 feet of inch-and-a-half line. The batteau crew consisted of six men, four at the oars, an anchorman and a steersman. The crew, at the exhortation of the anchorman, would bend to the oars and row down the lake like galley slaves of old until the cry "All gone!" came across the water from the headworks. This meant that the line was all out. At this signal the anchorman in the batteau shouted to his crew, "Head boat!" and the crewmen bent their backs with a renewed effort to take up all the slack in the line. It took split-second judgment on the part of the anchorman to flip the anchor overboard at the instant the line was taut. Choosing one side or the other of that instant could mean disaster.

Sam Jalbert, who acted as anchorman on many a Long Lake booming operation, recalled that Milton Savage, one of the batteau oarsmen, decided Sam had the easy job and that any dunce could wet an anchor. Sam finally had enough of such churlishness. He suggested that Milton try it. Milton did try it—just once. He flipped the anchor just a moment too soon. Instead of carrying clear, it stove a hole through the side of the batteau and the crew were forced to swim for their lives.

Once the anchor was overboard, the labors of the batteau crew had only begun. The crew rowed back to the headworks and all hands joined to man the capstan bars, two men to a bar, and begin winding in the straining warp. Inch by inch and foot by foot, the headworks with its tow of logs was wound up to the anchor. Then once more the anchor was boated out and the process repeated until the boom was safely across the lake.

There was no sleep for the weary when the boom was in the lake. Nights, tending to be windless, were favored for the operation. "With a contrary wind there was hell to pay," Sam recalled, "for once the logs started across the lake, they had to be moved, wind or no wind, and there was no rest unless we could find a lee. So we would hold a moist finger to the wind and look at the sky and pray for a calm night. If the boys prayed good we sometimes got a favoring wind. But it was work, m'bye, no matter."

The job of booming down the lake was a grueling part of the river drive, calling for endurance and dedication beyond the capacity of a common man. Of these loggers Fannie Eckstorm wrote that she would never again behold the likes of the men she saw as they came off a drive "White and Indian crisped almost to a blackness by the sun, baked with the heat, bitten by black flies, haggard, gaunt, sore-footed, so that once their driving boots were off, their parboiled feet could endure none but the softest kid . . . and above all sleepy, falling asleep while they talked to you, gaping from unutterable weariness, dropping into deep slumber if left for a moment."

The development of the steamboat as a beast of burden for use on the Allagash headwater lakes got its impetus from the sudden growth of the pulpwood industry. In the mid-1920s,

A. G. Hempstead, a chronicler of the Maine lumbering scene, visited Chamberlain Farm on Chamberlain Lake. What he saw were some ghosts of the brief and romantic era when steamboats played an important role in Maine's lumbering industry. He wrote:

> As our boat approached the shores of Chamberlain Farm the first impression was that of an old farm with a number of unpainted buildings, some cultivated land and a large hillside hayfield that is growing up in trees. On the shore were two steamboats, both dilapidated and fallen to pieces to such an extent that they can never be used again.
>
> The boats are interesting. Dave Hanna, who has lived at the farm for the past 13 years, explained this boat. The *W. H. Marsh* was partly frozen into the lake one fall. In order to protect the engine her stern was cut off just behind the paddle box and the forward part of her hauled up on the shore. When the ice went out in the spring the stern floated away and was lost.

Today, nothing at all remains to remind the present of a day when steamboating was a lively part of the lumbering scene on the Allagash waterway lakes. Saltwater men might apply the logger's term, "wood butcher," in the pejorative sense to these freshwater boatbuilders and use the term "straw sailors" in condescension when referring to bewhiskered woodsmen who handled these lake boats; but the loggers built boats that did the job and right there on the lake shores. Moreover, they managed to operate them with a competence that was more than adequate.

The *W. H. Marsh* was built at Eagle Lake in 1903 and she was used for five seasons towing boom to the Tramway, that ingenious Yankee contraption that conveyed logs on an endless belt across the height of land between Eagle and Chamberlain lakes. She was dispatched there to assist the *George A. Dugan,* another indigenous steamboat whose job it was to tow pulpwood booms down Chamberlain Lake to Telos Dam where the wood was landed in East Branch Penobscot waters to be driven to Grindstone.

The *Marsh* was a queen of sorts in her day, 91 feet long, 25-foot beam and equipped with a 150 horsepower engine and two wood-burning vertical boilers. She did her job tolerably well before the ice caught her fast and shortened her useful life.

The *George A. Dugan* was designed and built by O. A. Harkness, dubbed "The Admiral" and for good reason: he was the boatiest man in the woods in those opening decades of the present century. "O. A." was a hard man to locate for he was ever on the move covering the far-flung wilderness logging operations and keeping machinery going, be it fired by gas, wood or coal. His special passion was his inland fleet of boats, many of which he built and operated.

The *Dugan* was one of his first inland vessels and therefore he held for her a special affection. She was built in 1902 at Chamberlain Farm from timber cut at hand and in the astonishing time of four months. She was 71 feet long of 20-foot beam, twin-screwed and powered by two single engines and two vertical boilers which developed 150 horsepower. The *Dugan's* usefulness was roughly a decade, a respectable age for her and her sister ships which carried countless millions of cords of pulpwood across the lake before an era was done.

In the course of this period the batteau gave way to the "boom-jumper," and it was The Admiral who developed these powered workboats on the headwater lakes. He saw the need for a boat that could operate in water clogged with pulpwood. It took a special boat and a special man for the tricky job of jumping booms. Boats were designed for the job and there were men with a cowboy flair who soon got the knack of riding them.

When it was necessary to get inside a boom the boat was headed directly at the barrier, throttle wide open. The trick was to hit the boom with the bow up so that the boat would rise smoothly on her forefoot and slide over the obstacle in one splashing leap. Many of these boats were built on the coast according to Harkness's specifications. One special jumper was built in Brewer in 1916 by the Cobb Brothers. It was a round-bottomed craft with three keels that projected under the stern to form a box that guarded the propeller from floating wood and protected the screw as the boat leaped the boom. A good share of the construction and repair was done right on the Allagash lakes or at Greenville at the foot of Moosehead Lake, the jumping-off place for Maine woods adventurers and lumbermen alike.

The raw frontier town of Greenville had very little to recommend it. James Russell Lowell dismissed it as "a little village which looked as if it had dripped down from the hills and settled in a hollow at the foot of the lake." Before the coming of the railroad, stages carried the motley traffic that funneled into this bleak settlement which faced to a wilderness that extended north for over a hundred miles to the St. John.

Wrote Thoreau of his stage journey from Bangor to Greenville in 1857, "If you looked inside the coach you would have thought we were prepared to run the gauntlet of a band of robbers, for there were four or five guns in the front seat, an Indian's included, and one or two on the back one, each man holding his darling in his arms."

Moosehead Lake was simply "The Lake" to anyone north of Bangor and the name had a persuasive charm which attracted an adventuresome multitude, hunters, trappers, lumbermen, as well as wide-eyed tourists. It was an all-day run and often a day and a night from Bangor, depending on stopovers, freight and the sociability of the driver en route. The stage left from the Franklin House bright and early in charge of a driver whose qualifications were broad and functions various. The stage driver was a personage, his position Olympian; he was idolized, courted and, in the case of Jerry MacDonald, elevated to the peerage of God's noblemen.

Jerry MacDonald's arrival at the settlements along The Avenue Road, as the route was called, was the great event of the frontier day. There were packages, messages, many verbally transmitted and confidential, to say nothing of the snippets of news Jerry passed along from the outer world. Jerry was, they say, an index, catalog, price list, and dictionary, and even such delicate matters as proposals of marriage were entrusted to him. Needless to say, there were children aplenty named after him in gratitude for such good offices.

The stage fare was two dollars, one dollar extra for a canoe. Meals along the route were standard at twenty-five cents and a bed the same in the event a traveler was benighted. This price might even include an illicit drink if the customer knew how to go about it.

Thoreau, predictably, rejoiced in the coming of prohibition to Maine and remarked on his final wilderness trip that he trusted his own state of Massachusetts would have the good sense to follow Maine's lead. James Russell Lowell, whose Moosehead journey was roughly coincidental, was not quite so delighted. "We drove up to the grocery to leave and take a mail-bag, stopping again presently to water the horses at some pallid little tavern, whose one red-curtained window (the barroom) had been put out by the inexorable thrust of Maine law."

Nor did Lowell regard as admirable his driver's nonchalance toward his responsibility as mail carrier. "As we trailed along at the rate of about four miles an hour, it was discovered that one of our mail-bags was missing. 'Guess somebody'll pick it up' said the driver cooly: 'any rate, likely there's nothing in it.'"

Lowell was moved to comment. "Who knows how long it took some Elam D. or Zebulon K. to compose a missive intrusted to that vagrant bag, and how much longer to persuade

Pamela Grace or Sophronia Melissa that it had really been written."

As for the stage itself, it was a cumbersome rig, large, long, with high wheels, usually of the same diameter fore and aft. It required almost a half-acre space to turn around and none but an artist could back the rig up. The teams were, for the most part, owned by lumber operators who liked to see them used during the summer and fall when they weren't needed in the woods. The stages were long enough to carry batteaux and with seats removed could accommodate as many as six of these nested river boats. Nor were there many "deadhead" runs on the return trip, for a swing could be made by way of Katahdin Iron Works to take a load of pig iron for Bangor's hungry foundries.

Beyond Greenville, the next stop for the wilderness-bound traveler was Northeast Carry, the most easterly prong of the forked bays at the head of Moosehead Lake. This was the traditional staging area for both lumbermen and adventurers. The Carry could be reached from either Mount Kineo or Greenville by steamboat during the more than half century that these vessels were a feature of the lively Moosehead scene.

The portage from the lake to the West Branch Penobscot was two miles and forty rods over the ancient Indian trail. It was an arduous passage, particularly in the mud season, a fact that Lowell attested to when he estimated the distance with a pack on his back at "eighteen thousand, six hundred and seventy-four miles."

There was no alternative to packing over the trail before 1847 when the Maine Legislature granted a charter to the Moosehead Lake Railway Company which was authorized "to locate, construct and maintain a railway with material of wood or otherwise, with one or more tracks, from the head of Moosehead Lake to the West Branch of the Penobscot River . . ."

The first foot road across the Carry had been constructed

early in the century by the state and served for some decades
as a link in the long trail from Moosehead to the Madawaska
settlement on the St. John. Jackson's party in 1837 found the
road in poor shape and "encumbered by fallen trees and
bushes, blocked by fallen trees and choked with alders."

The new "railway" had no more than a generic relationship
to the railroad that was yet to be dreamed of. The track was
made of straight pine logs fifty feet, and some sixty feet, long,
hewed on three sides, leaving on the upper side an outside
edge two or three inches wide to prevent derailing. Some of
the rails were hewed flat with a three-inch cleat nailed on for
the same purpose. The body of the car was a platform five feet
wide and ten feet long and it just cleared the tops of the wheels
and overhung them. The first wheels were wooden discs cut
from large pine logs, but these were soon replaced by iron
wheels cast in one piece, hub, rim and spokes. As the car
could not be turned around it was constructed on the ferry
principle, both ends rigged alike to accommodate the motive
power, an ox or a pair of horses in tandem.

In his *Life in the Open Air,* Theodore Winthrop related with
zest his experience in 1860 with this hybrid wilderness jumper.

> The steamboat dumped us and our canoe on a wharf at
> the lake-head about 4 o'clock. The wharf promised a settle-
> ment, which, however, did not exist. There was for popula-
> tion, one man and one great ox. Following the inland-point-
> ing nose of the ox, we saw, penetrating the forest, a wooden
> railroad, ox-locomotive, and no other befitted such rails. The
> train was one great go-cart. We packed our traps upon it,
> roofed them with our birch, and without much ceremony or
> whistling moved on. As we started, so did the steamboat.
> The link between us and the inhabited world more and
> more attenuated. Finally it snapped, and we were in the
> actual wilderness. I am sorry to chronicle that Iglesias here-
> upon turned to the ox and said impatiently, "Now then,
> bullgine."
>
> Corduroy railroad, ox locomotive and go-cart train up in

the pine woods were a novelty and a privilege. Our cloven-hoofed engine did not whirl turbulently along, like a thing of wheels. Slow and sure must the knock-kneed chewer of cuds step from log to log. Creakingly the train followed him, pausing and starting and pausing again with groans of inertia.

A very fat ox was this, protesting every moment against his employment where speed, his duty, and sloth, his nature, kept him bewildered by their rival injunctions. Whenever the engine-driver stopped to pick a huckle-berry, the train, self-braking, stopped also, and the engine took in fuel from the tall grass that grew between the sleepers.

It was the sensation of sloth at its uttermost. Iglesias and I, meanwhile, marched along and shot the game of the country, namely: one *Tetraco Canadensis,* one spruce partridge, making in all one bird, quite too pretty to shoot with its red and black plumage.

So, at last, in an hour, after shooting one bird and swallowing six million berries, for the railroad was a shaft into a mine of them, we came to the terminus. The chewer of cuds was disconnected, and plodded off to his stable. The go-cart slid down an inclined plane to the river, the Penobscot.

We paid quite freely for our brief monopoly of the railroad to the superintendent, engineer, stoker, switch-tender, brakeman, baggage master and every other official in one.

But who would grudge his tribute to the enterprise that opened this narrow vista through toward the Hyperboreans, and planted these once not crumbling sleepers, and once not rickety rails, to save a passenger a portage.

The "bullgine railway" as a facility was not for the ages. In his *Paddle and Portage,* Thomas Sedgwick Steele recounts his party's adventures at the crossing in 1881 when nothing remained of the brave and imaginative Yankee contraption except rotting logs all but lost in the encroaching wilderness.

Steele's party strapped its canoes and dunnage aboard a wagon drawn by a pair of horses which proved no more reliable than oxpower. Halfway over the Carry the team stopped and refused to budge and no amount of verbal and physical abuse could persuade the horses from their stubborn inertia. They finally responded to Steele's stratagem of holding a feed bag a yard from their noses. With Steele in the van with the teasing feed bag, and the rest of the crew pushing from the rear, the carry was eventually negotiated.

Lucius Hubbard, who made the carry a few years later, also had a few nostalgic words to say about the Moosehead Railway: "Before the use of modern conveyances was known to these wilds, the Indians carried their canoes on their backs over the portages, which then were but narrow paths broken through dense forests. In later years, the enterprise of the logger built a tramway across the Northeast Carry, over which supplies were drawn by oxen, to be distributed among the logging camps on the Penobscot. . . . But the tramway is no more. A destructive fire, which laid waste many acres of forest growth, ruined it as well. Its vestiges in the form of a few charred and decaying logs in the rank shrubbery at the side of the present wagon-road are hardly conspicuous enough to cause more than passing comment."

Hubbard noted that at the northern end of the carry was the farm of Joseph Morris, the last human habitation he would see for twenty miles. George C. Luce bought the farm a few years later and went seriously into the profitable business of running supplies and gear over the carry for sportsmen and lumbermen alike, charging what he advertised as "a reasonable price" and what many users called highway robbery.

What had been essential to the Indian a hundred years earlier—a light birch, a knife and an axe—had grown to a mountain of food and dunnage. Civilization had made the bare necessities of a wilderness trek a groaning wagonload. It was the "sporters" who were now journeying joyfully into the Allagash country in ever increasing numbers. They were to make the tote horse lean and the tolltakers, if not fat, comfortably larded.

ROMANTICS
AND RUSTICATORS

17

A T THE time of Thoreau's death only his loyal friends could imagine why anyone would want to read his Maine Woods Journals. Even Emerson qualified his enthusiasms, although he did suggest that once the work was published it would produce "a plentiful supply of naturalists."

Emerson was quite right. Along came John Muir, John Burroughs, Bradford Torrey, and a host of others less celebrated. Naturalists were not all the wilderness journals of the Concord recluse produced. It took a decade or more before Thoreau's preachments on the simple life penetrated the fertile soil of puritan New England; but once the message got through, there was an army of passionate and wide-eyed apostles booted and spurred for an assault on the Maine woods.

Perhaps it was not so much that Thoreau's neglected work found its time: the times found Thoreau. The children of the mauve decades had been cradled with Longfellow's *Hiawatha*, with its scent of Indian summer and the smoke of tribal campfires. The poet had spent his boyhood in Maine and the poetry of these ancient forest people was recaptured through the haze of his memory.

There was this land to the north, this paradise where the woods were filled with deer and streams swarmed with fish, a lost happy hunting ground awaiting to cleanse the soul of an age bowing before the false gods of European culture. Boston, New York, Philadelphia; they all had become civilized— "effete" was the word of the day. Had not Henry Thoreau struck the true note when he had turned his back on a chance to go abroad, proclaiming that no culture could atone for the loss of his woods and streams?

177

Thoreau was aided and abetted by James Fenimore Cooper who earlier had reshaped the Indian and his legends, purging him of malice and savagery. The noble savage walked in the warm glow of sunset, beautiful, innocent and heroic. It was to these haunted trails of the Maine silva that the eyes of the young bloods, born too late to open the West, were turned to gain their manhood and find the lost innocence of their pioneer fathers.

Captain A. J. Farrar, a lusty adventurer and even lustier scrivener, set the tone and beat the drums for life-in-the-open-air forces. Wrote the doughty captain in his Maine guidebooks, which were to run into countless editions and become the standard work for these wilderness converts:

"How a person can fritter away two or three months of pleasant weather at fashionable summer resorts, surrounded by false glitter and senseless show, when the lakes and the forests and mountains of the Pine-Tree State are smilingly beckoning them to explore their hidden mysteries, is something hard to understand. But many do not know that this vast wilderness, with its forests primeval, with its lofty mountains, many of whose summits have been untrodden by the foot of man, its mirrored ponds and lakes, its picturesque streams, broken by rapids and falls, its healthy and bracing atmosphere, redolent with the resinous perfumes of the pine and fir, is within two days' travel of the great metropolis of New England. And yet such is the fact."

The Captain wound up his 1890 edition of his guide with this titillating passage on the Allagash: "In leaving the old beaten paths of travel one is also most likely to meet with game, or to find waters where the trout have not yet learned to fight shy of artificial flies. Although the state has been pretty well covered, in their various trips, by hunters, lumbermen and surveyors, we still have no doubt of there being parts of the wilderness of Maine whereon yet the foot of man has ever trod."

Such was the hunger to learn all about this last frontier that practically anything on the subject found its way into print. Neither literary merit nor authenticity was a prerequisite to authorship. So great was the flood of overblown prose on the theme that Lucius Hubbard, in his own scholarly *Woods and Lakes of Maine,* was moved to write, "Their picture of forest life . . . is apt to convey, if not an incorrect impression, at least an inharmonious one, lacking in color and reality, detail and finish, qualities the ability to produce can only be acquired by seeking nature in her wildest haunts, and drinking at her fountainhead."

What Hubbard was trying to say was that he at least had gone into the woods he wrote about and that, along with the soul-cleansing experience, there were blisters, black flies and a Spartan diet that went with it.

Such caveats went unheeded. What were such niggling discomforts compared to the reward of seeing a majestic moose drinking at dusk at some wilderness stream? The Allagash was the haunt of the bear and cougar, the last stand of the timber wolf in the East (the last wolf was killed in Maine in 1860, but those who wanted to hear wolves howling, went right on hearing them).(*16*) Into the Maine woods they trekked, bag, baggage, gun and camera, all fired with the passion to hear sermons in the rocks and find regeneration in the bracing air and among the virgin pine.

To hire an Indian guide was, of course, an imperative. The Indian, for his part, knowing a good thing when he saw it, was not unwilling to fall into the plans of the crusaders. The trouble was that there were scarcely enough qualified Indian guides to go around, less romantic white men having seen to this a bit earlier.

Certain of the white settlers who had chosen to make a life for themselves in the remote wilderness were just as quick to see a grateful dollar in this unexpected turn of events.

The first man to establish a toting service at Mud Pond Carry, the door to the Allagash, was a Frenchman, Jules Thurlotte.(*17*) A giant of a man, he spurned the use of horses, carrying everything on his back. Thurlotte went blind at the age of thirty and sold out his rights to Ansel Smith for thirty dollars.

Anse Smith, the first settler of Chesuncook village, had come to the wilderness in 1849 with his wife and family. He saw he had a little gold mine right in his own backyard and was not slow to exploit it. He acquired a team and a "jumper" and continued the Frenchman's function of taking the pain and tears out of the boggy portage. His fee was six dollars, a price that Lucius Hubbard, for one, considered outrageous.

In the years before Smith set up his enterprise, the Indian guides avoided Mud Pond Carry, insisting there was nothing to see or shoot at Chamberlain and Eagle lakes. The Indians promoted the Caucomgomoc Lake route, a passage that involved two or three short carries and a two-mile stretch of hard poling, but eliminated the man-killing portage at Mud Pond.

The unanimity with which the guides changed their attitude, once Anse Smith had set up his service, was astonishing. Suddenly, the Allagash headwater lakes were paradises. This was the haunt of the noble moose, the gathering place of the black bear; in fact, any game that lived in Maine congregated about the lakes in incredible numbers.

The "sporters" as they were termed in that day (or sometimes, more delicately, "gentlemen tourists") were in no position to take issue with their Indian bearers. They paid Anse Smith's fee and they went to the headwater lakes. At the height of the season, in those waning decades of the last century, campfires encircled Eagle Lake. According to one witness, there were times when a man did not dare to fire his rifle for fear of hitting a neighbor.

The gentlemen tourists got reasonably good aid from the available supply of Indian guides considering the service they in their innocence sometimes demanded. Henry Red Eagle, a famous Allagash guide of that era, recalled an instance when one of his charges insisted on taking a two-hundred-pound trunk on his woods adventure. For days the guide speculated on the contents of the trunk his sporter so zealously guarded, even to the point of supervising its loading and unloading at the numerous portages. On the way out of the woods the party was caught on Chamberlain Lake in a driving rainstorm. They were windbound for two days on the shore of the lake. The gentleman used the time to open his trunk and dry out its contents, which included a full dress suit, patent-leather pumps and a silk top hat.

It was not only the guides and outfitters who saw hay to be made while the wilderness sun shone. By the mid-1880s, the railroads were packing tourists in and promoting the Allagash as the royal road to adventure. Tracks were extended to Greenville. The railroads put on special trains to accommodate wilderness-bound gentlemen and few berths went begging.

Captain Farrar's indispensable guidebook opened with these particulars: "Electing Boston as our starting point, the most direct route is by night train to Bangor. This train known as 'the Pullman' leaves Eastern Depot at 7:00 P.M., running over the Eastern Division of the Boston and Maine Railroad to Portland, thence over the Maine Central Railroad to Bangor, arriving the following morning about 6:00 o'clock, given ample time before the departure of the other train to take breakfast in the depot, first-class in every respect. Baggage is checked from Boston to Greenville."

The "baggage," much of it excess and ill advised, would have required a barge and a corps of carriers. It was, of necessity, reduced at the outset or gradually "forgotten" by the guides along the trail. Ardent spirits (that was the accepted circumlocution of the day, although the Indians were more inclined to use the term "W. I. goods," that is to say, West Indian Rum) were essential, of course, to defend the voyagers against the rigors and hazards of the wilderness. Commonly, though, the presence of "snake medicine" compounded the hazards for there was one myth that the gentlemen tourists were quickly disabused of: the Indian who didn't drink. As

one disillusioned sporter explained, "We hired our fellow because he said he never drank unless he was 'ver' ver' sick'; he
was ver' ver' sick every night."

Indian guides by no means monopolized the burgeoning
profession of ushering innocents into the wilds. The white settlers who exacted little more than a marginal living from the
woods were, almost to a man, available. By and large the
Mooseheaders were woods-wise and genial, but finding a good
all-round man, one who could cook, handle a canoe on a
scuffed-up lake, as well as snub a canoe with a setting pole in
quick water, make a comfortable camp and tell just enough
lies to keep his party asking for more, was not always a simple
matter.

Silas, Lucius Hubbard's Indian guide on one of his Allagash
trips, reported to his employer that he had come upon a well-
known Moosehead guide that afternoon sitting on a log with a
shotgun across his knee. This fellow told Silas he was on the
way down the Allagash with some gentlemen. The gentlemen
had sent him out to shoot a few partridges to relieve the mo-
notony of hardbread and pork.

"I'll be dod-buttered," he announced, "if I'm agone to chase
around them woods for them gentlemen." What he planned to
do was to sit on that log and wait for sufficient time to elapse
to go back to camp and tell his clients that game was "real
scurce."

And consider "Old Johnny" Plourde, a mythic man with a
human weakness. He took a party into the Allagash country
and the first day out he was asked if he would like a drink.
Johnny allowed that he wouldn't mind; but the drink wasn't
produced that day or the next, although the sport did mention
how old and how good the stuff was. In fact, it wasn't until the
day that Johnny carried around Allagash Falls and the trip was
all but over that he got the drink, and by that time his thirst
had become monumental. What was presented to Johnny at
this juncture was just about enough to fill a thimble.

Johnny looked at the offering from a number of angles and

finally remarked, "You say this is old stuff, eh? Hummm. By gar, he's pretty small fer his age, now ain't he?"

The price of guide service had gone up considerably since Thoreau had wangled his bargain of $1.50 a day from Joe Polis. The charge was closer to $4.00 a day, the guide supplying the canoe, tent and cooking tools. He also arranged for the supplies, and it was not uncommon practice to accept from the outfitter a little something in the way of a kickback.

One of the most famous outfitting establishments was D. T. Sanders & Son,(18) of Greenville, which opened its doors in 1857. The store quickly built up a reputation for carrying anything and everything a man might ask for. This wasn't as astonishing a performance as it might seem, for in those days one brand of anything was about all there was and a store was lucky to get that. The proprietors were merchandising pioneers of a sort. Unable to buy more than one brand of tobacco, Sanders decided to give his customers a little variety and began packaging the same tobacco under two different names, Johnny Horner and Lazy Tom. When the guides and loggers got tired of Johnny Horner, they got Lazy Tom the next time around.

This deception was successful for many years, until one day a logger, back at camp and resting at the deacon seat, took out his can of Lazy Tom. He looked it over carefully, sniffed it. Finally he drawled: "Y'know, I got a feelin' that you're an own brother to our friend Johnny Horner." And that was the end of that.

The Allagash guide, although given at times to the venial sin of doing no more than the situation demanded, worked hard for his dollar. And when hard money was scarce he had no objection to putting in some extra time for a little pecuniary reward. Old Ellis, a trail-toughened veteran of those last-century Allagash trails, was offered ten dollars for a prime bearskin by a client who had no intention of getting within ten miles of a live one.

Old Ellis picked up a track on the snow and followed the

trail for three days without closing in on his quarry. In final exasperation, he yelled: "Go right to it, old bruin, go to it while ye may! Ther ain't a hair on yer back that belongs to ye!"

Those who lacked the money or fortitude to take to the Allagash wilderness were regaled in fireside chairs by those who did. Magazine articles on the subject studded the periodicals of the day and books, written in a rollicking Rover Boy style, crammed the stalls. Charles West, in his *Aroostook Woods*, published in 1892, let out all stops with his golden prose. Who in that innocent day could have resisted his clarion call to the great outdoors: "Luncheon time in the depth of the Wildwood, after an easy stroll of a few miles over the hills through pure, bracing air, brings an appetite to be envied, and we would not trade our seat today beside the brook, for one of the best hotels."

Much of the torrent of pine-scented prose was more sound than substance. And little wonder since the guides, both red and white, saw nothing but good clean fun in foisting upon their innocent charges all manner of misinformation, much of which promptly appeared in print.

In many instances, folklore was offered as scientific fact. Armchair adventurers might read that the beaver was an animal with a most astonishingly social organization. Each tribe had its territory and a chief whose job it was to punish trespassers by cutting off their tails, indeed a dire punishment in view of the fact that the beaver's tail was his cart with which he transported mortar and stone and then used as a trowel in the building of his dam.

Hubbard's was not the only voice raised to deplore such palpable nonsense. Theodore Roosevelt, then emerging as an advocate of the strenuous life, was constantly being outraged by "wilderness fakery." His special target was Ernest Thompson Seton's *Wild Animals I Have Known*. John Burroughs supported Teddy's position, referring to this exercise in imagination as *"Wild Animals I Alone Have Known."*

The century's end was approaching and the rosy dreams of wilderness trails were beginning to collide with the reality. The romancers had somehow failed to mention the black flies and blisters, the diet of hardbread and the chilling rains. The incorrigibles continued to seek the lonely trails, but they were beginning to be outnumbered by members of the affluent society who demanded a bit more style and comfort and, above all, a place for their ladies.

G. Smith Stanton, in his turn of the century book, *Where Sportsmen Love to Linger,* was sounding the end of an era without realizing it when he reported that at Mud Pond Carry his group encountered nine moose and met up with "a party of New Yorkers among which were several ladies."

The summer rusticators were usurping the scene in grand style, basing their excursions at the famed Mount Kineo House, which was situated halfway up Moosehead Lake on a bold promontory of pure hornblende where for centuries the Indians had come to mine their arrowheads. Twice burned to the ground, the imposing hostelry assumed its final form in 1884 with rooms to accommodate five hundred and a baronial dining room that could seat four hundred.

Captain Farrar's guidebook offered the particulars. "The house is supplied with bath-rooms, electric bells, and all modern conveniences, is heated and lighted throughout with gas."

Another report of the time clearly indicated that Mount Kineo House was the place to go to meet the "right people." "The guests of Mount Kineo are generally agreeable and well-educated people, those whom it is a pleasure to know; and when you have staid long enough to get acquainted, nothing can be more entertaining than the social enjoyments which mingle with the out-door sports. . . . The walks in the twilight upon the piazzas, the groups of friends clustered here and there, the peals of laughter from the adjoining rooms, the universal movement of the place, the free intercourse of the guides with the sportsmen, that admitted privilege of anybody speaking to anybody if he chooses to, the chattering at every available point, make a joyous life whose like can hardly elsewhere be found."

G. Smith Stanton enjoyed the gracious hospitality of the Mount Kineo House before plunging into the wilderness en route to the Allagash and found the accommodations and service "equal to any on the coast." The night before his departure he admits to having disturbing visions of Indians, bears and bull moose. His chief guide he described as "a noble specimen of the red man"; but, nonetheless, he was moved to record his uneasiness. "How did we know but that these Indian guides would scalp and rob us?"

Stanton and his companion, a Dr. Hazelton, were further unsettled upon viewing the fragile birch canoes at the putting-in place on the West Branch Penobscot. Then he saw a logger who must have weighed close to three hundred pounds load himself into a similar craft, already burdened with two barrels of kerosene. The canoe sat so deep in the stream that it appeared to Stanton that the man and the barrels were floating on the water.

Stanton's plan was to achieve the St. John via the West Branch and the Allagash by way of Mud Pond Carry. Two days out the party began to tire of "embalmed meat" and suggested to their guides that they try their luck for game. The hunting season had not yet opened and the guides vetoed the idea, suggesting that the guns remain packed away until the party reached Churchill Lake. The advice proved sound. Camping at Churchill Lake outlet, the party was met by two game wardens with a prisoner who had not waited. They learned that the wardens had disguised themselves as "sports" and had been invited to share an evening meal with the unsuspecting hunters. The venison that appeared on the menu provided the evidence.

Stanton expressed outrage at such injustice. "The governing power acts the coward towards the Beef Trust but it sets the minions of the law on the trail of the poor guide

. . . who is trying to make a living from his sporting camp."

The next day at Churchill Lake the Indian guide gave the nod and the hunters shot a deer, hiding the meat some distance from the camp, "for," Stanton noted smugly, "the law requires you to be caught with the goods on."

The highlight of Stanton's trip was running Chase Rapids in a drenching downpour. "We doubt that this 11 miles has its equal for wildness in the state. . . . Towering banks with dense jungle; immense trees lean over the bank to grab you. The current runs like a mill race; great boulders are everywhere, alongside of you, under you, and you are lucky if some do not get on top of you. Canoes are constantly being swamped. Along the bottom of the river one catches glimpses of bakers, tin cans, kettles, bags of provisions—in fact all kinds of equipage lost by unfortunate canoemen."

The party made it through with no damage except to the sugar supply which was replenished by stopping off at the Harvey Farm(19) which, Stanton informs his readers, was the favorite stopping-off place for those who got drenched or swamped running the rapids.

At Allagash Falls the voyagers ran into another obstacle. A log drive had got hung up and logs were glutting the river all the way from Round Pond to the St. John. The delay at the falls led to further adventure. While one of the Indians was preparing the noonday meal, the other went off to gather raspberries. One shot was heard. The cook took up a knife and rushed off in the direction of the report. What he came upon was his fellow guide in hand-to-hand combat with a large she-bear. It transpired that the raspberry picker had found company in the raspberry patch and had fired the one shot in his gun, which had only wounded the animal. There was nothing left for the second Indian to do but join in the fray with his knife. The bear was finally dispatched, but not before she lacerated the chief guide to such an extent that he was of no further help on the downriver journey.

Stanton's Allagash adventure was crowned by one final surprise. Arriving at the frontier logging town of Fort Kent, the party was met at the hotel by "a bevy of young, handsome and frolicking girls." Moreover, several of the "young ladies" insisted on sitting at the same table with the guides and "kept up quite a flirtation with the noble red men."

It was to be no more than one generation that knew the Allagash under such gay and luxurious circumstances. With the advance of the new century, the sound of revelry died and the fires of the well-appointed campsites along the river went out. Slowly, the sedate dining room of the Mount Kineo House emptied as the fashionable forsook the wilderness trails for the sea. The Moosehead Lake steamboats were retired one by one; the trains stopped running and once again the Allagash was left to the hunters, trappers, the loggers, and the new breed of wilderness adventurers who sought no company but an aloneness that more and more was becoming a thing beyond price.

The romantic trek persisted no more than a half-century, but this exuberant and guileless army of wilderness seekers left its mark. But for those who carried the first banners, the Allagash might have remained merely a place: they made it a symbol and had a high time doing it.

MOOSETOWNERS, 18
SQUATTERS AND
HORSEBOATS

O N THE last stretch of his Allagash wilderness trip in the
early 1880s Lucius Hubbard and his party ran out of
food. It was a bleak October day and he recounted in his book
The Woods and Lakes of Maine "that all eyes pierced the
misty, frozen atmosphere, seeking the welcome smoke of some
settler's chimney."

What he sought that day almost a hundred years ago were
the outlying clearings axed out by the Allagash men who had
pushed upriver from the settlement at the confluence of the
Allagash and St. John rivers to wrest a living from the wilderness. Hubbard and his party were taken in by Finley Mc-
Lellan(20) and warmed by his fire. They were directed to the
Moores Farm a mile upriver where they were cordially wel-
comed and spent the night before carrying the falls and proceeding north to the St. John.

The outlying farms are gone and the clearings, for the most
part, have been reclaimed by the forest; but the old settlement
at the mouth of the Allagash is still there. It stands, alone and
hidden, facing south to almost two hundred miles of Maine
wilderness, appearing much as it did over a century ago when
it was the last outpost and the northern gateway to the roadless wilds of Maine.

The first settlers pushed up the St. John from the Maritime
Provinces, seeking land and a new life. English, Scotch-Irish,
Irish, they chose the spot where the tumbling Allagash River
joined the St. John and formed a tight little English-speaking
island in the land of the Acadian French.

189

"Moosetowners" they were called by outsiders, as if to suggest their backwoods isolation and predilection for the harsh wilderness life. And wilderness men they were—and still are; for although they brought with them seed potatoes and a yeoman's love of the land, what they met were trees and it was the trees that shaped their future. They were known then, as they are known today, as the finest woodsmen and watermen in the State of Maine.

The first of these Allagash people came from the Baie Chaleur. In the van were the Gardners who poled their laden boats up the St. John in the second decade of the last century. When they found the valley taken up by the Acadians, they pushed on to the mouth of the Allagash and settled on a river island as protection against the hunting wolf packs that infested the region.

There are few places in America that have remained so little changed over a century of time. A quiet, courteous people, they speak the language of their fathers and grandfathers, a speech cleansed of vulgarities, and their manners, too, have an old-world flavor. At a time when spruce was king and logs rode the rivers on the spring drives, the settlement hummed with a boisterous vitality. It seemed for a while that there was a future for this village at the meeting of the rivers. Logs, millions of board feet of them, were running the pitches on both the Allagash and St. John and drives and drivers met here at the junction before proceeding on to the mills at Van Buren and Fredericton.

At the front lines on the rivers were Allagash men, the Gardners, Moores, Kelleys, McBreairtys, Walkers, Haffords, Jacksons. Many were lost as the river took its toll of calk-booted men.

McGargle Rocks, a nasty piece of white water just below the falls, bears the name of one luckless Allagash river hog whose pike pole picked a jam not wisely but too well. He was lost in a grinding smother of logs when the jam went out.

And there is a nameless logger who contributed another

legend to the river. Thirty-three miles upriver from the St. John is Ghost Bar Landing. It was in the piney days that a great pine was felled and the axeman was crushed in its fall. The great pine was hauled to the river landing; but when it was found to have a rotten heart, there it was left to rot. Drivers passing down the river would see upon occasion a spectral figure in logging attire, standing by the abandoned pine in an attitude of beseechment. It was said that he could not rest in peace until the log was turned into the river.

A feature of the spruce lumbering era on the lower Allagash was the horseboats, the strangest of all river conveyances which plied the river to carry supplies to the upriver logging camps. The Allagash horse-drawn towboats were born of necessity. The few tote roads were impassable once the mud season set in and for most of the distance upriver there were no roads at all.

The horseboats were flat-bottomed craft, roughly forty feet long and of twelve to fourteen-foot beam. A long sweep was set in a notch in the stern to serve as a rudder and was manned by some brawny Allagash Charon. The sweepman was captain and his crew consisted of two bow men with piked setting poles, the halyard man, whose job it was to see that the lines were clear of rocks and other obstacles in the river, the cook and, finally, the "horse fly," or rider. The amphibious rig was drawn by a pair of powerful horses, the horse fly riding the off-horse and managing the nigh, or left horse of the pair. Some of the smaller boats were drawn by a team hitched to a tongue; but more frequently there was several hundred feet of line from the boat to the team, an arrangement that lent maneuverability and gave the rider sufficient scope to seek good footing in the river.

The rider had to know his horses; but, even more important, he had to know every hole and rock in his river. One pitch-black night, Joe Jalbert, riding a powerful white draft horse named Turk, found a hole he wasn't looking for. The horse went under and Joe struck out for the boat. Joe made it, but

Horseboat

Turk was drowned. Turk Island, thirty-three miles upriver from the St. John, marks the site of this misadventure.

Lucius Hubbard met up with one of these curious carriers on that final stretch of the river. He wrote:

On the way down the river we passed several flatboats or scows, drawn by horses, and loaded with hay and supplies for the loggers who were to operate up the river during the ensuing winter. Most of the carrying trade on the Allagash and St. John is done by means of these flat-bottomed boats, which seldom draw, even when loaded, more than eight or ten inches of water, and carry twelve and a half tons' weight, or one hundred and twenty-five barrels of two hundred pounds each. The horses which weigh from thirteen to fifteen hundred weight, walk in tandem, two to each boat, along the river bank, on tow-paths where there are any,

and, in the absence of these, in the water, their drivers in
the latter case often following them, even up to the waist.
This comes to be a severe strain on the men as well as the
poor beasts, when snow and slush of an early autumn freeze
about their legs. The latter often have to swim for five to
seven rods through stretches of deep water. They are
whipped up before they reach these places, the tow-rope is
drawn in and when the horse begins to swim, the rope is
slackened, and the headway gained by the boat enables
them to reach a footing before they must begin to pull
again. The drivers at these times stand on the horses' backs.
For these services the drivers get from fifteen to twenty
dollars per month and their food, which consists of tea,
bread, codfish, pork, beans and dried apples . . .

It was indeed a rough road up that swift and boulder-strewn
river. The rider on the lookout position had to be constantly on
the alert for trouble ahead. His shout to the boat crew, "Kee-
rister ahead!" meant but one thing—a boulder lay athwart the
path. As the rider turned the team to avoid the rock, the sweat-
ing pikemen leaped to the gunwales and, finding holding bottom for their poles, shoved hard on the danger side to veer off
from the forbidding boulder.

The upriver route was divided into two sections: one horseboat went as far as the falls where the supplies were carried
around the falls and loaded aboard a second horseboat which
would haul the cargo the remainder of the route to Long Lake
Dam.

Many of the boats were equipped with sails to take advantage of the open water at Round Pond. Two weighted planks
acted as leeboards. The horses were taken inboard, the sail
unfurled, and away this ungainly vessel would go across the
water. It took a half day to make the run from the Allagash
settlement to the falls and roughly three days for the relay boat
to make it to Long Pond Dam. On the return trip, the horses
were taken aboard for a well-deserved free ride home. The
crew enjoyed no such respite. Running home downriver, snub-

bing the awkward craft down the pitches, was a tricky and
hazardous assignment and one way a man could make a name
for himself, if he lived long enough.

One of the most renowned members of this colorful profession was Big Jim Fleury.(21) Six feet two and two hundred
pounds plus, he carried a pair of fists like demijohns which he
delighted to use, alike in joy and anger. Big Jim owned his
own fleet of horseboats and contracted with lumber companies
to deliver supplies upriver at so much per ton.

His crew, as gaudy a lot as ever sailed the Spanish Main,
included a lady cook known only as Ma, and little Alex Tidd
who served as horse fly. Ma made four of Alex, with something
left over, and heaven help the lubber who found fault with her
management of the floating cookshack.

Ma wore a pair of pants held up by three yards of towing
warp and she could knock out a snake's eye at ten paces with a
squirt of tobacco juice; but, all appearances to the contrary,
there was a soft spot in Ma's heart. She had a heart as big as a
barn and the best part of it yearned for Alex Tidd. And little
wonder. Alex was a dream on a horse, riding easy and graceful
as any circus bareback rider. He rode barefoot, singing lumbering ballads as he went. He sported pegged trousers, lopped
off high up on his ankles and held up by a pair of bright red
fireman's suspenders.

Unlikely Lorelei though she was, Ma was not one to give up
without a try. On the upriver haul, she would take out her
harmonica and the music she could wring out of the thing was
enough to melt a man's heart. Her favorite tune was *The
Merry Widow Waltz;* but if Alex got the idea he managed to
hide the fact. Then one day, home from the river, Ma made up
her mind. She just picked little Alex up, tucked him under her
arm and lugged him to a Justice of the Peace. Understandably,
it was a solemn wedding and as binding as any willing one,
but if it was a marriage made in heaven no one was ever to
learn. Last seen, the pair was headed up the St. John with Ma
in the seat of the tote wagon and Alex trussed up behind.

The usual compass orientation of north being "up" and south being "down" must be forgotten when considering the north-flowing Allagash. In the view of the Allagash people living at the confluence of the Allagash and St. John Rivers, the river begins at Churchill Dam.(22) When they speak of the "lower river" what they mean is the northern section of it that begins at Round Pond. The "upper river" is that piece of water from Round Pond south to Churchill Dam. When Allagashers go south they go "up" and when they go north they go "down." After all, a man poling against a swift-flowing river should know when he's going up, and if up happens to be south, this is the Lord's doing, not his to wonder why. The Allagash head-water lakes, Churchill, Eagle, and Chamberlain, are all "up" from the northern settlements along the St. John, the fact that the map shows them to be a good week's canoe run to the south, notwithstanding.

The Allagash people have not forgotten to this day that the Bangor lumbermen stole their Allagash water in the early 1840s when they installed the lock dam at Chamberlain Lake and the canal at Telos and caused water from the Allagash headwater lakes to flow south into the Penobscot watershed. They insist now, as they did then, that it was their own God-given water and designed to flow north. And it was only with the connivance of rascally politicians that the black deed was accomplished. Who were these Penobscot scoundrels to say they needed that water more than the Allagashers who had their own logs to float to market?

All the Allagash pine, and later the spruce north of Churchill Lake, went north to the St. John. Thus, Churchill Lake was the traditional line that separated the two great lumbering enclaves, one centered around Bangor and the other along the St. John. It also separated the Allagash men and the "Bangor Tigers," two distinct breeds of loggers who left, each in his own style, an indelible mark on Maine lumbering history.

And the Allagash spruce was flowing north and downriver to the St. John in rollicking hordes by the mid-1860s. Woods horses had superseded oxen and the sawdust of crosscut saws covered the snow where once the white chips from flashing axes had gathered. The big trees crashed, to be twitched to the yards, and then two-sledded on the snow to the river landings.

Here on the St. John watershed there was never the problem of revising the provisions of nature. The Allagash flowed into the St. John and the St. John flowed on to the sea. Allagash logs, once sent afloat on this endless belt, had reasonably good expectations of arriving sooner or later at their markets. The critical and limiting problem was getting enough water over a sufficient period of time to accommodate the traffic. Obviously, the river had not been originally designed to carry logs for the benefit of timberland owners. It devolved upon the land-owners to modify the river's natural behavior better to serve man's needs.

In 1907, the St. John Lumber Company acquired the charter for the Allagash Improvement Company with the idea of har-nessing the river and controlling its water to facilitate late spring and early summer log driving. The dam was built at Long Lake. The original dam was seven hundred feet long and held a fifteen-foot head of water. On the river below the dam, rocks and ledges in the quick water were dynamited.

The improvements helped. The Allagash, however, was not easily amenable to taming. These pigmy adjustments failed to take the curse out of such dread trouble spots as McGargle Rocks, Schedule Brook Rapids, and Allagash Falls. It was said of Moosetowners that they could throw a bar of soap into a pitch of white water and walk across the stream on the bub-bles. And when the logs were in the river there were Allagash "bubble-walkers" at their stations. And they were needed, for seldom did a drive go according to plan. The river had a mind of its own.

Will Cunliffe lost a drive in the early 20s that all but broke the St. John Lumber Company. He was a hard man and a tight-fisted one, and it was his meanness, they say, that caught up with him. Any man who ever worked for Will had a story to

River Drive

fatten the legend of his unpopularity. One logger who went out of the woods to attend church on Sunday was asked upon his return what the priest had given him for penance. The reply was prompt and wickedly telling, "To go into the woods and work for Will Cunliffe."

Will had a habit of having special food served to him at the logger's board. Fresh eggs were hard to come by and, in Will's view, much too expensive to serve to the crew. When a pair of fried eggs appeared in front of the boss that morning, a logger, with more gumption than good sense, reached for them. "I like my eggs as well as the next man," he announced. He ate the eggs, but that was his last meal at Cunliffe camp.

Long Lake Driving Dam

It was this natural meanness that lost him the drive. Will just couldn't abide seeing men standing around at their stations, leaning on peaveys and pike poles. He ordered the crew to begin turning the logs into the river before the gates were open to give him a head of water. When the water came, the logs jilpoked(23) and quickly a jam began forming below the falls. Men were called in from all along the river. When it appeared that pike poles and peaveys were unavailing, a towboat was dispatched to fetch up a load of dynamite. In the dynamite crew were Sam and Ned Jalbert, Willy and Martin White and Tom Harvey. They blew the jam in grand style, but all that was left of seven million feet of spruce logs was a hundred thousand feet of merchantable timber.

It was on one of Cunliffe's last Allagash drives that Fred Marquis fell into Bruno Paradis's beans. Bruno, the cook on that drive, was famous for his beans. They were slow-cooked in giant pots and carried to the men along the river in the wangan boat. They were snubbing the boat down the Horserace, a bad pitch on the Musquacook which enters the Allagash just below Round Pond, when Ernie Savage at the stern got a floating log under his sweep. With no leverage to work it, the boat began yawing out of control. Ernie yelled for Fred in the bow, and Fred, realizing the nature of the trouble in an instant, took one leap over the pile of gear and blankets amidship and landed knee-deep in the beans, one leg in each pot. Fred's boots must have added a special something to the dish. The driving crew, which never learned about the misadventure, averred that they were the best beans Bruno had ever cooked.

Among the famous landmarks along the lower river that recall the great lumbering past is Michaud Farm, just above the falls. It was settled by Michael Michaud shortly after the Civil War, and at one time the clearing supported a dozen or more families. Here hay was grown for the woods horses and horses were summer pastured. It was here that Joseph Michaud was born and where he learned the lumbering trade that was to stand him in good stead when he became a lumber king in his own right.

Joe Michaud, known as "One Eye," was as good a man in the woods as the Allagash ever produced. Joe's smartness stopped at the sight of a woman. He was as ugly as sin, a fact that goes a way toward explaining his four wives and the fact that two of them were acquired with the help of newspaper ads.

Gabrielle, his number three, clearly had something else on her mind besides a loving husband when she responded to Joe's public appeal. She agreed to share his bed and board, but only on the condition that he put all his property in her name before the nuptials. When Joe returned from a river drive shortly after the wedding, Gabrielle was gone and so were Joe's liquid assets. Undaunted, Joe advertised for number four. This lady, no kinder, decamped with most of what Joe had left, which by this time was hardly worth the trouble.

Another personage who enlivened the scene on the lower Allagash was Sarah Taggett. Sarah, among her other talents, was a "Medicine Woman"; that is to say, she could midwife a baby, sew on a lumberman's ear or remove bottle glass from a logger's skull. What Sarah lacked in medical knowledge, she made up in enthusiasm. She drove a team like a mule skinner and swore like a trooper. Her chief recognition marks were a pair of old pants and a pipe that was ever in her teeth.

Matches were a prime necessity for Sarah. She stopped by at the Cunliffe store in Fort Kent of a summer day and bought a replenishing supply of sulphur matches from Vin Cunliffe. Back in the woods on her rounds, she went to light up her pipe, only to find that she couldn't get so much as a fizzle out of the danged things. Sarah was in a sputtering rage when she went storming into the store a few days later.

"Now, these matches of your, Vin," she roared, "they ain't no jeezely good, you jumped-up, bandy-legged jilpoke!"

"Now there, Sarah," Vin soothed, "not a thing's wrong with them matches, I declare." And to make his point, Vin smoothed down a section of the fabric at the stern of his pants and, with a bold stroke, set the match alight.

"Humph!" Sarah snorted, "what in the name of whistlin' Kee-rist you 'spect me to do? Come all the hell and gone way to Fort Kent to strike a match on your fat backside, every time I've a mind to light my pipe?"

And there are Moosetowners still alive who remember Charlie Nadeau and the day he brought the earthly remains of Jean Paradis home to St. Francis from an upriver logging camp. Charlie was a toter. With a team and sled he made a living running supplies into the camps; hay, boom chain, peaveys and anything else that was needed in a hurry. Charlie's service was swift and he prided himself on it. He never stopped at the side of the trail to boil his tea, but built a fire right in the sled under the seat and took his lunch on the run.

There was a very good business reason for Charlie's haste. The first tote team into camp often got a return load at the going rate. What Charlie got that winter day in the way of a consignment was the frozen body of Jean Paradis to deliver to St. Francis. Charlie got the stiff aboard and, lashing it on snugly with a chain and snatch-hook, off he went. And all might have gone well except that it was bitter cold and Charlie stopped off at the settlement at Allagash and bought an illicit pint to warm him on the last stretch of his run. Tippling as he went, he clean forgot to check his load on the run downriver. The way they tell the story, Charlie came roaring into town, singing at the top of his lungs, with the board-stiff body of Jean Paradis skating along behind the sled at the end of a length of logging chain.

At the height of the river driving days on the Allagash as many as 1,500 men were used in the spring to drive the Allagash, St. Francis and St. John rivers, and most of them hailed from the settlements strung along the St. John from Allagash to Grand Falls, New Brunswick. The driving period on the Allagash was little more than a month, although water storage improvements early in the century lengthened this period somewhat.

To take advantage of the early spring high water, driving crews started upriver at the first indication of the ice breakup. Once holding booms were established, logs were turned into the streams from the landings. Batteau crews were stationed along the main river at about ten-mile intervals to tend the shear booms which were constructed at bad places in the river to keep the logs from hanging up. It was their job, as well, to take up a clean rear and help turn logs into the river from the landings. If difficulties arose at any spot along the river, the crews were diverted to the trouble area. All efforts were directed to keep the logs moving while there was a drivable pitch of water. For the men it was a matter of pride; for the owners it was the difference between profit and loss.

Once water storage improvements were set up, driving was extended into the summer, but it was a tricky gamble. In the summer of 1909, some sort of record was set when logs were driven from Round Pond on the Allagash to the St. John in five days, only to have the logs hung up on the main river.

Again, in 1915, a drive to Van Buren was saved only by diverting water from Chamberlain Lake into the Allagash. By this expedient they were able to raise the waters of the St. John at the mouth of the Allagash two feet and maintain that level for several days.

Before the telephone was adapted to woods use, communications were maintained on some river drives by a code of colored flags. Messages were relayed down the line much as the early Indians used smoke signals. The showing of a red flag meant, "Danger! Stop logs!"; black, "Shut off water"; a white flag, displayed once, meant, "Let water come," displayed twice, "Let logs come." For the driving boss, getting logs to the booms was a heavy responsibility. It was a job few men envied.

When the St. John Lumber Company failed in the early 1920s, Ed Lacroix acquired the river rights and title to the extensive lower Allagash properties. Unlike Will Cunliffe, no one ever had a bad word for Ed. He paid well and fed well, and the high respect he had for the men who worked for him was returned. His Madawaska Company developed an elaborate set of depot camps along the river and he constructed the first motor truck road into the wilderness from Lac Frontier in Quebec Province to the depot supply camp at Churchill Lake on the Allagash.

With the coming of logging roads into the heart of the wild lands, the end of the driving days was in sight. In the last long drive(24) on the Allagash in the mid-1930s, Ed Lacroix drove thirty million feet of long log spruce, cut on Big Pleasant and Churchill, to the mill at Van Buren.

Other factors contributed to the passing of the river drive. More and more land was being cleared and this, together with extensive cutting, fires and budworm devastation,(25) was thinning the forest canopy. Trees stored moisture and root structures held back the runoff. Now, prodigal use of the land was demanding the price of quick spring rises of water and early runoffs. Where once there had been a small variance between high and low water over an extended period, there was by the early 1930s a difference at Van Buren of thirty-five feet between spring freshet high water and summer low water levels. Despite water control improvements, lumbermen were lucky to get the upstream end of a drive to the booms on the available water. Many a drive in those last years was hung up by low water and abandoned to go out with the ice the following spring.

To further cloud the logging picture on the lower Allagash, the century-old trouble between Canadian and American lumber interests flared up once more. The trouble began with the development of the St. John Lumber Company near Van Buren which by 1907 was the largest milling operation in New England with a daily capacity of 250,000 feet of boards, 160,000 laths and 350,000 cedar shingles. The Canadians claimed violations of the Webster-Ashburton Treaty of 1842, alleging that the Americans were not authorized under the treaty to maintain sorting booms, piers and other installations for the purpose of stopping logs for manufacture, although the Canadians were doing just that at Fredericton and at other points on the St. John. The main objection from the Canadians was that log jams of as much as 100 million feet of logs accumulated at the sorting booms and clogged the river.

Verbal exchanges quickly were translated into action and violence broke out along the river. Armed watches were maintained at the shear booms on both the Canadian and American sides of the river and only the hasty appointment of an International Commission prevented the situation from deteriorating into another full-fledged lumberman's war.

For a hundred years or more the timberland owners had been fighting another sort of war in the Maine woods. It was a quiet, unpublicized war, fought without lethal weapons, except in a few special cases, and a minimum of bloodshed. It was a sort of cat and mouse war, David and Goliath war, a pesky deer fly and horse war, which is to say that the antagonists were ill matched in both numbers and power. This long and unsung war arrayed the timberland owners, on one side, and certain unauthorized persons known as squatters on the other.

At one time or another the Allagash country knew a variety of squatters, for if one thing may be said about this parasitic breed there were no two of them alike. What they did have in common was a lack of sensitivity in the matter of property rights and a staunch wish to be alone. The landowners were all pretty much of a mind in that they were unanimously of the opinion that squatters were pests and should be routed out whenever and wherever they were found. The owners, lacking the manpower facilities to keep a constant surveillance of their vast holdings, seldom uncovered the trespass until after the interlopers were entrenched and living happily off the land.

At first blush it would appear that a simple directive would have served to banish the squatter from his illegal squat. On the other hand, the squatter usually was quite aware of his

nuisance value and possessed of sufficient animal shrewdness
to realize that no timberland owner could afford to go around
making enemies when a match could wipe out, in a glimmering, a multimillion dollar investment. It wasn't blackmail exactly if an offending squatter in his catbird seat might suggest
by way of passing the time of day that the standing spruce
over yonder was as pretty a tract of timber as a man was ever
likely to see. In such situations the landowner was inclined to
diplomacy, which usually meant that the fellow got a lease for
a token sum and continued to live on nature's bounty for the
remainder of his natural life.

The majority of squatters never amounted to much, nor did
they strive to. Anse Hanley(26) was an exception in that he
did a lot better on borrowed land than most did with a paid-up
mortgage. Anse might be called King of the Allagash squatters
and his story a rags-to-riches tale. He drifted into Fort Kent
one day from nowhere with nothing but a thirty-thirty rifle and
was leading a huge barefoot woman and two ragged children.
It appeared he had a little stake, for he bought a second-hand
canoe and a few supplies before heading upriver.

He was next heard from when river travelers noted his
squat. They couldn't very well miss it. He had cleared about
twenty acres of land and planted it to potatoes and oats. It
wasn't long before he was doing a lively business selling his
oats and potatoes to lumber jobbers and investing his profits in
pigs, chickens and milch cows. He was in a particularly strategic position on the lower river, for sportsmen were usually
running low of supplies by the time they reached there. Anse
sold them eggs, milk, green vegetables, and maple syrup at a
handsome price and conveniently was forever without change.

Anse's helpmate Josephine—that there was a marital status
was never satisfactorily established—had grown to huge proportions with her prosperity. So great was her size and
strength that she soon gained the name of "Two Sled Jo." Her
brood over the years increased to fourteen or so. Anse was

never quite certain of the house count, or, for that matter, of his personal responsibility in every case.

Once when someone asked Anse how many children he had, he drawled, "Ain't quite sure 'bout that tow-headed 'un. Might a been downriver too long fer a spell."

Nothing bothered Anse Hanley except possibly the fact that he wasn't taking full advantage of his opportunities. After all, there were long winter evenings when he had time on his hands. With the idea of improving each shining hour, he went downriver by canoe to the settlements and fetched back a keg of molasses, a copper boiler and coils. The still he contrived was well researched. It sat on the stove and from it the copper tubing ran out through the cabin chinking, took a vagrant course through the snow, and then back to the camp. Sitting with a pipe in his teeth, Anse could fairly hear the drip, drip of dollars. It was like money in the bank.

He called his special brew "Banticook Rum." The sportsmen and guides bought all he could produce, and those who survived the introduction to Anse's witch's brew, and clearly could not be killed with a poleaxe, even came back for more.

Anse was too smart to drink his own product, but he stood by tolerantly while Jo knocked off a pint or more a day. "Helps with her milk fer the young 'uns, don'tcher know," he would say.

But Anse was still not satisfied that he was covering all the bets. One day on the trail that ran from the Allagash to Seven Islands on the St. John River, he met up with some Canadian smugglers from St. Pamphile. He was soon engaged in the lucrative business of trading American guns, cigarettes and tobacco for fine Scotch, Irish and Canadian whiskies for which he had a ready market among the well-heeled sports who couldn't stomach his private stock. And to make the bushwhacking doubly worth while, he ran a trapline the length of the trail and, in and out of the open season, picked up what he termed "a little extry."

Sooner or later there was bound to be trouble in Anse Hanley's paradise. It came to Anse when the lumber company decided to dispense with jobbers and do some cutting on their own. Needless to say, they were astonished, not to say outraged, when they saw Anse's spread on the company land.

Anse appeared undismayed by the sudden crisis. When representatives of the company arrived to deal with him he brought out stools and called for Two Sled Jo to break out jug and dippers. And while the lumbermen were trying to get the Banticook past their Adam's apples, Anse spoke glowingly of the fine timber along that piece of the river.

"Don't want ter be mindin' yer fellers' business," Anse drawled, coming to the point, "should think though you'd be needin' someun hereabouts to sorter keep an eye out fer fires an' sech. Me an' the boys we'll make it right sure you won't have a mite o' trouble."

Anse got a lease. More than that, he contracted to sell them all the hay and produce they would need when the camps opened in the fall. And for a little something extra, he guaranteed *not* to sell any of his Banticook to the company crew.

Unlike many another squatter, Anse was never known to resort to violence or engage in any unseemly feuding. He even got along reasonably well with game wardens, taking such good care of those that came his way that they seldom bothered to take more than a casual look around. There was only one occasion when Anse lost his gentlemanliness. A shiftless professional lumber camp hunter, by the name of Flint, kept hanging around the place trying to wangle a jug of Banticook. When Anse refused him, Flint, who was a dead shot, picked up his rifle and pointed at a moosebird perched on the tiptop of a nearby spruce. He took a quick aim and fired.

As a rain of feathers drifted to earth, Flint rested his hand on the porch post and turned to Anse. "You wouldn't like now to be a moosebird, would you, *Mister* Hanley?"

"Nope," Anse said in his usual calm manner. He reached for the axe that leaned against the camp and brought the razor-keen blade down upon Flint's trigger finger, severing it neatly at the first joint.

Then he did offer Flint a potion of Banticook. He bandaged his wound and, leading him to the edge of the clearing, booted him on his way.

Anse Hanley became an old man before his time. He died of hard work rather than of old age. It was rumored that he left something over sixty thousand dollars, and he made it all on land he borrowed for his lifetime. Anse wasn't the last of the Allagash squatters, but he surely was the last of the squatter greats. After Anse moved on, better timber cruising, more efficient forest and game warden service, and the coming of the airplane, dealt a crippling blow to squatters and squatting. There are yet a few here and there in the Allagash woods, but it's unlikely that there will ever be another with Anse's talent for gentle larceny and his flair for improving each shining hour.

The passing of river driving on the Allagash hastened the decline of many lively enterprises along the river. The settlement at the meeting of the rivers languished. Today, the settlement of Allagash stands all but forgotten at the end of the road. Log cabins, weathered old houses, are scattered about; not hugging the road, but facing the wide bow of the river which was the only highway before the road came through from Fort Kent and the French villages along the St. John. Until several decades ago, the road ended at the river and the only link to the outside world was the ferry operated for fifty years by Nazaire Pelletier. A highway bridge now spans the river carrying route 161 from Fort Kent to this last outpost of the nineteenth century.

Just across the bridge on the river side of the road, lives Tom Pelletier—"Pelkey" is the way the name is spoken by Moosetowners. Tom—and before him his brother Nazaire—once ran the ferry. Tom displays models of the ferry and the Allagash horseboats he has whittled out in the hope of attracting strangers. But strangers seldom pass his door.

Nor do many strangers come this way to listen to the sounds of another century. Of an evening, "Come-all-ye's" may still be heard, such lusty ballads as "The Lumberman's Life" and "The Jam on Garry's Rock," which told of brave deeds and stirring events of the lumbering past. The quilting bees and country dances, which once helped to pass the long, lonely winter nights, persist to carry on an all but forgotten way of life.

Today, Allagash is a plantation, in Maine the first step in political organization from unorganized territory. Moreover, it has the distinction of being the largest in area of any plantation in the state, taking in four wild land townships, or a total of 144 square miles. These extensive bounds were arranged when it seemed that a city might grow at the meeting of the rivers. Instead, the population dwindled.

Tom Pelkey might tell you that "them as could afford to, moved away and them as could not, remained." But his slow smile and the set of his old eyes as he looks up the river seem to betray the truth that those like himself refused to move on simply because, for an Allagash man, there could never be another home.

Now, suddenly there is hope that the future, so long delayed for this settlement caught in a back eddy of the past, may be realized. The villagers speak of "The Dam" as the coming of salvation. On the St. John, just upriver from Allagash, is the site of the proposed Dickey Dam. The giant development, with its millions in Federal spending, will bring a new prosperity to the river people and with it will go one of the last repositories of a vanishing past.

When river driving ended on the Allagash, the restricting dams were abandoned. The dams at Churchill and Long lakes fell into disrepair. Spring freshets took them out in the 1950s. The ancient river shook free of its bonds and, returned, once again, to its wild and primitive state.

WILDERNESS WARDEN

" A ROUND DEPOT Lake, the wardens have found the
bones of about one hundred moose that have been
killed within two years. It is unmistakable that indiscriminate
slaughter has been carried on there for years, and the only way
to prevent it is to keep a line of wardens from Baker Lake to
the Allagash."

The above paragraph appeared in the 1904 Report of the
Commissioners of Inland Fisheries and Game of the State of
Maine. The Commissioner was pleading for more money. The
total state appropriations for the department that year was
$25,000, the balance of $28,000 coming from license fees and
fines. The game protection personnel for this wilderness territory consisted of six underpaid wardens and the problem of
controlling poaching with such a lean staff was presented in
the Commissioner's brief.

"With a good pitch of water it takes a warden, working
hard, a full week to pole and paddle up the river from Fort
Kent to Depot Lake. So it will be seen how futile it is to
undertake to protect game in that region without wardens on
the ground all the time."

For that lonesome, unloved, overworked and underpaid little band of men, it was indeed a discouraging and all but
hopeless assignment. The Canadian side of the border was
settled right to the frontier making it a simple matter for Canadian poachers to slip in and out of the Maine woods with
illegal game, fish and fur. Roads penetrated into the south and
east Maine woods from the settlements. Hundreds of maple

211

sugar camps and logging operations run by Canadians, which brought legitimate traffic to the Maine wilderness, tended to cover the proliferation of game violations.

The wilderness wardens, a few years earlier, had put an end to the career of the notorious Pete Fountaine, whose traffic in moosemeat and fur must have equaled the total legal kill; but Pete's liquidation served only to whet the appetites of the hungry, avaricious and lawless. The wardens, on their rounds, found clear signs every day of illegal activity, but nine out of ten reports ended with the laconic statement: "No prosecution instituted for lack of evidence."

Cassius Austin, whose long career as a poacher's nemesis was to span a large part of the first half of the present century, learned early that a warden's lot was not a happy one. His father, Frank, was one of the first in the state to be invested with the full-time authority to enforce the game laws of the state in that far-flung wilderness. Cash was still in his early teens when Frank Austin got word that a fellow warden had been gunned down in cold blood.

Young Cash, already showing promise of the two hundred pounds of hogshead bulk and bull muscle that was to awe, restrain, and sometimes deter the lively and unreconstructed poaching fraternity which for generations before his advent had considered game wardens little more than a casual nuisance, was ready and willing.

The killer was taken into custody. A confession was obtained. The motive was simple and, in the context of the times, reasonable enough: he didn't like game wardens. True, six wardens for the ten million acres of wilderness was equal roughly to no wardens at all; yet even such minimal vigilance was regarded as an affront. With every other man and boy in the settlements on both sides of the Maine-Canadian border a poacher, active or potential, any warden at all was regarded as one too many. At the nub of the frontier thinking lay the sturdy conviction that the wilderness was there to be used and the game therein for "them as could take it." Any interference

Cash Austin

with the God-given right was not only impertinent but possibly unconstitutional.

Things being as they were in the dawning years of the present century, a man who would accept the job as game warden was foolish enough; but actually to work at it was regarded as sheer madness. A frontier man himself, Cash had no illusions about the life of an enforcement officer. In this border region which was 90 percent French and where families of fifteen were accepted as normal, just about everyone was somehow related. It was to be said of Cash Austin that he would arrest his own grandmother. This was just barely an exaggeration. Cash, whose mother was French and his father of English descent, had relatives on both sides of the language barrier; thus, not arresting a relative was much like trying to make scrambled eggs without breaking an egg.

To seek the source of such unswerving dedication to the cause of protecting wildlife requires a harkening back to Cassius Austin's formative years and the influence of his warden father. At a time before "conservation" had any meaning in a context of preserving natural resources, Frank Austin took nature's side against the prime predator, man. Guide, sportsman, woodsman of high repute, he was one of three guides chosen to show Teddy Roosevelt the Maine woods in the future president's youth.

One particularly cruel and ruthless act perpetrated by poachers during his father's warden years made an indelible mark on young Cassius. He was a mere fifteen when, traveling in the Allagash wilderness with his father, the pair came upon the tracks in the snow of three men and a moose. It appeared that the men had chased the moose for two days. They had only axes and, upon coming up on the exhausted animal, had put upon him with these crude weapons. Next they had punched out the beast's eyes with sharpened sticks and enclosed him in a corral of sticks and branches until they could return with rifles to finish him off.

In Cash Austin's first phase as game protector he worked part time as a temporary warden. As was the case with 90 percent of the population of the border settlements, his regular vocation was logging and guiding. Although such dawn-to-dark endeavors produced little more than a marginal living, the warden service was even less attractive, offering a base pay of two dollars for a twenty-four hour day, with fringe benefits of a good night's sleep when and where you could grab it.

In this matter of sleep—or lack of it—Cash recalled that his father Frank, after going without sleep for two days, finally caught a man poaching salmon on the spawning beds. He took the miscreant into custody and ten miles through the woods to jail. He was ready to drop from sheer exhaustion. On a hunch, he started right back to the scene of the arrest to catch the same man in the same illegal act. The poacher, after paying his bail, made the mistake of figuring that a warden, being only mortal, had to sleep sometime.

With this background in mind, Cash Austin was not immediately responsive when an attempt was made in the early 1930s to recruit him as a full-time warden. To give him further pause, he had by this time got himself a wife and was starting a family. The depression was in its darkest hour and poaching activity had reached such a brazen height that there was real danger of a total collapse of the enforcement agency. Cash already had built up a reputation as a hard, tough and tireless officer, traits that were sorely needed if any sort of law was to be restored in the woods.

Cash recalls that the appeal was not designed to overwhelm him with eagerness. "I was told I could retire one day on half pay; that is if I didn't get shot first."

His reluctant decision to assume the risks and the responsibilities of full-time wardenship was in no small way prompted by the fact that he, himself, was down to his last peck of potatoes. He passed the examination and was forthwith assigned to what was undoubtedly the toughest and most lawless district in the Maine woods, then or since.

The worst troubled area lay between the towns of Stockholm and Van Buren along the right of way of the Bangor & Aroostook Railroad. A gang of poachers with dog packs were raiding the winter deer yards, and such was the unrestrained slaughter that the tracks for miles ran red with blood. Not only were the outlaws flouting the law, they were mocking it, impaling the heads of their animal victims on poles along the roadbed.

Cassius Austin barely had the chance to flex the stiffness out of his new uniform before he had his first test of nerves. One of the gang accosted him on the street of the village. "Cash," he said, "you better get this straight. We don't like game wardens. If you get messing around in our way, I'm going to shoot you."

Cash didn't bat an arctic-blue eye. He said: "Then you better get *this* straight. If you shoot at me, your shooting better be good, because you'll never get another chance."

Thus, having served notice, the fledgling warden went to work. First off, he acquired a sled and dog team, composed of a German shepherd and a collie, and set out to patrol the deer yards in several hundred square miles of snow-blanketed wilderness. His plan was to go into the woods and stay in for up to two weeks at a time, sleeping when and where the night overtook him. It meant covering up to fifty woods miles a day and checking out every snowshoe track he crossed. For him it was a matter of simple pride that wherever poachers could go he too could go—and faster.

To travel fast was to travel light. Cash's grub list, in the light of what a woods traveler today considers basic necessities, amounted barely to survival rations. "What I packed for two weeks on the trail was a two-pound square of salt pork, a little flour, molasses and a fistful of tea. I made pancakes with the flour and soaked them in the pork fat. You'd be surprised how long frizzled pork sticks to a man's ribs."

Such Spartan austerity and dogged perseverance soon produced results. Late in January of that first year, he tracked down a band of marauders and their dogs holed up in a camp at the foot of Long Lake. There were only two men in the camp at the time. Suspecting others were involved, he stood guard over his prisoners and waited.

The wait was brief. Just before dark two men appeared in the clearing, dragging a buck deer. There were a few in that scantily populated wilderness region Cash didn't know by their first names. When Joe Hebert stepped into the darkened camp,

Cash said softly, "Joe, that looks to me like deer blood on your hands."

Startled, Joe turned and faced the last man in the world he expected, or wanted, to see at that moment. "Maybe," Joe said. "What are you going to do about it?"

"That's easy," Cash replied, "I'm going to take the bunch of you out of the woods and to jail the first thing in the morning."

As it turned out, it wasn't that easy. It was four to one. Cash took all the snowshoes for assurance that with four feet of snow in the woods the men wouldn't attempt a break. He confiscated the guns to reduce the odds against him further. "But that meant," Cash recalled, "I had to stay awake for another twelve hours."

It was just about the most agonizing night he ever spent. "They tried for me once. But only once," he added succinctly.

On the way out in the morning he called his supervisor, Levi Dow, from a Forest Service woods phone. His orders were to release the men with instructions to appear in court in Frenchville Monday morning. Cash followed instructions. Monday came and the culprits failed to appear. It fell upon Cash to set forth once more and usher the men to court.

His first call was at the home of Magloire Pelletier. Magloire had no intention of going to court, and to make his position clear, he barricaded the door and threatened to shoot to kill if an attempt was made to enter. Cash responded by laying his shoulder against the hinge side of the door and carried the door into the house with Cash behind it. The surprised poacher reached for a hammer. Cash parried the blow aimed at his head, with his arm. Somewhat incapacitated, Cash was forced to resort to his sidearm, settling the matter with a well-placed shot through the uncooperative poacher's foot.

All four poachers drew jail sentences, sixty days for killing out of season and another sixty for hunting with dogs. The most serious charge of felonious assault got lost in the shuffle. It wasn't so much that Warden Austin lacked evidence to convict, it was simply, being a frontier man himself, Cash considered resisting arrest normal behavior and a certain amount of physical abuse a part of the job.

In the course of his industrious career as a wilderness lawman, Cash was shot at perhaps a dozen times, struck over the head more times than he likes to remember and, on one occasion, was willfully run down by a poacher's car. In all but a few instances he pressed only the game violation charges. One of the exceptions was the case where the poacher ran him down. Being shot at was one thing, being knocked into a ditch by an automobile was something else again. On his back in a ditch he shot from the hip and balked the man's escape by shooting out his windshield.

Unlike Western folk heroes, Cash had a decided reluctance to use his sidearm. Although he was required to carry the standard thirty-caliber revolver, his awesome natural equipment usually rendered any show of it redundant. In the event a malefactor failed to respond to either French or English, Cash was inclined to accept the challenge on the man's own terms on the sound enough theory that it was not so much the badge of authority as the man behind the badge that commanded respect.

One fall day he caught a poacher in the act of netting salmon on the spawning beds. The poacher suggested that there were not enough wardens in the state to take him in. Cash quickly and efficiently demonstrated the fellow's error by hogtying him and lugging him out of the woods.

Once the ice went out of the lakes and streams in Maine's north country, the waterways became the highways for the wilderness wardens. Access, although somewhat simplified, was no less arduous. It was upriver work all the way battling the north-flowing Allagash and St. John, and the job was particularly daunting when the spring freshets were rampaging down the pitches.

As a waterman, Cash had few peers and the few, more often than not, were on the wrong side of the law. However, after that first year as a full-time warden, Cash Austin was getting his message across. He had established a reputation as a warden who played for keeps and buttressed the claim by making more arrests and getting more convictions than all the rest of the wardens in the North Woods division put together. The lawbreakers who continued to operate paid Cash the left-handed compliment of tending more toward caution and the employment of wile. Camps were camouflaged, trails covered and canoes carefully hidden.

Although Cash was influencing people he was making few friends. That first fall he came upon an illegal gill net set at the mouth of a spawning brook. He was in the process of taking up the net when a rifle cracked back in the neighboring woods and lead struck a few inches behind him. He legged it in the direction of the report. He didn't find his man, but what he did find was a single mitten, left in the assailant's haste to depart. A further search uncovered a hidden canoe. In a region where a canoe held much the same status as a horse of the Old West, establishing the ownership of the craft was no great problem. It belonged to a man who had threatened to kill him and had very nearly succeeded.

The man faced with the accusation, stubbornly denied he had been anywhere near the spot at the time of the incident and, moreover, he had friends who cheerfully supported his alibi. Cash, never one to be obstructed by legal forms, walked straightway into the man's home and searched it from top to bottom. He came up with the mitten that matched the one he had found. And he got his man.

Although this one-man crusade to bring law and order to a region largely populated by unabashed sinners was not making Cash a host of friends, his relentless pursuit and the impartiality with which he exercised his authority was gaining him a grudging respect. In those laissez-faire days there was no great onus attached to the avocation of poaching. The crime was to get caught. To be caught by Cash was to be caught by the best, a fact that tended to dilute the humiliation.

Sam Spencer cheerfully gave the devil his due. Sam and his boys, beaver poaching in the Allagash region, were run down that winter of 1941 in a memorable battle of wits and endurance, an operation that took two weeks and covered over a thousand miles and fifteen wilderness townships.

"Sure, I got caught," Sam admitted some decades later at a mellow seventy-eight. "But it took that so-and-so Cash Austin to catch me."

The duel began on the morning of October 13 when Warden Austin drove from Fort Kent to Lake Umsaskis by way of Canada and the LaCroix lumber road. There he met Warden Harold Dow who had come up the Allagash by canoe, a stratagem decided upon to allay suspicion that might be aroused by two wardens traveling upriver together.

The two then canoed downriver to Round Pond where they cached the canoe and struck out across country in the direction of First Lake Musquacook. In the course of several days' cruising they discovered a good supply of beaver, but no signs of illegal trapping. They arrived back at Round Pond at dusk. As they were about to launch the canoe, Cash grabbed up his binoculars. What he had seen was a canoe sliding along the west shore of the lake. On the field of his glasses he saw what happened to be two men working a gill net.

After dark the wardens crossed the pond and, after eating a cold supper, crawled into sleeping bags. At dawn, the suspicious canoe appeared again, and this time they were close enough to see the two men harvest a boatload of trout and whitefish from the net. This was in itself a violation; but the wardens were convinced there were others involved. And what they were seeking was evidence to make the illegal beaver charge stick. They allowed the canoe to continue toward Long Lake.

The first break came that day. A systematic search of the feeder brooks at the head of Round Pond uncovered both beaver and mink sets, the latter baited with whitefish that showed indications of having been gill netted. Returning to the pond, a further search produced a hidden camp and a fresh beaver pelt.

At this juncture, the pair decided to split up, with Dow keeping the camp under surveillance and Cash staking out near the gill net. The action came to Cash first. The second day of the vigil the canoe appeared on the pond with a load of beaverskins and headed for the camp. Cash's stakeout was a good mile from the camp. He was never clocked for the mile, but he's convinced he broke some kind of record for bush-whacking that day. He arrived at the camp just in time to alert his partner and waylay Sam Spencer and his son, Patrick, coming ashore.

Sam, long famed as an Allagash guide, cook and woodsman, was an old friend of Warden Austin's; but it was no part of friendship that prompted Cash to forego arresting the poachers on the spot. That would have meant a long trek back to civilization, by which time the others in the ring would most surely have made themselves scarce. In the face of Sam's protest, Cash confiscated the outboards and canoe to make certain the Spencers wouldn't warn the others. He then got quickly to a Forest Service phone and called his supervisor, asking for a plane with which to search the vast area.

The remaining members of the poaching ring were eventually corralled, but it was another week and a few more hundred miles of bushwhacking and waterwork before the Great Poacher Hunt, with its all-star cast, was wrapped up and left for the storybooks. It took a woodsman's eye to spot that trail from the river. There was some dry-ki on the shore that didn't look quite right to Cash. There had been a heavy frost the night before but, curiously, the driftwood had no coat of rime upon it. Once ashore the answer was simple; the driftwood had been put there a few hours earlier to hide the trampled grass and the trail that led to the poachers' hideaway.

In the days before a policy was established that gave the wilderness warden authority to accept bond from game violators apprehended fifty miles or more from a court, it was frequently the unenviable job of the arresting officer to usher the miscreant out of the woods along with the necessary evidence. This was no mean task, particularly if the warden was outnumbered two or three to one, the evidence a dead deer, and the distance from court several days' foot journey. Such was the case of the Lizotte brothers, Albert and Pierre.

Cash caught the pair red-handed. It seemed a proper part of justice to Cash that the punishment fit the crime. Since he needed the dead deer for evidence, he saw no reason why the perpetrators should not assume the burden of producing it. He ordered the pair to start dragging the deer. This was midwinter with a perilous wind honking out of the north. Cash started ahead to break trail. The poachers, after dragging the evidence a number of miles, sat down and refused to budge another inch.

Cash didn't say much. He tossed off his pack and, digging a hole in the snow, prepared for the night. "Boys," he said cheerfully, "there's a camp a few miles from here, but if you don't mind sleeping out tonight, I don't. I'm used to it." The two Frenchmen took up their burden.

Cash Austin's zeal sometimes created problems. After one particularly efficient event, he was chagrined to learn that he had taken up all the available space in the border hoosegows. He wasn't stumped for long. It was well after midnight that Warden Supervisor Levi Dow was aroused from his bed to find Cash at the door with three prisoners.

"Levi," Cash announced to his groggy-eyed superior, "you've got nothing much to do tonight. You can stay up and guard these fellows until I can find a place for them in jail."

There were innumerable occasions when Cash felt that no good purpose could be served by clapping a man in jail. Engaged in taking a wilderness census for the Federal Government, he and two fellow wardens dropped in on Fred Deschaines, the genial hermit of Seven Islands on the upper St. John. They got the vital statistics they wanted and, in the process, uncovered sixteen illegal fisher and sable skins.

"Hell," Cash recalled, "the old fellow didn't have any money and putting him in jail would have killed him." What Cash did was to arrange with a lumberman for whom Fred worked occasionally to take something out of his pay to satisfy the law.

Not such a genial fellow was the Mad Frenchman, so-called for his habit of shooting windows out of wilderness camps. It was shortly after the war that a guide named Porter stepped out of his camp one evening to fall dead with a bullet through his head. This senseless crime triggered one of the greatest manhunts in the annals of the Maine woods, a chase that involved the State Police, several Sheriff Departments, the Warden Service, guides, woodsmen, and just about everyone else with any knowledge of the area.

In the course of the massive operation, the killer was variously described as a monster eight feet tall and a half-man-half-ape who swung from trees. Cash was leading the posse that finally brought the fugitive to bay. It was the brother of the killer's victim who put a bullet through the man's leg. Cash, the only man in the posse who could speak French, interrogated the "monster" before he died from shock and loss of blood.

From the beginning, Cash had been somewhat scornful of the mass hysteria, feeling, as wardens do, that a few good woods-wise men are more effective in a search than an army of eager amateurs. "The fellow had no idea he'd shot that guide, let alone killed him. He said he was looking for food and wanted to scare anyone that might be around. Hell, he wouldn't have gone one-hundred-twenty pounds, soaking wet!"

It was shortly after Cash Austin had been appointed to the post of Warden Supervisor, upon the death of Levi Dow, that he very nearly remained in the woods for keeps. The first phase of this poacher hunt was routine enough. Flying over his wilderness division with a warden pilot early in December of 1946, he spotted some strange snowshoe tracks north of Al-

lagash Lake. Both the hunting and trapping seasons were
closed. Such tracks meant but one thing to Cash: poachers at
work. He got in touch with Warden Curtis Cooper and together they started in by canoe.

In the region of the St. John headwaters they nabbed two
Jackman trappers between Ross Lake and Desolation Pond.
The two poachers were flown out, along with the evidence of
twenty beaverskins. Convinced there were others involved,
Cash had four additional wardens flown in. The wardens proceeded south to Baker Lake and, sure enough, two more illegal
trappers were flushed out. They, too, were flown out to jail.

By this time the weather was deteriorating and a big freeze
was imminent. It was a question of whether to continue on and
attempt to bag two more violators he suspected were operating
near upper Knowles Brook, or to get out while the getting was
good. Cash, no man to call it quits before a job was tidied up,
opted to proceed. The gaunt and trail-weary wardens poled
their battered canoes deeper into the wilds, breaking ice as
they went. The sortie was successful and the last two poachers
were apprehended.

It was clear now that Cash had played this one too close.
Winter shut in like a slamming door, locking the waterways
with ice. There could be no help now from the air, for the ice
on the ponds rendered pontoons useless, and the ice wasn't yet
thick enough to support ski-fitted planes. Digging in and waiting for help wasn't a happy solution, either. Three weeks in the
woods had all but used up their food.

The unattractive alternative was to attempt to break out
before winter locked all exits. It was a hard, rough go, reminis-
cent of Benedict Arnold's ill-starred wilderness trek to Quebec
in the general region two hundred years earlier: but make it
they did, breaking ice for four solid miles on one stretch of
water.

Not long after this grueling adventure, Cash Austin reached
the mandatory age of retirement. Needless to say, there were

those who shed no tears when Cash turned in his badge and returned to lumbering.

On the other hand there were others, and among them not a few who had felt the pressure of Cash Austin's hard, enforcing hand, who knew they were witnessing the passing of the last of a breed of wilderness wardens.

There were other men, and good ones, to take his place; woods-wise, diligent and incorruptible men such as David Jackson, Leonard Pelletier, Curtis Cooper, who carried on the tradition and responsibility of game enforcement in the Maine wilderness.

Today, the Allagash wardens get the job done without resort to Cash Austin's rough-handed methods. It may be argued that his tactics served no useful purpose, that more can be done to encourage respect for the game laws by making friends than by making enemies. Yet no one can deny that he accepted a challenge at a time when there were few willing to face it. And he got the job done.

As a measure of his impact on his time, not even his detractors succeed in cutting Cash Austin down to size. At least, Cash would have accepted as a compliment the summing up of one contemporary who remarked with warm conviction: "It'll be a long time before you'll see another so-and-so like Cash Austin in the woods."

KING SPRUCE 20
AND SOME
YANKEE MECHANICS

FEW WERE aware that the legendary age of pine was
dying when fifty million feet of long log spruce, mixed
with pine, arrived at the Penobscot booms in the spring of
1851. Maine's "piney days" did not die with a bang. Nor did
King Spruce assume the throne with a roll of drums. When the
end was in view the most surprised of all were the prophets
who had said that the great pines were forever.

For several hundred years the great pines were the jewels
set in the matrix of the vast spruce forest. What remained
when the pine began running out was a wasteland destined, it
seemed, to be left once more to the wild beasts and trappers.
Prior to 1845, no spruce was cut for market. The few who
began to consider the idea were dismissed as a bit mad or, at
best, addlepated.

The line between madness and vision has ever been tenuous.
When in 1850, the East Penobscot was first cruised for spruce
and the first spruce loggers began operating around Mattawamkeag, the pine men were no more than tolerant. Spruce
was a weed tree. Could you make a silk purse out of a sow's
ear?

The madmen, unabashed, pushed their quest for spruce into
the region of the Allagash. By 1855, 78 million feet of spruce
arrived at the booms, as against 123 million feet of pine. After
that, the gap closed steadily. By 1861, only 48 million feet of
pine went down the river. That was the first year that spruce
logs outnumbered pine. The piney days were over.

So the madmen were not fools. The market, which once

would settle for nothing less than clear white pine, began clamoring for spruce. It was discovered that spruce, both red and white, was soft, close-grained and eminently suited for cutting into boards. True, the spruce fell far short of the awesome grandeur of the pine, seldom going over three feet in diameter breast high, or exceeding sixty feet in height. But spruce stood clean and straight and it was there in a quantity that defied comprehension. Moreover, spruce reproduced and flourished with incredible vitality. It was nigh indestructible.

What this new breed of timberland man had noted was that you could cut down a spruce stand, but you couldn't keep it down. They had seen land cleared in the trees for pasture and hay, only to grow back into forest again in a generation after the fields had been abandoned. Clearly, the spruce was the tree that "belonged" in the Maine woods.

This truth, so reluctantly accepted, was to change the face of the Maine lumbering industry and revolutionize its thinking. And once the realization penetrated that spruce was the timber of the future, the scramble was on. Fortunes gained by pine timbering in the first half of the nineteenth century enabled the sons of the pine barons to become spruce barons in the last half.

The assault on the pine had been a war of maneuver, a hit and run affair. The pine stands were spotty, islanded; a crew moved in, mopped up and moved out again, taking first what was handy to water and extending supply lines no deeper than the economics of the situation permitted. There were no roads(27) except those which a swamper crew could bush out for ox-drawn sleds. Ten miles was a mighty long haul to water. But they took the best of the pine, for the finest stands stood hard by the waterways. What pine the loggers failed to reach was left to succumb to old age or to stand as targets for lightning strikes.

Harvesting the spruce presented an entirely different proposition. There it waited in solid ranks, inviting frontal attack on a grand scale. Where once a crew of forty men was ideal, now

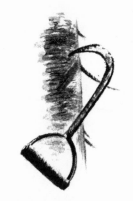

Pulp Hook

a hundred or a hundred and fifty men could be used handily. And now for the first time saws began to replace the axes, much to the bitterness of the old-timers who used their double-bitted tools with the artistry of a painter with his brush and were not about to see their precious axes junked without a battle.

It was a losing fight. The new technology was making its impact all along the line. The times and the job dictated new approaches, new weapons. Yankee ingenuity was marshaled to meet the challenge.

In the spring of 1858 Joseph Peavey dreamed up the tool that was to make his name a part of the language. A blacksmith from Stillwater, Maine, he was endowed with that Yankee knack of finding practical solutions to prickly mechanical problems. The story is told that Joe Peavey was lying on the bridge that spans the Stillwater branch of the Penobscot watching river hogs attempting to break a log jam. The drivers were using a swing dog, a short pole upon which hung an iron collar. Attached to the iron collar was a hook, or dog, used for rolling logs. It was a pretty poor rig Joe opined, awkward and dangerous. Joe Peavey, of a sudden, saw a simple answer. He hastened home to his shop and directed his son, David, to fashion a tool according to his specifications. What David produced was a pole with a rigid clasp at its business end, with lips on one side drilled to take a bolt that would hold the hook in place, allowing it to move up and down but not sideways.

As a crowning touch, a sharp iron spike was driven into the end of the pole.

Thus, in one afternoon, the improved cant dog, better known as the peavey, the logger's tool that was to roll uncounted billions of logs from Maine to the Pacific was born.(28)

The speedup, spurred by fierce competition that accompanied the opening of the spruce era, was reflected in the increased irascibility of the walking bosses and even in the manner of turning a crew out of bed in the wintry predawn. The bull voice of the cookee was replaced by a tin horn or, more commonly, the gut hammer. This last invention of the devil was a piece of iron, usually a triangle, which hung just outside the cookshack. When struck smartly with another piece of iron, it was extremely difficult to ignore.

As was the case with the cult of the axe-lovers, there were those stubborn sentimentalists who refused to renounce the old ways and continued to perform their sadistic chore with vocal virtuosity. One famed tormenter, with a voice that rocked the forest, was wont to chant: "Get up, get up, get up—dyin' old Christ, ain't you goin' to get up?"

Whichever way the spruce logs went, north to Canada or south to Bangor, they rode the rivers high, wide and handsome. They took the pine where they found it but no longer did they seek it out. King spruce rode the wave of the future.

The spruce stood solidly ranked as far as the mind could reach. Waste was a by-product of haste and urgency to feed the insatiable maws of the mills, themselves in the throes of a technological revolution that was trebling their capacity to produce boards. Trees were cut at snow level and trimmed to

Peavey

an eleven-inch top diameter.(29) Everything under eleven-inch diameter was classed as batten and sold for next to nothing, or left in the woods to rot. The wide main logging roads destroyed young growth. Nor was much care taken in cleaning up the rear of a river drive, with the result that thousands of feet of good timber were left on the banks, or hung up in bogans to rot.

There was yet no glimmering of the idea of forest management as the assault on the spruce forest began. The forest was there to be cut and as quickly and completely as possible. So at it they went, cutting the trees, rolling the logs into the rivers for the river hogs to drive to the mills. The sawmills ate them up and whined for more.

The great bulk of the Allagash spruce went north with the flow of the river to the St. John and the Canadian mills. The Bangor men battled to get their share of the Allagash timber from the Allagash headwater lakes and to drive it south into the Penobscot watershed and to the booms on the main Penobscot River. What success they had could never have been achieved without a strong mixture of Yankee ingenuity and imagination.

The Kennebeckers, too, were in the thick of the battle. They had not forgotten that their efforts to get Allagash timber into their own river had been finessed by the Bangor lumbermen at the time of the Telos Canal controversy. This time they didn't make the mistake of going ahead first and attempting to appease the politicians afterward.

In 1893, J. S. and F. T. Bradstreet, who owned a large sawmill at South Gardner on the lower Kennebec, succeeded in having an act passed by the State Legislature to incorporate the Seboomook Dam Company. As in the case of the earlier canal proposal, the idea was simply to get logs from the West Branch Penobscot into Moosehead Lake, thence down the lake to Kennebec where logs could be driven to mills downriver.

Advanced technology offered a more sophisticated approach to the logistical problem. Under the direction of Ira Peavey, a sluiceway-conveyor was constructed. The first conveyor, operated by a steam engine, took the logs from Carry Pond by means of an endless chain, fitted at intervals with iron dogs. The logs were then dumped on a second conveyor and delivered to the sluiceway which was two miles long. The sluiceway was V-shaped like a great hog trough and was supported by X-shaped horses hewed out on the spot. The whole ingenious contraption worked like a charm. There were inherent weaknesses in the rig, however. The operation required forty men: twenty men were needed along the sluiceway alone to keep the logs running. A disastrous fire destroyed the installation the second year of operation. Rebuilt, a second forest fire swept over the region and, despite the valiant efforts of the crew who attempted to keep the wooden sluiceway watered down, the planking was charred for a quarter of a mile.

The Yankee rig operated in all about eight years and managed to carry eighty million feet of logs into Moosehead Lake(30) before it was abandoned.

Prodded perhaps by the success of the Kennebeckers' conveyor, the Bangor lumbermen put on their own Yankee thinking caps in the hope of solving another logistical problem. Between Eagle and Chamberlain lakes there was a height of land a mere 3,000 feet wide that separated the St. John and Penobscot watersheds. A conveyor system that could jump that barrier would, they saw, save all kinds of fuss and money.

In 1901, an engineer by the name of Fred Dow was dispatched to the region by Marsh & Ayer of Bangor to study the situation. Dow failed to find any serious obstacles and he was given orders to proceed. Nothing quite so ambitious had ever been attempted a hundred miles back in the sticks and when the Taylor Iron and Steel Company, of Highbridge, New Jersey, delivered the conveyor at Greenville the sight of tons of cumbersome machinery was enough to discourage even the most sanguine proponents.

The heaviest equipment went up the lake by boat to Northeast Carry that fall. The rest was hauled over the frozen lake by teams. The cable alone weighed fourteen tons. The first attempt to take it into the woods literally bogged down at Smith's halfway house on the West Branch Penobscot. The cable was cut into two pieces and, by luck and exhortation, it finally arrived at the site.

Dow and his crew at the base at Eagle Lake were having their own problems. The crankshaft on the large engine had arrived broken and Dow was forced to fall back on a small donkey engine to run his rotary saw. And once the equipment was assembled in the woods, enough bugs developed to challenge the most resourceful haywire mechanics.(31) For one thing, the 4,800 ⅞-inch bolts that fastened the 600 clamps and 600 trucks .o the cable were not threaded down far enough. Each bolt had to be removed and threaded down with a hand die.

The feat of setting up this contraption back in a roadless wilderness was astonishing enough, to have it finished and operating in a year represented an incredible performance. In addition, the towboat, the *George A. Dugan,* the seventy-one-foot craft that was to haul the logs across Chamberlain Lake, was built right on the spot in four months. O. A. Harkness, the towboat's builder, wrote this description of the tramway in operation:

The steel cable of 1½ inch diameter was 6000 feet long and fastened together so that it was endless and reached from Eagle to Chamberlain Lake. At intervals of 10 feet the trucks were clamped on. These trucks consisted of steel saddles on which the logs rested and two 11 inch wheels which ran on two tracks 22 inches apart. There were two tracks, one above the other. The loaded one went on the top track and the empty one returned on the lower track. Half way between the trucks there was a steel clamp. Both the clamp and the truck fitted into the sprocket wheel which was nine-feet in diameter and situated at the Chamberlain Lake end of the tramway. The sprocket wheel made nine revolutions per minute which made the logs travel 250 feet per minute. Wood was used for fuel for the two boilers which furnished steam for the engine. It took a lot of power to start the machinery moving but it rolled easily once it was in motion.

Things were moving fast during this the most active period in the lumbering history of the Allagash. The tramway was used only six seasons before another Yankee invention took the bloom from its wonder. In that brief span, working from 4 A.M. to 8 P.M., it moved an average of 500,000 board feet a day and a total of 100 million feet of timber.

There had never been any doubt that it was cheaper and quicker to haul logs directly to Chamberlain Lake if means could be found to get them there. It fell upon A. O. Lombard, son of a Springfield, Maine, blacksmith, to find the means, making in the process one of the most significant and revolutionary contributions to the technology of the age.

For six thousand years man had moved on wheels. It took a bit of imagination, to say nothing of a strong charge of audacity, to consider an alternate possibility. What was needed in the woods was a mechanical log-hauler. A wheel was no good at all on snow; it was round and offered insufficient traction surface.

A. O. tucked the problem in the back of his mind for a spell. Then one night he locked himself in the den of his Waterville home and commenced to scribble. In just twenty-four hours he had the first crude drawings for the most famous of all lumbering inventions, the Lombard steam log-hauler. Lombard had no idea that his basic idea of the caterpillar tread was to mother the military tank and the farm tractor, but once he had constructed a wooden working model at the pattern shop of the Waterville Iron Works, he realized he had something, not only new for the woods, but new under the sun.(32)

The first Lombard steam log-hauler was dubbed *Mary Ann*. Built in the form of a wood-burning locomotive, it carried tractor treads at the stern and a sled forward. The original idea was to use a team of horses to steer the rig. When this failed to

Lombard Steam Log-Hauler

satisfy him, Lombard designed a mechanical steering device.
There was another critical bug to iron out. He had designed
the pistons of the steam engine to work up and down together
instead of alternating. On her trial spin, the *Mary Ann* did a
dervish dance, much to the amusement of the doubting-
Thomas audience. A. O. lost no time in correcting that mistake
and in short order the first Lombards were ready to revolutionize the logging industry.

The response was something less than ecstatic. What worked
in favor of the log-hauler's acceptance was the desperate need
for some sort of power conveyance that could get to the more
remote timber and move it to water. In 1907, the Allagash
region saw the first of these chuffing monsters when it was
decided to try one out in Township 6 Range 14. A twelve-mile
hauler road was constructed from this area to the mouth of
Little Allagash stream. In the course of that winter, three
Lombards were used, to the satisfaction of some and the in-
dignation of others who observed that the steam-haulers spent
more time in the repair shop than they did on the road.

There was more than a little truth in this charge. The early
steam-haulers would not stand much abuse and abuse is what
they got. Many of the parts were of cast iron, which becomes
extremely brittle in frosty weather. Installations of costly
pumping stations were required in order to fill the boilers on

each trip. The pumps were used also to fill the horse-drawn sprinkler tank that traveled on runners and sprayed the road each night. There were three-inch holes in the rear of the tank, so arranged that the water would flow into the runner tracks and freeze.

These iced tracks served the belching monsters very well on the level or on an upgrade, but when the iron beasts, which weighed from ten to thirty tons, began picking up speed on a downgrade there was many a bad moment for the steersman until snubbing systems were devised. At best, the Lombards called for a dauntless crew. The conductor rode the train, which consisted of as many as eight to ten laden sleds, and it was his job to communicate with the engineer in the cab, a function he accomplished by means of a wire strung on stakes.

On the locomotive, besides the engineer, were the firemen and the steersman, the latter having the roughest job of all. He sat on the sled ahead of the crawler and guided the fearsome beast with a large iron wheel that was supposed to direct the runners on the turns. He was right under the stack and the least of his hazards was a good chance of having his clothes set afire by live cinders. Later, when a housing was installed for him, he fared somewhat better but this protection in no way eliminated the ever-present danger of being caught at the wheel with the iron horse going hell-for-leather and out of control on an icy downgrade. As one Lombard engineer recalled, "When she hit the grade and wouldn't behave, you first prayed to the Lord, and when that didn't help, you just hung on for dear life and took the Lord's name in vain . . . and if *that* didn't work, you jumped."

The Lombard brought a new and interesting office to the Maine woods, the dispatcher. In that first log-hauler operation this dispatcher had his office at Russell Brook. He sat at a desk facing a chart of the route, the straight line indicating the main road and the crooked line the "go-backs." At each of ten crossings were telephones where the engineers called in for instructions so that the dispatcher could arrange to keep the road clear for loaded trains.

The Big Boss, John Kelley, wasn't the most popular man in the woods, and the day John hitched a ride to the log landing was just the day the Lombard engineer had been waiting for. The steam-hauler was plowing snow that day and the boss elected to ride the plow. The engineer knew every stump and bump in the road, but there was one particular stump he had in mind and he took it at high speed. John Kelley went high into the air and landed headfirst in a snowbank. That particular engineer was not at his job the next day. He allowed as how he was going to quit anyway.

The steam log-hauler era was as brief as it was dramatic. The internal combustion gasoline engine was reaching a stage of development where it could be adapted to the log-hauler, resulting in far greater efficiency. The steam-hauler, drawing eight sleds, averaged 40,000 board feet per load and on occasions hauled as much as 100,000 feet of long logs. The gas-type hauler's average was nearer 20,000 feet, but the running time was shorter and the faster trips meant less of an investment in sleds. Also, the steam Lombard required costly 18-to-20 foot roadways, while the gasoline rig could operate on a much narrower roadbed.

Although it was established quickly that one Lombard could do the work of sixty horses, the huge capital investment, repair costs and delays caused by breakdowns cut deeply into any savings. Many of the old-time loggers refused to be convinced that the day of the woods horse was over. When the Great Northern Paper Company decided to give the gas-powered tractor a try on their Soper Brook operation, Al Edgerley, the superintendent, was one of the headshakers. As the chugging tractor started into the woods from Greenville, Al followed with a pair of driving horses, muttering to himself. Finally, Al had enough. He got out of his pung, hitched his horses to the mechanical beast and walked ahead of the procession with a lantern.

The log-hauler era lasted roughly ten years. Ed Lacroix, one of the most famous of all Allagash lumbermen, used Lombards as late as 1929. Few tears were shed when the steam log-hauler blew its final whistle in the Maine woods, but those who had lived through that colorful era found it hard to forget. As one old logger put it, "To meet one on a still, bitter night deep in the woods, the head lamp cutting through the darkness, chugging and rocking as it towed a train some 500 feet long— blowing steam and smoke and fire to the treetops, was something indeed to remember."

While the Lombard had come and gone in one brief decade, the gasoline engine and Lombard's caterpillar tread were beginning to blaze new trails and shape the dawning age of modern lumbering.

Steam power was to have one final fling in the Allagash before modern haul roads and fleets of trucks assumed the logging burden. The day of pulpwoods, with its fresh imperatives of speed and efficiency, was emerging. At first, there was stout resistance to this direction from the landowners who feared the cutting of smaller trees might depress timberland values. Diminishing sawlog markets, coupled with the devastation caused by the spruce budworm infestation, which ravaged great areas of the Maine and Canadian wilderness, softened this initial opposition. A massive cutting operation was called for if the trees in the infected areas were to be salvaged. Once more, the timberland owners were faced with the problem of penetrating the remote areas and getting timber and pulpwood into the Penobscot watershed.

The idea of building a railroad back in the wilderness was every bit as audacious as the Telos Canal or the tramway. Water was still the cheapest way to get logs to market, but the timber was not always handy to water and, when it was, the water frequently flowed in the wrong direction for the Maine timberland owners. In 1925, the Great Northern Paper Company decided to explore the East Branch Penobscot route. In the spring of that year an exploration party that included Ed Lacroix and O. A. Harkness along with some seasoned Chesuncook guides, notably Ansel Smith and Nick Mulligan, investigated this possibility for a route to tap the timber resources of the Allagash. Finding the obstacles too formidable, alternate possibilities were studied. The route from Eagle Lake to Umbazookskus was finally settled upon. Later, the route was extended to Chesuncook Lake.

Here again, heavy equipment was brought in across a wilderness and Yankee mechanics were pressed into service to meet the problems that arose every foot of the way. The route went across Allagash stream at the foot of Chamberlain Lake, which necessitated a trestle 1,800 feet long. The responsibility for pushing through the upper eleven miles of track—the section from Eagle Lake to the head of Umbazookskus—fell upon Ed Lacroix, while the Great Northern assumed the job of constructing the lower five miles. Ed MacGregor, one of the great railroad construction family, took charge of the construction for Great Northern. He hired Ed Ronco, guide, woodsman and one of the most knowledgeable Allagash hands in Maine. When cedar was needed, Ed Ronco knew where to find the best. If culvert timbers were needed, the call went out for Ed who seemed to know every tree in the Allagash. On hand too was famous "Dynamite" Murphy who ordered eight tons of explosives and began to use the stuff with his special brand of joyous artistry.

A man would have been hard put to find a college degree on that wilderness job. This was just as well, for with no precedents, nothing went by the book. For example, when the problem arose of graveling the roadbed there was nothing in the way of mechanical equipment to expedite the job. It didn't take a couple of headscratchers long to devise a rig to accomplish the purpose. Gravel was dumped on a string of flatcars by a diesel shovel. A snowplow was placed on the end car and connected to the locomotive by a cable. When the rolling stock arrived at the section of road to be graveled, the locomotive was uncoupled and the flatcars braked. The locomotive then proceeded alone, dragging the plow along the flatcars and neatly sweeping the gravel off the cars and depositing it where it was needed.

When the road was being hewn out of the woods, crews based at the Tramway prepared the equipment to be used on the hauling operation. The work included the erection of loading conveyers and the remodeling of cars for the special job of hauling and unloading pulpwood. Practical men, who had never heard the word "automation," were faced with the task of finding ways and means of eliminating costly manual procedures. At the terminal at Umbazookskus Lake a trestle that reached 600 feet out into the lake was constructed with a six-inch cant toward the unloading side. The cars themselves were built with a twelve-inch slope on the same side and the cars' sides were hinged at the top so that once the side was raised at least two thirds of the load tumbled into the water without human aid.

A major difficulty arose before the right-of-way was completed. When MacGregor completed his five miles, he was asked to continue on to meet Ed Lacroix's crew working down from the north. By then, the fall rains had begun and the intervening bogs were quickly a morass. But the job went on and the wilderness railroad was completed in the incredible time of four months.

That day in August of 1927 was a day for rejoicing. That was the day the 90-ton steam locomotive, which had been converted from coal to oil, drew its first load of 100 cords of pulpwood. Full efficiency wasn't achieved immediately on the run, with only 1,800 cords delivered at the end of that first week. The Yankee mechanics went to work and soon 6,500 cords were being handled by the "pulpwood express." Success was achieved at tremendous financial cost. With its span of usefulness envisioned at twenty years, the heavy investment was considered justified. As with the tramway, this figure was an overestimation. It was nearer ten years that the wilderness railroad served its purpose of landing Allagash pulpwood in the Penobscot watershed.

Pulpwood, the stepchild of the lumbering complex, was about to become a mainstay and the darling of the industry. The power chain saw, with its banshee cry and flashing teeth, had burst upon the scene and was quickly beginning to eat its way beyond the existing limits of economic transportation.

Pulpwood as a product and the chain saw as a tool coupled to force a new way of thinking upon the timberland owners. The distances between stump and mill were growing ever longer. The ancient Aztec cities had withered because the land close by was not replenished, forcing the necessity of traveling farther and farther to support the centers of consumption. The prophets who had said that the Maine timber would last forever had been proven false. The time had come to consider alternatives to unrestricted looting of the public domain.

A few on the management level had already been thinking in terms of the future. David Pingree, Jr., son of the Allagash pine baron, a husbandman by nature, had managed to recoup the fortune his father had lost in imprudent leather speculation. Pingree *fils* was giving some thought to the curious idea of growing trees as well as cutting them. The bull voice of Austin Cary, the father of forest management, began to be heard and heeded. The hard-nosed Yankee lumberman listened to Cary. A Maine Yankee himself, self-made and self-educated, a woodsman in the logger's sense, Cary spoke a language the timberman could understand and he spoke out loud and clear. The gospel Cary had been preaching since before the century's turn was beginning to make good sense and those exotic phrases "selective cutting" and "sustained yield" were no longer dismissed as mouthings of visionaries.

It was the primacy of pulpwood as a forest product that dictated the policy of long-term thinking and resource hus-

Chain Saw

bandry. Gone were the days when a sawmill could set up shop with a small capital investment, reap a quick harvest and get out. Converting wood into paper required stability and the investment of millions in plants, equipment and timberlands, capitalization that could not be amortized on any short-term basis. Planning for the future suddenly became a prerequisite of successful enterprise.

"Conservation" remained a suspect word in the mind of the timberland owners. It was associated too closely with the "preservation" concept with its implication of hoarding and withdrawal from use. They preferred the term "forest manage- ment" with its suggestion of intelligent utilization. The con- servation forces were not completely disarmed by the sudden espousal of "multiple use" by the landowners, suspecting, not without some justification, that the industry's conversion to the principle of sharing the wilderness with the public was moti- vated largely by a wish to improve the corporate "public image" and an even more fervent desire to present an alterna- tive to the growing public demand for the preservation of national resources implicit in the "forever wild" concept.

There are, today, clear signs that the gap of mutual suspi- cion that has existed so long between private landowners and the conservation-oriented public is beginning to close. What appeal to conscience failed to bring about, enlightened self- interest appears to be achieving as the realization has pene- trated that the vast wilderness under the stewardship of pri- vate ownership is not a mine to be exploited and exhausted, but a storehouse and a pantry filled with a bounty to serve both the present and the future.

THE LONG
ROAD BACK

I N THE fall of 1966 an act creating the Allagash Wilderness Waterway received the blessings of the people of the State of Maine and became law. It became, moreover, the first such wilderness river preserved in America.

In the body of the act the state policy was thus enunciated. "Whereas the preservation, protection and development of the natural scenic beauty and the unique character of our waterways, wildlife habitats and wilderness recreational resources for this generation and all succeeding generations; the prevention of erosion, droughts, freshets and filling up of waters; and the promotion of peace, health, morals and general welfare of the public is the concern of the people of this State, the Legislature declares it to be in the public interest, for the public benefit and for the good order of the people of this State to establish an area known as the Allagash Wilderness Waterway."

Admittedly extravagant in its hopes, the act nonetheless clearly shows a will and brave intent to hold the line against encroachments that day by day across the land are gnawing deeper into the remaining repositories of our natural resources.

The enabling act brought to pause the long, and frequently bitter, controversy that had been bubbling along ever since Henry David Thoreau in his Maine Woods Journals announced for national preserves where wildlife need not be "civilized off the face of the earth."

More recently, it was the National Park Service that took up the cudgels and brought the question into the arena for final decision. Recognizing that time was running out, the Park

243

Service made a series of proposals, all of which were resisted, not only by the private timberland owners but by a large segment of the Maine citizenry as well.

At the same time, other proposals were made that would have eliminated the controversy by eliminating the river. Proposed were power dams, one in connection with the old Passamaquoddy scheme and the other by private power promoters. Both would have flooded the Allagash region and destroyed the river forever. Another danger threatened as pressure was mounted by an Aroostook citizen group to build a road across the heart of the region.

With the Federal Government pressing for action, it behooved the state to present its own proposal, which was to acquire a corridor along the waterway 400 to 800 feet wide. Overall, about 200,000 acres were involved to be placed under state control and administered by the State Park and Recreation Commission. Timber harvesting would be regulated, not only along the riverbanks, but in contiguous areas as well.

The United States Department of the Interior pulled back its own proposal, but implicit in its forbearance was a "do it or else" warning. To further encourage action, the Federal Government offered matching funds for acquisition of land. It was this state proposal that received the blessings of the people of Maine. The fact that the final stages of negotiations took on the aspects of a shotgun wedding in no way diminishes the ultimate victory.

Throughout the long controversy the cast was standard and the positions of the protagonists predictable. Arrayed on one side were the timberland owners, who traditionally resist any sort of regulation, and their supporters who view such public pressure as a threat to the sacred right to own and manage land.

On the other hand stood a stout and vocal band who considered the future of the Allagash too important to be entrusted to the uncertainties of private and commercial ownership and who saw only catastrophe if the inexorable cannibalization of our natural resources be allowed to continue.

Inevitably in the heat of battle divergent positions tend to become extreme and rigid as each side fabricates its own special demons. The specter of confiscation and public ownership was paraded on one hand, the bugaboo of rapacious private interests on the other. It was left to reasonable men to sit down together and decide what best might be done.

At the outset there were disagreements within the opposing positions themselves. This was particularly evident within the conservation camp where the very nature of the concept "wilderness" was involved. There were those partisans who saw no salvation unless the region was restricted both in recreational and commercial activity. A wilderness that is "developed" ceased, they contended, to be a wilderness. Others insisted that forests, waters and wildlife become recreational assets only through use. There was general agreement, however, that unrestricted access and use would most surely destroy the avowed purpose of the wilderness preserve.

The timberland owners have not relinquished their original position that the Allagash region, far from being a wilderness untouched by man, has in fact been in continuous use for three hundred years. At the very core of the landowners' brief for continued private control was the contention that under their stewardship the region has indeed been preserved and, further, that it has been open freely for public recreation.

The argument at first blush was persuasive. In the middle of the last century, Thoreau wrote of the Allagash, "what is the most striking in the Maine wilderness is the continuousness of the forest, with fewer intervals or glades than you had imagined. . . . The aspect of the country, indeed, is universally stern and savage." The Allagash Thoreau saw is still there. One hundred plus years of use have not altered its essential character.

The conservationist argument was equally cogent. They asked: "What assurances do we have that this wilderness will continue to be managed prudently? By the very nature of profit-oriented industry wouldn't practical considerations always take precedence over aesthetic values?"

Here again was a semantic impasse. "Aesthetic value" resists definitive bonds. Along with the concept "wilderness," it lies in the realm of the emotions and is subjective by its nature. To many, indeed to most, a shaggy, unkempt wilderness is not very beautiful. Thoreau attempted to anatomize this very Maine wilderness. He asked himself what was the essential difference between the Allagash wilds he met and his own combed and tended Concord countryside. "It has lost," he noted, "its wild, damp and shaggy look, the countless fallen and decaying trees are gone."

Then Thoreau, with his perceptive mind, put his finger on the very quick of the matter. "Civilized man not only clears the land and cultivates open fields, but he tames and cultivates to a certain extent the forest itself. By his very presence, almost, he changes the very nature of the trees as no other creature does."

Man has become a positive ecological factor in the complex interrelationships of nature, and more and more has he the power to alter and modify the environment in which he lives. Ecologists themselves have been prone to ignore man, dismissing him as a nuisance and a disturbing factor in the search for pure and stable situations for investigation. Admittedly, a "wilderness" is a region least disturbed by man's presence and management. Yet not even a wild land can escape the agency of man nor deny him a place in the economics of nature. Today, no wilderness can be understood, let alone "preserved" except within this larger framework.

It should be accepted then that the Allagash cannot be "preserved" in the sense of keeping it forever fixed in time like a fly in amber. The wilderness was changing before man's coming. Man's guns, axes, his mere presence, have quickened the pace, altered the habitat and added new complexities to the already complex interrelationships. It is this complexity, this variety of

nature which should be conserved and treasured. It is to this
end that wilderness-lovers should direct their efforts and seek
some wise and working principle of co-existence.

A living wilderness should and can be used so long as use
involves enjoyment rather than mindless consumption. Intelligent use depends upon restraint and a qualitative rather than
quantitative utilization. It is much too soon to say that the
Allagash has been "saved." Clearly, the Allagash cannot
provide outdoor recreation for the multitude without im-
pairing its natural values.

Massive use would be as destructive as a plague of locusts.
As there are places on earth for broad public use, there should
be places on earth for the appreciators who accept that rewards must be earned and that without effort there can be no
true appreciation.

This then is the promise and the challenge. And it is only in
the fulfilling of this promise that the Allagash can remain special and for the future.

Nor is public ownership any final guarantee of eternal salvation of these wild lands. Sixty years ago, the State of New
York drew a line around five and a half million acres of Adi-
rondack forestland, decreeing that they should remain "forever-
wild." Today, pressures are mounting to accommodate the
mass recreation by building roads into the fastness and leasing
sites for motels.

There is little doubt that managed harvesting of mature
trees is a part of intelligent land use. The danger lies in provid-
ing access to a multitude of wilderness-destroying angels. Once
the doors are open to a wilderness, the wilderness evaporates
and leaves in its stead another trammeled place.

Inevitably, there will be pressures upon the Allagash country
from those who wish to exploit it, as well as from those who
wish, in the name of public recreation, to sacrifice its special
qualities by making of it a playground rather than a sanctuary.

Somehow, through good luck, providence and the imperatives of hard economics, the Allagash has survived three hun-

dred years of use without losing its essential wilderness character. That it will so remain cannot yet be taken for granted. Nor
will its integrity be safe until its users, both private and public,
join with the same vision and work together to realize a common good.

Clearly, man has arrived at that critical point in his evolution where he is reaching the limits of his power to control the
world he has made. In reaching for the moon he has wandered
too far from his biological roots. In the mindless destruction of
the last remnants of his wilderness domain, he is most surely
shutting the doors on the long road back.

It is in this context that the Allagash stands as a challenge
and a test.

NOTES

(1) This is Lucius Hubbard's translation. He suggests that Allagash is a contraction of *Allagaskwigamook* the Indian name for Allagash Lake, the source of the Allagash. Its Indian meaning, according to Hubbard, is "bark-cabin lake." It has also been translated, "camp on lakeshore." Over the years the river has been variously rendered "Allequash," "Alequash," "Allegash" and finally "Allagash." Thoreau, who favored the rendering "Allegash" offered the translation "hemlock-bark," giving William Willis (*On the Language of the Abnaquies*, Maine Hist. Coll., Vol. IV) as his authority. This would appear to be an error for hemlock was, and still is, scarce to nonexistent in this region of the Allagash country.

(2) It was from Gyles's account that we first learn the early Indian name for Katahdin. In the early Indian usage it was "The Teddon" or "The Hill," much as the Indians and later the white settlers of that region, referred to Moosehead Lake as "The Lake," as if to say, "what other lake is there?"

(3) A dam built over a hundred years ago at the foot of Chesuncook Lake raised the water, and the meadow river with its soft shores and grassy lowlands was flooded back to a hard shoreline. Each time the dam was raised in subsequent years, the shore and the trees were further encroached upon. Later, with the building of Ripogenus Dam, the region was further flooded.

(4) In recent years, John Sinclair, Woodlands Manager for the Pingree Heirs, came upon an old-growth pine in the Allagash region that was nine feet at the butt. It was a crotched tree and no doubt was spared by the early lumbermen because of this defect in its conformation. Pine is still reproducing in some sections of the Allagash, particularly in situations where fires and logging activity have removed the surface "duff" and exposed mineral soil.

(5) Also spelled "dri-ki." It is generally accepted that this is an English approximation of the Indian word for driftwood. Dry-ki is a feature of Maine

lumbering lakes. This spectral thicket of standing or fallen dead and weathered trees which rings these lakes was caused when dams raised the water level and drowned the lake perimeter. When the dams went out the water returned to normal levels and the dead trees remained.

(6) This was William H. Smith, another Allagash landowner who had a stake in getting Allagash timber into the Penobscot watershed.

(7) Of this gaudy lady, Stewart H. Holbrook wrote, "Fan Jones was a woman of wide vision, looking both landward and seaward. There was a huge chimney on the outside of her place and this she caused to be painted sky blue, the blue of the brightest sky ever seen. It was never allowed to fade, but was repainted twice a year, brighter and more lovely each time. And this chimney was so placed that its heavenly color served as a landmark for woman-hungry loggers coming downriver from the woods, and as a promise of snug harbor to the sailors coming upriver. If a man got lost in Bangor, whether by land or by sea, it was no fault of Fan's. . . ." The great Bangor fire, which spared Fan's emporium, occurred in 1911.

(8) Wangan, also spelled "wanigan" or "wannigan," referred to a number of entirely different things. First, it meant the logging camp commissary or store, and the payroll deductions for goods bought at the store. It also was the spot where the driving crews made camp for the night. The wangan boat was the craft that carried food and supplies to the men on the river drive. Doubtlessly, the word is an English corruption of an Indian word although the derivation is obscure.

(9) Thoreau spelled the name "Aitteon." Fannie Eckstorm, who wrote an account of the death of Thoreau's guide, stated that the name which appears on his gravestone is Joseph Attien. This spelling indicated both the pronunciation and the derivation, for the word is not Indian but an Indian variation of the French Étienne or Stephen.

(10) Up until well into the twentieth century, many Maine hunters made a living killing game for the city markets, a practice that is now illegal.

(11) Hiram Leonard, a Bangor man, was indeed a noted sportsman. He was also a market hunter and an old Allagash hand by the time he was 30. Leonard frequently stayed at the Molunkus House, a hostelry near Mattawamkeag, a stage stop on the Bangor-Houlton run where Thoreau himself stayed overnight on his Katahdin ex-

cursion in 1846. Leonard spent several weeks each fall at this inn where he was charged $3.00 a week for board. It was his habit to sit on the porch with his gun by his side and read the paper, his chair tilting back against the house. He would glance up occasionally and cover the surrounding landscape with his eyes. When a deer appeared in the field he would take up his gun and, without rising from the chair, bring the game down. He supplied game to the Bangor market and always succeeded in taking back a wagonload of venison. Leonard knew the Allagash wilds as well as any white man of his time.

(*12*) In error, Thoreau placed Pillsbury Island on Heron Lake. It might well have appeared so on his maps which were, to use his words, a "labyrinth of errors."

(*13*) Many modern naturalists have suggested that Thoreau was not always entirely reliable as a naturalist. Curiously, he went through life without ever connecting the familiar ovenbird with its song.

(*14*) Thoreau had a special fondness for the word "saunter" and he was the first to employ the word in its accepted modern sense of walking while meditating. In his paper, "*Walking*," Thoreau goes into the possible

derivation from wanderers in the Middle Ages who claimed to be going "à la Sainte Terre" —to the Holy Land. Some of the pilgrims found the going rough and instead of continuing became vagabonds. Thus the term "saunterers" came to have the connotation of idlers on the way.

(*15*) John Gardner, small boat historian, gives the spelling *batteau*, and plural, *batteaux*, as the English adaptation of the French *bateau*, which is the French word for any small boat. The double "t" spelling was the rendering of this particular class of double-ended river boat. Fannie Eckstorm maintains that *batteau, batteaus* was the accepted usage by Maine lumbermen.

(*16*) In the 1898 issue of *In The Maine Woods*, a promotion publication put out by the Bangor & Aroostook Railroad, the "grey wolf or timber wolf" was included in the list of Maine fauna. It reported that several wolves had been killed that year near Moosehead Lake in the township of Monson. The following note was added to instruct sportsmen in the event of an encounter with a wolf. "Should a sportsman ever run face to face with one, let him be sure to keep in an upright position, and not stumble or fall in the face of the wolf, for if he does, the wolf will be on him like a flash. But should he face and get up before the wolf reaches him, directly the hunter is in a standing position again, the wolf will crouch on his belly close to the ground, and very often he will allow the hunter to go quietly up and knife him without offering the slightest resistance."

It is quite doubtful if many sportsmen encountered a timber wolf during those waning years of the last century and even less doubtful if any of those so honored took this procedural advice. In recent years, however, there have been several sightings of wolves by responsible woodsmen. These sightings have been near the Maine-Canadian border, which suggests that northern Maine has become a casual range of these predatory animals.

(17) Jules Thurlotte was the "blind Canadian" Thoreau's guide Joe insisted on visiting on Thoreau's woods jaunt in 1857. There was a tragic story that Thoreau might have learned if he had been interested. The Frenchman had a wife who shared his life in the woods until he was stricken by blindness. A few years after Thurlotte lost his sight, a one-time friend slipped into the woods from Canada and stole his wife, leaving him alone and helpless. Thurlotte was found by a passing lumberman and taken out of the woods. He

sold his rights to the toting service to Anse Smith before he left.

(18) D. T. Sanders & Son is still in the family and still doing business at the same old stand in Greenville.

(19) The Harvey Farm, now abandoned, was one of the landmarks on the lower river in the last century. The farm had been built and land cleared by John Harvey who came upriver in the 1880s with an axe and a pair of oxen. Old memories describe John Harvey as six-by-six, thin as a splinter and ugly as a meataxe, with a little tuft of chin whiskers that trembled as he talked. He married an old squaw and had a dozen or more children by her. Once he was asked if all the children around the place were his. "Spect so," John replied, "leastways they was all caught in my trap."

(20) Hubbard, in error, wrote the name "McLennan." He could only have stopped off at the farm of Finley McLellan which stood a mile below Michaud Farm. Finley Bogan, a marshy spot where McKinnon Brook enters the river, is named after him.

(21) The story of Jim Fleury and his crew was drawn from an account in *Down East* Magazine (Oct. 1961) by William Fowler. Allagashers tell me that

the story is substantially correct, but that the names are fictitious. Fowler must have had his own good reasons for cloaking the identities of these characters, but I see no good reason why it should not be reported that certain living Moosetowners suspect that the horseboat captain Fowler had in mind was "Big Jim" Gardner.

(22) The dam at Churchill Lake was built in 1925 by the Great Northern Paper Company in cooperation with the Madawaska Company. It held a seventeen-foot head of water and was used principally to facilitate booming pulpwood across Churchill and Eagle lakes for further transportation into Penobscot watershed rather than for driving purposes. For a period a thriving little logging settlement which supported a bilingual schoolteacher, was there. Helen Hamlin in her warm little book, *Nine Mile Bridge,* gives a good account of the settlement.

(23) Jilpoke, sometimes spelled gil-poke, is an old logging term for a log that gets in an awkward position. A jilpoked log is a log angled in such a position that it can't readily be floated. By extension, a jilpoke is an awkward or recalcitrant fellow.

(24) It was during this period that the long log driving ended all over the state. Some pulpwood still runs down the rivers and in recent years long logs were still being driven on the Machias River; but the days of river driving might be said to be over and not likely ever to return.

(25) The spruce budworm is an insect associated with spruce and fir forests in New England and eastern Canada and across the conifer belt to the Pacific Northwest. The budworm feeds on the foliage and pollen of mature trees. Always present in the northern forest, the budworm becomes epidemic from time to time, destroying vast areas of standing timber. In recent years, a controversy has raged over massive aerial spraying by timberland owners. Conservationists contend that the toxic agents wash into the streams and are responsible for extensive fish kills.

(26) The facts bearing on Anse Hanley's career were gleaned from an account by Arthur Fowler that appeared in the Rangely weekly newspaper some years ago. Fowler covered the whole breed of squatters, of which Anse was certainly the most memorable.

(27) Actually there was one road across the Allagash country at the opening of the spruce era. The so-called "California Road," which cut across the Maine wilderness, was established before the Revolution

and served as the single link between Eastern Maine and Canada. It also served as a shortcut between the French Provinces in the Maritimes and Quebec. The road, no more than a wagon trail, began at Washburn and went almost due west, crossing at the outlet of Musquacook Lake. It crossed the Allagash at Harvey Farm and the St. John at Seven Islands at the Fitzgerald Farm. The road crossed into Canada along the Little Black River, just south of St. Pamphile and continued on to the St. Lawrence. Presumably it was called the "California Road" because it went west for 350 miles and was the most direct route from Maine to the West. Most of the old trail is grown over today, but sections of it are still used as lumber roads. The course of the old road can still be distinguished from the air, for the road during one period was cleared with grub hoes which removed much of the topsoil with the consequence that the swathe supported little but stunted growth.

(28) Stewart Holbrook offers a version of why Joseph Peavey failed to take out a patent on his invention. Joe Peavey liked his rum as well as the next man, perhaps a bit more. He was on his way to the post office in Bangor with his drawing for the patent office when he stopped by at the home of a blacksmith friend in Orono. Warmed by rum and feeling communicative, he showed the drawings to his friend. One round led to another and the upshot was that, when Joe came to, his drawings were on the way to Washington submitted by his friend.

(29) It wasn't until 1903 that logs began to be topped at an eight-inch diameter.

(30) When the installation at Seboomook was bought by the Great Northern Paper Company early in this century, the conveyers were dismantled and subsequently a forest fire completely destroyed the sluiceway.

(31) "Haywire" is one of the few authentic logger terms that has been accepted as a part of the American language. Under conditions of extreme weather and general abuse, logging machines and equipment were constantly breaking down. It was in many instances literally haywire that kept things moving. Wire was used to bale the hay for the woods horses and it was jealously saved to repair anything from a busted hame strap, a split axe or peavey handle to a boom chain or a steam log-hauler. A notoriously poor logging camp was referred to as a "haywire outfit." The usage spread to mean broken, no good, or plumb crazy.

(32) Lombard's mechanics were better than his law. He failed to get a "means" patent for his revolutionary invention. What he filed was a specific account of what he intended to build neglecting to protect the principle involved in his crawler tread. Western farm tractor companies began producing mechanical farm equipment using this tread almost immediately. One company acknowledged Lombard's basic invention by offering to settle any claims he might have had for $60,000. Lombard accepted this token figure and went fishing.

BIBLIOGRAPHY

Adney, Edwin and Howard H. Chapelle, *The Bark Canoes and Skin Boats of North America.* Washington, D.C., The Smithsonian Institution, 1964.

Averill, Gerald, *Ridge Runner.* Philadelphia, J. B. Lippincott Company, 1948.

Barnes, Francis, *The Story of Houlton.* Houlton, Maine, 1889.

Brooks, Van Wyck, *The Flowering of New England.* New York, E. P. Dutton and Company, 1936.

Cary, Austin, *The Woodsman's Manual.* Cambridge, Massachusetts, Harvard University Press, 1932.

Coolidge, Philip Tripp, *The History of the Maine Woods.* Bangor, Maine, 1963.

Eckstorm, Fannie Hardy, *The Penobscot Man.* Bangor, Maine, 1924.

Farrar, Captain Charles A. J., *Guide to Moosehead Lake.* Boston, Lee and Shepard, 1890.

——— *The North Maine Wilderness.* Boston, Lee and Shepard, 1890.

Gyles, John. Narrative of his captivity, reprinted in *Tragedies of the Wilderness,* ed. Saml. G. Drake. Boston, 1846.

Hamlin, Helen, *Nine Mile Bridge, Pine Potatoes and People.* New York, W. W. Norton, 1954.

Hempstead, Alfred Gear, *The Penobscot Boom.* Orono, Maine, University Press, 1931.

Holbrook, Stewart H., *Holy Old Mackinaw.* New York, Macmillan, 1944.

Houpt, William Parry, *Maine Long Logging and Its Reflections on the Work of Holman Francis Day.* Ann Arbor, University Microfilms, 1964.

Hubbard, Lucius L., *The Woods and Lakes of Maine.* Boston, 1884.

Jackson, Annette, *My Life in the Maine Woods.* New York, W. W. Norton, 1954.

Lowell, James Russell, *Fireside Travels.* Boston, Ticknor and Fields, 1864.

257

Marriner, Ernest, *Remembered Maine*. Waterville, Maine, Colby College Press, 1957.

Mattiessen, Peter, *Wildlife in America*. New York, Viking Press, 1959.

Mitchell, Edwin Valentine, *It's an Old Maine Custom*. New York, Vanguard Press, 1949.

Parkman, Francis, *Count Frontenac and New France Under Louis XIV*. Boston, Little, Brown and Company, 1908.

Platt, Rutherford, *The Great American Forest*. Englewood Cliffs, New Jersey, Prentice Hall, 1965.

Smith, Edgar Crosby (Editor), *Moses Greenleaf, Maine's First Map-Maker*. Bangor, De Burians, 1902.

Speck, F. G., *Penobscot Man*. Philadelphia, University of Pennsylvania Press, 1940.

Springer, John, *Forest Life and Forest Trees*. New York, Harper & Bros., 1851.

Stanton, G. Smith, *Where the Sportsman Loves to Linger*. J. S. Ogilvie, 1905.

Steele, Thomas Sedgwick, *Paddle and Portage*. Boston, Estes & Lauriat, 1882.

Thoreau, Henry David, *The Maine Woods*. New York, W. W. Norton, 1950.

West, Charles, *The Aroostook Woods*. Boston, 1892.

Williamson, William C., *History of Maine*, Vol. 2. Hallowell, Maine, 1839.

Willoughby, Charles C., *Antiquities of the New England Indians*. Cambridge, Massachusetts, Peabody Museum, 1935.

Winsor, Justin, *Narrative and Critical History of America*, Vol. 6. Boston, 1884.

Winthrop, Theodore, *Life in the Open Air*. Boston, 1863.

Wood, Richard G., *A History of Lumbering in Maine*. Orono, Maine, University Press, 1935.

Magazines, Reports, Bulletins, Records

A Big Game Guide. Published by the Bangor & Aroostook Railroad, 1898.

Bulletins. Appalachian Mountain Club, 1924–1926.

Deer in Maine. Game Division Bulletin #6.

Down East Magazine. September 1954; March 1962; October 1961.

Forests of Maine. Bulletin. 1932. Austin Wilkins.

Harper's New Monthly Magazine. March 1860.

In the Maine Woods. Publication of the Bangor & Aroostook Railroad, 1900–1957.

The Northern. Published by the Great Northern Paper Company, 1921–1928.

A Preliminary Survey of the Munsungan-Allagash Waterways. Bulletin VIII. Robert Abbe Museum.

Report of Commissioners of the Inland Fisheries & Game of the State of Maine. 1904.

Report on Public Reserve Lots. Maine State Forestry Department, 1963.

Report on the St. John River, William T. Nash. Frazer Company, Ltd., 1938.

Second Annual Report on the Geology of the Public Lands Belonging to the Two States of Maine and Massachusetts. C. T. Jackson. 1837.

Second Annual Report upon the Natural History and Geology of the State of Maine. C. H. Hitchcock. 1862.

Sprague's Journal of Maine History, Vol. 13. Maine Historical Society Collections.

State of Maine Land Office Records, Vol. 81.

INDEX